MW01257056

Cooking with Feeling

Pat Haley

PAT HALEY

Copyright © 2012 Pat Haley
All rights reserved.

ISBN-10: 1456367722
ISBN-13: 9781456367725
Library of Congress Control Number: 2010917499
Createspace, North Charleston, SC

Table of Contents

THAT WELCOMING FEELING: AN INTRODUCTION

When I first discovered that my family and friends enjoyed whatever I cooked, I began to trust my own feelings about food. I never set out to be a food expert. In fact, the emotionally sterile food labs at college seemed more like a setting for Orwell's 1984 than a celebration of food.

My early dinner parties were served on the floor. Something I did not learn in home ec. But there was no money to furnish that Manhattan studio apartment, once the rent was paid. So I spread my future mother-in-law's red and white checked tablecloth on the floor. Pillows served as chairs. My hungry and equally impecunious friends feasted on spaghetti and meatballs served in the shadows of a candle stuck in a wine bottle.

Cooking for my friends and family seemed to be the expedient thing to do. Here was a fast, cheap, informal and effective way to bring together the people I loved. Nothing fancy; just love.

Long before I had a kitchen of my own, I was fascinated by anything that had to do with food. In Woolworth's where little girls were supposed to be dazzled by doll houses and coloring books, I studied gold-edged gravy boats and ruby red glass tumblers. I filled my mother's recipe drawer with Woman's Day formulas for birthday cakes. I was always the volunteer for the mile hike to the pastry shop to buy jam-filled tarts for dessert. Food always had to do with feeling good.

Mothers are the first to teach us about feelings. "Never ignore a good impulse," my mother said. When she made her annual batch of fastnachts, she dispatched us to the neighbors with warm, fragrant plates of these festive German doughnuts served only on Shrove Tuesday. Self-consciously, we hoped we wouldn't meet playmates who were sure to poke fun. But when a neighbor ooooohed over the unexpected gift on a cold February night, we learned what Mother was trying to tell us about feeling.

When a good feeling takes over, there's no telling what may happen. I am likely to top an autumn cheesecake with a bunch of frosted grapes. Or I might garland a steak and kidney pie with pastry leaves. I thrill to the doing of it just as much as the compliments. When I discover a new splash of color in a pasta salad confettied with vegetables, I have to show it off right away. I risk spilling the dish--and my marriage--by running upstairs to my husband's cloistered study. But the love washes back to me right away.

If people respond to your gifts or meals, that very response exorcises the myths that intimidate beginners. For example, the First Commandment of entertaining reads: Thou shalt serve guests only those dishes you have tried before. But to me inviting people to dinner is the occasion to try something new. If every cook obeyed the conventional wisdom, the only dinner entree would be scrambled eggs.

It is true that an unfamiliar recipe may surprise you when you are most vulnerable. That's why I studied all the recipes available for coulibiac before I made it for our book group. (We read The Brothers Karamazov). I was prepared for the many steps it takes to cook and assemble this complex salmon dish. But I never expected to spend six hours on the coulibiac--finishing just 15 minutes before the guests arrived. And this was the speedy version from a food processor cookbook.

Later, when I was accepting compliments for the coulibiac's extraordinary taste and texture, I blurted out that making the dish had taken most of the day. To my immediate regret. I hoped my friends didn't feel I blamed them for all the time and trouble.

When I entertain, I want my guests to feel welcome. I do enjoy the intricate preparations but I don't want people to feel they caused me extra work. When I slice lemons for the water glasses or tuck a fresh flower into a napkin ring, I am at my most private self. I do these extras for me.

My husband too has learned not to say, "I think you are doing too much." When he sees me in a frenzy of pepper-mill filling, table-setting and napkin folding between pot-stirring and rug-shaking, he takes a walk.

When guests feel nurtured and satisfied, conversation flows. Watch people relax as the meal unfolds. The talk is richest when friends are sweetened by dessert and lounging over second coffees in the soothing candlelight.

Cleaning up after a company dinner is something I prefer to do alone. I need a solitary sorting of leftovers, emotions, responses, glasses and silver. I also savor the feeling of being connected to my mother as I clean and polish the special dishes she has passed down to me.

Of course, not all food feelings are sweet and loving. Negatives abound, too. When food is abused as a drug to quiet uncomfortable feelings, serious illness results. Obesity, anorexia and bulemia occur when unresolved food feelings rage out of control.

I am always saddened when food is served with a helping of hostility. When I was a reporter, a woman complained to me she was depressed by a legal problem she said was inspired by violence. When I finished the interview, she insisted I stay for coffee. With a look that dared me to refuse, she plopped before me a huge pastry smeared with bright yellow goo. That sugar bun told me something about her depression. Her look told me something about violence.

And there was the self-proclaimed natural foods expert who served me lunch with such anger and paranoia that I fled to the nearest Mounds bar to neutralize--somewhat homeopathically--the poison of a not-so-natural mind.

If the food I make fails, it can also mean a relationship is floundering. The guest is no longer welcome but I don't know that yet. When an old friends from another time and place moved to town, I invited them to dinner. In the days when our friendship bloomed, Edward and I and the two of them had marvelous evenings over wine and simple good food. But on this night of the reunion dinner, my bread failed to rise, my stuffed mushrooms shriveled and the chicken breasts in Champagne lacked sparkle.

I can't even remember the dessert. I do remember feeling relieved when they left-- our very good friends. It later turned out I should have trusted my food feelings; the friendship sputtered and died.

As for my very best friend--good Edward--I can still warm a cold March night for him with the startling fragrance of a new soup. And I can coax him onward to the fresh excitements of Mexican, Japanese or Hungarian delights historically denied the be- nighted palates of New Hampshire natives. Food and its wealth of feelings have shown me how to renew our friendship, at just about every meal.

NEVER THE SAME MEAL TWICE

A Foreword By Edward Sullivan

If I have been asked once, I have been asked a hundred times: "How does it feel to be the husband of a cookbook author? You must dine pretty well."

It feels just fine. What else can be said of endless raptures like Chicken Tarragon, Filet of Sole Champagne or Scallop Bisque? A regimen of Chocolate Chestnut Torte and Macadamia Nut Rum Banana Bread, taken in moderation, has to sweeten anyone's days.

It's fun just to be in the company of someone taken up in the passion of any art. I salivate when I can actually watch happiness at work. My nostrils quiver to the fragrances that drift from her kitchen. I hear music when others can only hear mixers grinding, steamers whistling, oven doors booming.

But of course there has to be a flaw in every life. Imperfection persists in the world, sages say, for the perfection of the just.

Yes, it feels uncommonly good to husband a cookbook author and I dine very well, thank you, but there remains an abiding predicament: I never get to eat the same meal twice. A food writer is constantly experimenting, proving, testing, creating. There aren't enough meals in a year for a first-rate innovator. There is no time for repetition; no looking back. The artist is consumed by this unrepeatable moment. To be the immediate live-in victim of all that testing may seem hazardous enough but the real hazard is that, once I have tasted a new delight, I will never be permitted such gladness again. She is already in pursuit of the next innovation.

Now, if you wanted to torture someone, which would be crueler: denying a gratification altogether, or letting the wretch taste it just once with the dire certainty of never, never tasting it again?

———◆———

I think it can be fairly stated that I helped discover the real Pat Haley. She was not allowed to cook at home. Though a graduate home economist, she never actually soloed in anyone's kitchen until she met me, a boon denied her until her aging twenties.

I can remember the very night. She was sharing an apartment in New York with four other flight attendants newly fledged. I don't know how I deserved it but I was admitted to this bower of nymphs for supper, a reward I never expected in this life.

Alert to my pedestrian tastes, Ms. Haley chose as her entree a hamburger. Yes, a hamburger. But this was no ordinary hamburger. Where I come from, a hamburger was a fistful of red-dyed gut slopped on a grease-blackened grill, fried to an acceptable gray and served on chemically contrived bread. To kill the taste, it was usually smothered in catsup, onion, mustard or relish. It fills the belly. It also fills arteries, surgeries and graves.

Ms. Haley's inaugural hamburger actually seemed strange to me. Hefty, substantial and nutty brown, it was presented open-face on a warm, crusty, seeded, wheat-loving roll from the German bakery around the corner. There was also some sort of pickle garnish. And a side salad invisibly dressed.

Here was a hamburger that invited a delicate, caressing touch. It responded with a gush of fragrance. Slowly, tentatively, I raised it to my–

In that moment, life, pleasure and the meaning of food was changed for me forever. Later, when deemed worthy, I learned the ingredients included chopped onion, a dash of Worcestershire, a dollop of chili sauce, and even *an egg*, for goodness sake. What's more, it wasn't fried at all; it was broiled. Most of the killer fat was drained away.

But the recipe does not tell the whole story. Her sorcery was confirmed when my brother was also invited to her table. He too had been raised in a household where more was always considered better, where obesity and television were not yet understood as diseases.

I asked him, "How do you think she does it?"

"It's no mystery," he shrugged. "She cooks with feeling."

———◆———

Of course. That's the ingredient in every dish she prepares. A feeling: welcome, generosity, friendship, sympathy, gratitude, wonderment, celebration, even healing– pick any one of them and you will find it in a Haley recipe.

And she hardly knows the power of it. To this day, she expresses surprise when people throb with excitement at one of her buffets or even one of her simple bread-and-soups.

I have not had the same meal twice because it is impossible for Ms. Haley or any other artist to have precisely the same feeling twice. She may come close to repeating the same recipe but she inevitably veers toward some new condiment, a different herb, an altered sequence, a dash of the inevitable something-else-for-a-change–each of them inspired by a novel, spontaneous feeling.

When we are hibernating under the New Hampshire snows and both hunkered into our writing, she will sometimes mount a Soup-of-the-Week on the stove to sustain life. But Friday's soup is not the soup that started out in the same pot on Monday, because of course she tinkers with it all week. "I would get bored–distracted, really–if I had to repeat exactly the same thing."

And she has to perform these marvels in a very tiny kitchen. This house was built in a century that did not provide space for running water, refrigerators and food processors. Her kitchen is about the size of a toll booth. So I help her out whenever I can by calling it a galley. It is really a very large galley.

But now that Ms. Haley's heartfelt vittles are immortalized in cookbooks, other possibilities are opening for me. It is likely that discerning cooks among you will dare to reproduce her wonders.

Mind you, they are warranted to bring you to new heights of feeling, even compassion, and you are now aware of the plight of food writers' spouses. Your kitchens too will clang and grind and whistle and boom. Your tables will be set, your candles lit, your peppermills freshly charged with feeling, feeling, feeling–and you can mercifully invite me.

A SENSE OF BEAUTY

The act of cooking gratifies all the senses. Even the mysterious sixth sense visits my kitchen. How else can I explain the seasonal craving for a Blue Hubbard squash? Or the urge to nourish the beloved or a good friend? As I prepare any meal, one by one the five senses reveal themselves. I savor the aroma of roasting peppers, the sizzle of frying onions, the smooth-as-a-baby's-bottom yeast dough, the gritty, bitterness of the arugula plucked from the muddy soil of spring.

Such sensory pleasures reward the cook but in the end, the dish must also please the eye. A dill sprig, a red nasturtium, a flower carved from a carrot–each evokes visual pleasure. Sometimes, in the rush of the evening, I suddenly realize that the chicken breast, roasted potatoes and corn on the cob are all the same color. Quickly, I sauté a handful of julienned orange, red and green bell peppers. The sweet pepper ribbons grace the dinner plate and the food becomes a feast for the eye.

Food in Bloom

A s every gardener knows, flowers nourish the spirit. As every decorator knows, flowers civilize the house. But few cooks take the next step: using edible blossoms to decorate or flavor the dishes they present.

True, recipes for nasturtium salads do not appear in the ordinary cookbooks. The common day lily–unlike chocolate, wine and even the potato–has no newsletter of its own. Tropical exotics like kiwi and breadfruit may be available in the supermarket, but dandelions and elder flowers have yet to bloom on the produce counter.

This is because flowers are fragile and no one has yet figured out how to endow them with that profitable quality called shelf life. But if you have a garden or even a prolific lawn, you can afford the luxury–and the pleasures of cooking with flowers.

Yes, some flowers are poisonous. Others taste terrible. But there are many that will add a touch of beauty to your menu, from the violets of early, spring through the chrysanthemums of autumn. A good way to learn the lore of edible flowers is by asking local cooks about their favorites. When I settled into the New Hampshire countryside, one neighbor suggested tossing dandelion buds into an omelet. Another gathered clover blossoms to make jelly from her grandmother's recipe. A third mixed a few geranium leaves in her green salads. By the time the garden club put on an entire edible flower luncheon–from marigold mousse to cakes garlanded with candied pansies–I was convinced: a flower is indeed more than just a pretty face. Shaker cookery called for chive blossoms and rosewater. Nowadays even celebrity chefs are discovering flower cookery. How about "pasta primaflora?" That's linguine tossed with sautéed rose petals, day lilies and violets and a creamy pine nut sauce. How about a salad of crisp and greens with a splash of nasturtiums?

As novel as such dishes are, flowers are traditional fare in other countries. In Ireland, dried clover petals add a taste of honey to fresh bread–and perhaps a bit of luck.

Violets are still crystallized by hand in southern France. The candied violets taste like perfume and are delectable with anything chocolate. If you would rather sip your violets, Toulouse also exports a violet liqueur.

In the Middle East, orange blossoms and roses flavor desserts. In the Far East, major feasts call for chrysanthemum petals; day lily buds are for everyday.

At the Iowa State Fair in Des Moines one year, crowds seeking relief from the sweltering August heat headed for the air-conditioned Food Building, for a session in flower cookery and related arts. There, a horticultural expert demonstrated "Cooking, Crafting and Landscaping with Scented Geraniums" surrounded by a display of blue-ribboned cakes, cookies, pies, jellies, jams, muffins and preserves.

How to begin your own flower cookery? It's easy to decorate sautéed zucchini with its own bright yellow blossoms. Or surround a chocolate-glazed cake with a border of pale creamy marigolds.

Nasturtiums are a good choice for beginners because they are versatile and easy to grow. They thrive in poor soil and tolerate most pests and the weather. For about a dollar, you can buy a packet of blooms in sunset orange or pale yellow splashed with deep maroon.

The leaves of the nasturtium plant resemble cress—with a peppery bite. Add a handful of the leaves to salads that call for larger amounts of milder-flavored greens. The nasturtium blossoms add a bright color and sharp flavor to salads. Float the blossoms on the surface of a chilled summer soup or embed them face down in aspic, gelatin salad or ice ring.

For nasturtium vinegar, loosely pack a quart jar with blossoms and fill with cider vinegar. Cover and let stand for a month. The flavored vinegar will add a subtle bite to salad dressings.

You can also use large mature nasturtium leaves as you would grape leaves. Stuff the leaves with seasoned rice, steam and serve as finger food. When the nasturtium blossoms fade and seed pods appear, pickle the pods and use like capers to add a piquant note to sauces for fish or poultry.

Roses are another versatile flower. The petals may be used to make rose tea, rose butter and rose jelly or jam. Scatter a few in the bottom of a cake pan before adding the batter. Add the chopped petals to omelets or pancake and muffin batters. Ice cream flavored with rose petals and champagne is one of the most sensuous of summer pleasures. Candied rose petals add a festive touch to any dessert.

Marigold petals are often substituted for saffron, an expensive spice. Of course, if you do have access to the real thing by all means, use it. And be aware that this luxurious spice itself originates in the stamens of the autumn crocus. No saffron? Rinse and drain a marigold blossom. Separate the flower into petals and spread on a tray. Cover with a paper towel and put in a warm, dry place until the petals are dried. Crush the petals and store in a tightly-covered container. When preparing rice, for example, add a teaspoon of dried marigold petals to the cooking water for a gold color and pleasant pungent taste.

For a dramatic dessert, consider fritters made with white elder flowers. Dip the clusters in a beer batter, deep fry, and dust with powdered sugar and enjoy. The white elder flower may also be used to make vinegar and syrup. Not to mention the elderberry wine served by the maiden ladies in the play *Arsenic and Old Lace*. Just one glass of that brew sent their lonely gentlemen boarders to an early reward.

Using flowers as containers is a simple way to include them in a menu. Fill hollyhocks, tulips, or gladiolus with individual servings of shrimp salad for lunch or fill the blooms with a variety of dips for the cocktail hour.

Candied flowers and petals are another festive way to serve the blooms. But time and patience are essential ingredients in this craft. Choose flowers with simple shapes and work only on a day when the humidity is low. In New England, late May is probably the best time to make candied flowers. Even in early June, we can be blanketed with soggy air. For the coating, add 1-1/2 teaspoon fine granulated sugar to an egg white and beat until frothy. Dip rosebuds, pansies or violets into the mixture. Then dust with more fine granulated sugar. Using tweezers, transfer the flowers to waxed paper and dry until brittle. Store in a tightly-covered container.

Even if you don't have a flower garden, look to your lawn for edible blooms. Toss a few violets into a salad or make dandelion fritters. And if dandelion is not your cup of wine, consider varying the recipe by substituting rose petals, violets or orange blossoms.

Before you cook with flowers, it is a good idea to learn which are poisonous. They include azalea, crocus, daffodil, foxglove, iris, oleander, mountain laurel, rhododendron, jack-in-the pulpit, lily of the valley, poinsettia and wisteria. If you are not certain whether a flower is edible, check with an authority like the county extension service. Do not use flowers that have been treated with pesticides.

Harvest flowers just after the morning dew has evaporated. Rinse them in cool water. Drain well. Store in a covered container in the refrigerator.

When using flowers such as roses, marigolds and chrysanthemums, trim the bitter white bottom from the petals. Grasp the flower in one hand and trim the flower as you would slice the bottom end from a bunch of celery. Remove the pistils and stamens from flowers such as hollyhocks and daylilies.

Cooking with edible flowers is a lot like gardening. If you count on anything, you may be disappointed. But when you least expect it, there will be a pleasant surprise. Flower cookery is still a random thing—like blossoms in a meadow.

To learn more about the art of cooking with flowers, here a bouquet: of classic works on the topic.

The Edible Ornamental Garden, by John E. Bryan and Coralie Castle, 101 Productions, San Francisco, 1974. 192 pages. There are still a few of these books available but publisher does not plan to reprint the book soon.

The Best of Shaker Cooking, by Amy Bess Miller and Persis Fuller, Macmillan Publishing Company, New York, 1985.496 pages, $19.95. General cookbook that includes some flower recipes.

Rose Recipes from Olden Times, by Eleanor Sinclair Rohde, Dover Publications, New York, 1973. 94 pages, $2.95.

The Forgotten Art of Flower Cookery, by Leona Woodring Smith, Pelican Publishing Company, Gretna, Louisiana, 1985, 180 pages, $10.95.

The Scented Garden, by Rosemary Verey, Van Nostrand Reinhold Company, New York, 1983, $14.95, 168 pages. A general gardening book that includes a chapter on cooking with roses.

Nasturtiums in shades of orange, gold, red and burgundy are a pretty addition to any garden. They are easy to grow and both the leaves and the flowers can be added to a salad. The flowers are also a handy garnish. And when the season ends, you can pickle the seed pods to make mock capers.

MOCK CAPERS

1 cup nasturtium seed pods
1/2 cup cider vinegar
1 tablespoon black peppercorns
1 teaspoon salt
1 garlic clove, peeled
1 onion slice, separated into rings
1 dill sprig

Pick the pods while they are still green and not yet yellow. Rinse and drain. Place pods, onion, garlic and dill in a clean pint jar. Mix vinegar, peppercorns and salt and heat to a boil. Pour into jar. Cover and store in refrigerator. Age for a month before using.

Makes 1 cup.

CHICKEN WITH VIOLETS

3 whole boneless chicken breasts
6 tablespoons freshly grated Parmesan cheese
3/4 cup coarsely chopped violet or pansy petals
1 cup all-purpose flour
1 cup milk
4 tablespoons butter
1 chicken bouillon cube, crushed
1 cup dry white wine
Salt and freshly ground pepper
1/3 cup heavy cream

Cut chicken breasts in half lengthwise. Put 1 tablespoon each of Parmesan cheese and violet petals on each breast. Starting at the short end, roll up the breasts and secure with a toothpick. Dip the breasts in milk and then roll in flour.

Melt the butter in a skillet. Add the chicken when the butter foams. Cook over medium heat until golden on all sides. Stir in bouillon cube and 1/2 cup wine. Season to taste. When wine is reduced by half, add remaining wine. Reduce heat, cover and continue cooking for about 15 minutes or until chicken is fork tender. Turn chicken several times during cooking. Add more wine if sauce looks too dry.

Remove chicken to a warm platter. Increase heat and add cream to skillet. Stir to dissolve any meat bits attached to bottom of skillet. Taste and adjust seasoning. Spoon sauce over chicken and serve immediately.

Makes 3 to 4 servings.

CHAMPAGNE ROSE PETAL ICE CREAM

1/2 cup pink rose petals
1 tablespoon sugar
1/2 cup Champagne or dry white wine
1 pint vanilla ice cream, softened
4 candied pink rose buds

Trim the bitter white base from the rose petals. In a blender or a food processor, whirl the rose petals, sugar and Champagne until smooth. Stir rose petal mixture into ice cream. Pour into a shallow pan and return to freezer.

Freeze for about four hours stirring once or twice to break up ice crystals. Top each serving with a candied rose bud.

Makes 4 servings.

When broccoli slips to 88 cents per bunch at the local supermarket, it is difficult to resist. If you grow nasturtiums, use the first blossoms to garnish this special soup.

GINGER BROCCOLI SOUP

1 bunch broccoli
1/4 cup olive oil
1 cup onion
1 tablespoon finely-chopped ginger
1-1/2 teaspoons *garam masala*
1 teaspoon grated lemon zest
4 cups chicken broth
1 cup half-and-half
1/2 cup milk
Salt and fresh-ground pepper to taste
Fresh chopped chives or nasturtiums for garnish

In a large saucepan, sauté onion and ginger in oil until onions are translucent. Stir in spices, zest. Add broth and bring to boil. Add broccoli pieces. Cover and simmer about 20 minutes. Cool and puree through food mill or in food processor. Reheat and add milk and half-and-half. Heat gently but do not let boil. Correct seasoning. If serving cold, cool at room temperature and chill. Garnish each serving with a sprinkling of chopped fresh chives or chopped nasturtiums.

Makes four to six servings.

Note: *garam masala* is a blend of spices from India. You may substitute 1/4 teaspoon each cloves, cinnamon and nutmeg.

Pearness

Is there any more compelling dream than your own fruit orchard? What could be easier? You plant a few trees. You savor the petals' bouquet. You harvest the fruit. When we moved upcountry, we inherited a pear tree over by the stone fence. We didn't have to lift a spade. When the tree burst into blossoms the following May, I forgave New Hampshire for winter.

I couldn't know that two weeks later the pear tree would again be draped in white. But not creamy, fragrant flowers massed on shiny dark leaves. No, this time our pear tree wore heavy, wet snow–on May 25, for goodness sake. It broke a record, of course. But I longed for spring–not records.

It turned out that our pear tree's blossoms that year were its final crop. The tree was dying and had to be cut down. Inspired by nursery catalogs promising fast fruit, we ordered a single dwarf pear tree.

We city folks did not know you must plant two trees for cross-pollination. Without it, there is no fruit.

We planted the new pear tree in the shade and anticipated the September harvest. I pictured myself canning a few bushels of pears for winter desserts like my mother had done. Our tree produced a few leaves and then died. Being a woman, I assumed it was my fault. I didn't know that a reliable nursery would have advised us this particular dwarf pear tree cannot survive in Northern New England. And that every fruit tree needs full sun.

Eventually, I did preserve pears but we bought them from a farmer who grew full-sized trees in a real orchard.

I wanted to show the children how to preserve food for uncertain times. Peter, Andrew, Miriam, Christine and I selected our pears and filled baskets with yellow fruit tinged with red. This wasn't work, we said. This was fun. Hah!

Then we came to the canning part. I had forgotten about scrubbing and sterilizing jars; boiling cauldrons of water; the messy, sticky, tedious paring and slicing, the instant browning of peeled fruit and the supermarket runs for ever more sugar.

My mother had taught me the canning that helped her through two world wars and a Great Depression. In grade school in the 1950s, we were taught that canned goods in a backyard bomb shelter would help us survive a nuclear attack. Hah!

So here I was, canning pears in the 1970s rage for self-sufficient natural foods. I led my own platoon of Green Revolutionaries. The children and I tied up our farmhouse kitchen for hours. Dinner was never on time that summer. The floor and the tables were covered with a permanent coating of goo. (I didn't know that white sugar–essential in canning fruit–was ideologically unacceptable.) Edward was patient with all of this self-sufficiency. Occasionally he retreated to the local burger palace.

When the children retreated to New York that fall, I had a shelf filled with the summer's labor–blueberries, tomatoes, peaches, zucchini pickles, raspberry jam and 17 quarts of canned pears. The problem was the pears tasted just like canned pears in heavy syrup, a taste I had outgrown.

I was ready to discover the exquisite taste of a fully-ripe pear eaten at room temperature. At its best, pear flesh has a buttery, melting feeling in the mouth. Just a hint of tartness balances the pear's high concentration of levulose, the sweetest of all sugars.

Perfect pearness requires effort and patience. To begin with, the ordinary pear, *pyrus communis*, is picked when it is mature but not yet ripe. Left to ripen on the tree, pear flesh takes on the color and texture of sawdust. Growers and grocers hold the unripe pears in convenient chilled storage.

To ripen pears at home, begin with a brown paper bag. Punch a few pencil-size holes in the bag to admit fresh air and discharge carbon dioxide. Pears breathe like people.

Bag the unripe fruit. Store at room temperature. Check the bag daily. Pears will ripen in two to five days. To hasten ripening, add a ripe apple or banana.

Bartlett pears turn yellow when they are ready. Most other pears do not change color. Test them by touch: when the stem end yields to a slight pressure, they are ready. You can store them in the refrigerator in a plastic bag for another week.

Or you can try a fruit-ripening bowl. Developed by the University of California, this clear plastic container lets you monitor the ripening of up to five pounds of fruit. The same ripener costs anywhere from $10 at a supermarket to maybe $30 mail-ordered from a so-called "chef's wholesale outlet." And I predict that if you are patient, you can pick up a fruit-ripening bowl for 50 cents at a garage sale where it will be displayed among the rejected exercise bikes, electric hair curlers and 20-year-old college textbooks.

———◆———

In the wild, pears are small, bitter and hard. And that's how they stayed until Louis XIV declared the pear his favorite. Lucky for us, the Sun King's flunkies competed to produce new varieties for His Majesty's pleasure. The superb French pear, *Cuisse-madame,* 'my lady's thigh,' was one of many new varieties.

To this day, Parisian gardeners grow their pears on trellised trees to coddle them in extremes of wind and temperature. Called *espalier,* this method assures a consistent crop. In the Loire valley, gentlemen farmers encouraged further species. Hence the Anjou and the Comice.

Many pears have French names for the same reason as wines–they are passions of the French. To marry these pleasures, they, of course, pack a whole pear in each narrow-necked bottle of *eau de vie,* a clear, light pear liqueur.

This ship-in-a-bottle feat is simple if you know how. When the pear is tiny, a bottle is placed over the fruit and its branch. The bottle becomes a greenhouse. When the pear is mature, the bottle is cut from the tree and filled.

Most of Europe's pear crop–it's larger than America's–is pressed into another drink, a cider called perry. European chefs serve cooked pears with game or even in the classic Hamburg eel soup.

Although one Oregon orchardist has produced a crisp, dry pear wine, most of the American pear crop is eaten as hand food. Of the 3,000 varieties cataloged, only eight are available here commercially. Here is an abbreviated guide:

BARTLETT. Named after Enoch Bartlett, a Massachusetts innovator. Comprises 75 percent of the American pear crop. Sweet and juicy for eating; good for cooking and baking. In season, July through December.

COMICE. Also called the Christmas Pear or the Fruit Basket Pear. A wonderful eating pear with excellent flavor. October through June.

ANJOU. A spicy, juicy, eating pear also ideal for tarts, purees and pies. The pear of choice late in the season. October through June.

BOSC. A long-necked pear for eating and cooking. Holds its shape when poached or baked. October through June.

FORELLE. A small pear that is good in salads or preserves. November through March.

SECKEL. The smallest of pears, the only American native variety. For eating and pickles and chutney. October through December.

For a simple but elegant dessert, combine a good eating pear with a cheese such as gorgonzola, brie, camembert, blue, Gouda or cheddar.

Pears also combine with vanilla, cinnamon, ginger, chocolate, red and white wines, Marsala, port, sherry, walnuts, pecans, chestnuts, almonds, apples, sweet potatoes or horse radish.

What's the future for pears? Color it red, say the growers. The red versions of Bartlett, for example, are more resistant to blight and command higher prices than the ordinary Bartletts–although the flavor is comparable. Red Anjou and Comice are also in the works.

And like the song says, partridges really do roost in pear trees.

They flutter around the pear orchard of my fantasies. And I am really trying not to believe those mail-order catalogs that promise Anjou, Bartlett, Comice and Duchess and Gorham pears all on one tree. Hah!

This is a warming soup with the flavors of late autumn and early winter. Serve with a fresh whole-grain bread, a sauvignon blanc and a Vermont cheddar.

PEAR PUMPKIN SOUP

2 tablespoons butter
1 ripe Bartlett pear, peeled, cored and chopped
1/2 cup chopped celery
1/2 cup chopped onion soup
6 leaves fresh sage or 1/2 teaspoon dried
1/2 teaspoon ground cinnamon
1/4 teaspoon nutmeg
1-1/2 cups pureed fresh or canned pumpkin puree
3 cups water
1/2 cup heavy cream
Salt and freshly ground pepper to taste
2 tablespoons grated Parmesan cheese
2 tablespoons chopped walnuts

Melt butter in a large saucepan. Add pear, celery, onion and sage. Cook over low heat until onion is tender and transparent, about 12 minutes. Stir in cinnamon, nutmeg, pumpkin and water and simmer gently for 15 minutes.

Cool slightly and puree in food processor. If desired, prepare to this point and refrigerate overnight. Reheat soup over low heat. Add cream and taste. Season with salt and pepper to taste. Ladle into warm bowls. Sprinkle with cheese and walnuts.

Makes 4 servings.

This is one of my favorite homemade cordials because it is light and fresh tasting. In France, this pear cordial is called eau de vie or "water of life" Be sure to use ripe pears for the best flavor. To ripen pears, place them in a paper bag at room temperature for a few days. Pears are ripe when they give slightly when pressed at the stem end.

PEAR CORDIAL (EAU DE VIE)

1/4 cup water
1/2 cup sugar
2 ripe pears
2 cups vodka

Mix water and sugar in a small saucepan. Place over low heat stirring until the sugar is dissolved and the syrup is clear-about 5 minutes. Remove from the heat and cool.

Quarter the pears lengthwise and place them in a wide-mouth quart jar. Pour in the sugar syrup and vodka. Stir gently. Cover and store in a cool, dark place. Allow the cordial to mature for eight weeks, carefully inverting the jar once a week.

Strain the cordial mixture through cheesecloth or paper coffee filter and pour into a glass bottle. Cork or cap and store in a cool, dry place. Makes 1-1/2 pints.

Every time I roast a big bird for the holidays, I like to try a new stuffing recipe. I may be the only one who does that. My friends tell me that Thanksgiving, would not be Thanksgiving without the same stuffing at the family table year after year. Here is one of my recent discoveries. I prefer to cook the stuffing separately to save energy. But some cooks like to roast a stuffed turkey so that the dressing will absorb the flavorful juices.

SAVORY PEAR STUFFING

¼ cup butter
1 cup chopped onion
1 cup chopped celery
6 cups slightly dry bread cubes
¼ cup brandy `
2 cups ripe pears, chopped into ½-inch pieces

½ cup chopped walnuts
1 teaspoon fresh ginger
1 teaspoon minced fresh sage
1 cup chicken stock as needed
Freshly ground pepper, salt

Sauté onion and celery in butter until soft. Transfer to a large bowl. Add bread cubes, brandy, pears, walnuts ginger and sage and toss lightly to mix. Add as much chicken broth as necessary to moisten the stuffing. Taste and season with salt and pepper. Makes about 8 cups stuffing for a 12-pound turkey. Or spoon into a well-greased baking dish. Cover with foil and bake At 350 degrees for 30 minutes or until heated through.

PECAN PEAR BREAD

1 cup sugar
1/2 cup cooking oil
2 eggs
1/4 cup sour cream
1 teaspoon vanilla
2 cups flour
1 teaspoon baking soda
1/2 teaspoon salt
1/4 teaspoon ground cinnamon
1/4 teaspoon ground cardamom
1/2 teaspoon finely grated lemon peel
1-1/2 cups coarsely chopped peeled pears
2/3 cup chopped pecans

Preheat oven to 350 degrees. Grease and flour a 9-by-5-inch loaf pan.

Combine sugar and oil in a large bowl, beating well. Add eggs beating well after each addition. Stir in sour cream and vanilla.

Sift together flour, soda, salt, cinnamon and cardamom. Add to batter and mix well. Stir in lemon peel, pears and pecans. Spoon batter into pan. Bake for about 1 hour or until bread tests done.

Turn out onto a rack and let cool completely before slicing.

Makes 1 loaf.

CHEDDAR PEAR PIE

9-inch unbaked pastry shell
2 pounds ripe Bartlett pears (about 4 large)
1/3 cup sugar
1 tablespoon cornstarch
1/8 teaspoon salt
1/2 cup flour
1/4 cup sugar
1/2 cup shredded sharp cheese
1/4 cup melted butter

Peel, core and dice pears to make 5 cups. Stir together the pears, 1/3 cup sugar, cornstarch and salt. Turn into pie shell.

Preheat oven to 425 degrees. Combine ½ cup flour, ¼ cup sugar, cheese and melted butter until crumbly. Sprinkle on top of pear mixture. Bake on the bottom rack of oven for 25 to 30 minutes or until pears are tender and crust is golden. Serve warm.
Makes 1 9-inch pie.

The Sweet Pepper Rainbow

One of the most glorious smells of late summer is the roasting of peppers. I regret I waited so long to discover this delight. But I was put off by a couple of things. First, for a while there was a media frenzy over roast peppers. I react negatively to hype. The breathlessness of this publicity signified to me another food fad, like kiwi or fake baby carrots.

And the hype on roast peppers always kept talking about peeling peppers. Peel peppers? Why? Potatoes, yes. Tomatoes, sometimes. But peppers?

Then—the killer frost was three weeks late that year—I had a bumper crop of fat green bells so I tried this pepper-roasting business.

It turns out that when peppers are roasted until they are charred, the skin does slip off. But that's not the point. You roast peppers because they taste so smoky, so mellow and so much better than peppers cooked any other way. I use the broiler, turning peppers as they blacken. In season, I use the grill.

Some cooks roast the peppers over a gas flame using a long fork. Others roast them on an outdoor grill and torture their neighbors with the tantalizing aroma. One determined cook told *The New York Times* that he uses a propane torch to do the job "in a quarter of the time for uniform blackness." Speed and uniformity do count, I suppose, but a propane torch?

And of course, even a simple matter like roasting peppers has at least two schools of thought. The first suggests putting the just-roasted peppers into a plastic bag for ten minutes to steam off the skin. And there is a no-bag school that just rinses the skin off under cold running water.

Baggers and no-baggers agree on the rest: stem, halve, seed and slice. The first dish I made with roasted peppers was *Chiles Rellenos*—cheese filled, batter-dipped fried peppers. This is satisfying lunch or light supper for two or more. For my solitary brunch, I prefer hummus spread in a warm pita topped with chopped fresh basil and slices of roasted sweet pepper. Yum! So this is what those pepper roasters have been trying to tell me all along.

Before my conversion to roasting, I grew peppers because they are Edward's favorite vegetable. He picks them as needed for an omelet or stir fry. Peppers keep well on the vine so there is no urgency about harvesting them until the frost threatens. Even then, I extend the season by draping the pepper plants with a gauzy white agricultural cloth. As the white veil balloons with the wind, covering the plants makes me feel like the artist Christo draping the world.

Eventually, we face the fact that one more growing season has slipped away. Then Edward slices the peppers and freezes them in zipper plastic bags. That's all. No blanching. No parboiling. No mystery.

For me, sweet peppers are a simple and satisfying crop to raise. When I set out the seedlings in late May, I plant a couple of coffee stirrers close to each stem. This stops the cutworms, which must encircle the stem in order to sever it from the root. Anyone whose entire pepper crop has been leveled overnight by cutworms has a few fantasies involving total extinction of this species.

Every July, something nibbles at the leaves of my adolescent pepper plants but it is easily discouraged by a mixture of one pint of water, two minced garlic cloves and one tablespoon cayenne. Whirl in a blender, strain and stir- in three tablespoons dish detergent. Make sure the blender cover is secured. When you spray this solution on the leaves, the pest takes off so fast that I, for one, have never had a chance to get better acquainted. When harvesting peppers, I have learned to cut—rather than tug—the fruit off the plant. Too strong a yank, and you'll end up with an entire branch in your hand.

———◆———

Both sweet and hot peppers belong to the botanical genus *capsicum* which is Latin for box. Indigenous to the tropical forests of Central and South America, the pepper was misnamed by explorers to the New World. Columbus brought the fruit back to Europe noting it was "a pepper more pungent than that of the Caucasus." Actually the capsicum peppers are no relation to the black pepper berries (*piper niger*) that are the source of ground pepper.

The Portuguese traders carried the New World peppers along their routes. In Europe, selective breeding created the sweet varieties such as bell and pimiento. India and China favored the hotter peppers.

In those countries, as in Mexico, hot peppers became a traditional way to treat colds. And with good reason, says an American doctor. "Chiles loosen up the mucous in throats and lungs," Irwin Ziment told *The Wall Street Journal.*

"A lot of the over-the-counter drugs don't have any more proven clinical abilities" than the chiles do," said the UCLA School of Medicine professor. Dr. Ziment routinely prescribes peppers to patients suffering from colds and coughs.

The active ingredient in the hot pepper cure is Capsaicin (cap SAY ih sin). This alkaloid chemical gives the chili its heat. If you have ever broken out into a sweat after one forkful of four-alarm chile con carne, you already know about the air-conditioning effect of the hot pepper. That may explain why hot peppers are popular in torrid climates.

Scientists also have discovered why folk medicine uses red pepper extract to relieve a toothache. Capsaicin, explains the British medical journal, *Lancet*, blocks a pain transmitter heading for a dental nerve.

Our New England soil and climate cannot readily produce the proper pungency for such cures. So I am content to buy hot peppers from California at the supermarket.

At the local garden shops, my search for bell pepper seedlings in color is fruitless. The response is as predictable as the appearance of Japanese beetles in July.

The garden shop clerk tells me that left alone, my green pepper will ripen to red, orange or yellow. But we are talking Northern New England. We are grateful when half the green pepper crop grows large enough to pick before the first frost.

Or another helpful clerk says, "I have exactly what you want." Once again, I mentally arrange a red, green and yellow roast pepper salad on a contrasting white plate.

That's as far as it goes. Come August, the plants hang heavy with tiny lime-colored banana peppers. Well, I have learned to live with disappointment. This is Red Sox country, after all. But even if I never ate a single bell pepper, I would still grow them for the pleasure of looking at the shiny bright green fruit. And yes for the tang of sweet peppers crackling on the grill.

DOUBLE SWEET PEPPER SALAD WITH GOAT CHEESE

2 sweet red peppers
2 large yellow peppers
8 ounces goat cheese
2 tablespoons fresh basil leaves, slivered
1/4 cup ripe olives, sliced
Vinaigrette

Slice peppers and goat cheese. On four salad plates, arrange alternating strips of red and yellow peppers and goat cheese. Spoon vinaigrette over salad and garnish with olives. Sprinkle with basil.

Makes 4 servings.

Vinaigrette

2 sweet red peppers
1/2 cup olive oil
3 tablespoons red wine vinegar
1/4 teaspoon dried thyme
Salt
Fresh ground pepper

Roast peppers until charred. Place in a paper bag and let steam for 10 minutes. Peel and seed peppers. Put into a food processor bowl and add oil vinegar and thyme. Process until smooth. Taste and season with salt and pepper. Process to just to blend in seasonings.

RAINBOW CHICKEN WITH HOISIN SAUCE

1 whole boneless chicken breast
3 tablespoons low-sodium soy sauce
3 tablespoons dry sherry or apple juice
1 tablespoon vegetable oil
1/2 cup chopped onion
1 clove garlic, chopped
2 tablespoons minced fresh ginger
3 bell peppers, 1 each green, red and yellow, cut into strips 1/4" wide
1/4 cup water
1 tablespoon hoisin sauce
8 ounces uncooked linguine

Cook the linguine in a large pot of salted, boiling water. Drain and keep warm.

Slice the chicken diagonally into 1/4-inch slices. Doing this step when the breast is partially frozen makes it easier. Place the chicken into a shallow bowl and add the soy sauce and sherry. Mix gently.

Heat the oil over medium-high heat in heavy skillet. Add onions, garlic, ginger and peppers. Cook and stir about four minutes, until onion begins to soften. Push vegetables to one side of skillet. With a slotted spoon, remove chicken from marinade. Add chicken to skillet and cook and stir until chicken loses it pink color–about three minutes.

Stir in marinade, water and hoisin. Cook and stir two minutes longer. Serve on bed of linguine. Makes two servings.

When we lived in Jerusalem, our friend Monsignor Gianni Rotunno was our guide to the more remote Holy Land sites. We walked over the ground at Jericho, site of the oldest city on earth. We walked about Bethlehem in the pink light of early evening. Best of all, Monsignor always brought a picnic.

The name of one dish–*Pasta Al Forno*–sounded exotic to me. That was long before the word pasta made us feel better about macaroni and cheese. We ate the *Pasta Al Forno*–baked pasta–at a temperature just a little hotter than warm. What a satisfying way to top off a day of sightseeing.

FOUR-CHEESE PASTA AL FORNO

12 ounces linguine
1 teaspoon salt
3 tablespoons olive oil
4 tablespoons butter
1/2 cup Parmesan cheese
3 medium zucchini
6 medium tomatoes
2 cups chopped onions
1 red bell pepper
1 green bell pepper

4 garlic cloves, minced
8 fresh basil leaves or 2 tsp. dried basil
2 tablespoons fresh oregano or 1 tsp. dried
½ teaspoon thyme
freshly ground pepper
12 ounces cream cheese, cubed
1 pound mozzarella cheese, shredded
1 pound provolone cheese, shredded
¼ cup fine bread crumbs
5 medium eggs, beaten

Add the salt and 1 tablespoon olive oil to a large pot of boiling water. Add the linguine and cook and stir until al dente, about 7 to 8 minutes. Drain and toss with 2 tablespoons butter and 1/4 cup Parmesan cheese.

Chop 1 zucchini into a small dice. Slice the remaining zucchinis into 1/4inch slices. Cut each of the tomatoes into four slices. Reserve sliced zucchini and tomatoes for final assembly of the dish.

Heat 2 tablespoons olive oil in a large frying pan. Over medium heat, cook and stir the onions, peppers, garlic, and chopped zucchini. Cook about five minutes or just until the onions are translucent. Stir in the basil, oregano, thyme, pepper and cream cheese. Remove from heat. Stir until cream cheese melts. Set aside.

In a large bowl, lightly toss the mozzarella and provolone cheeses until mixed. Generously butter the sides and bottom of a 13-by-9-inch baking and serving pan. Mix 1/4 cup Parmesan cheese and the dried bread crumbs. Coat the baking pan with the bread crumb mixture.

Stir 1/3 cup of the cheese-vegetable mixture into the beaten eggs. Then stir all of the egg mixture into the remaining cheese-vegetable mixture. Mix thoroughly. Cook and stir until mixture just begins to bubble.

Pre-heat oven to 325 degrees. Put half of the linguine into prepared pan.

Cover with 1-1/2 cups shredded cheese. Spread half of the vegetable mixture over the shredded cheese. Cover with 1 cup of shredded cheese. Top with 12 tomato slices. Cover with 1 cup shredded cheese.

Repeat layers: linguine, 1-1/2 cup shredded cheese, remaining vegetable mixture, 1 cup shredded cheeses and tomato slices. Top with sliced zucchini and then sprinkle on remaining shredded cheese. Cover with well-buttered foil. Bake at 325 for 50 minutes.

Uncover and bake about 10 additional minutes until light golden. Remove from oven and let sit 10 to 15 minutes before serving to ease cutting. Makes 12 servings.

Steve's chiles rellenos is not exactly fast food but when the craving for something Mexican strikes, this stuffed pepper dish is just right. To speed up the cooking, substitute prepared salsa for the tomato sauce and stuff the chiles with shredded cheese. If you cannot get the mild, long green California chiles, use green bell peppers.

STEVE'S CHILES RELLENOS DE QUESO

2 tablespoons olive oil
1 cup finely chopped celery
1 garlic clove, minced
1/2 cup finely chopped parsley
8 tomatoes, peeled, chopped
½ teaspoon dried oregano
½ teaspoon dried basil
1/8 teaspoon curry powder
½ cup whole wheat flour

1 teaspoon ground cumin
½ teaspoon salt
½ teaspoon red pepper flakes
6 fresh California chiles, or
1 7-ounce can whole green chiles
4 ounces Monterey Jack cheese
3 eggs, separated
oil for frying

To prepare the tomato sauce, sauté celery, onion and garlic in 2 tablespoons olive oil over medium heat until onion is translucent. Stir in parsley, tomatoes, oregano, basil and curry powder. Lower heat and cook 10 minutes, stirring occasionally. Keep warm.

Stir together flour, cumin, salt and red pepper flakes. Cut a small slit in one side of each chile to remove seeds. Leave stems on. Pat chiles dry with a paper towel Cut cheese into sticks 1/2-inch wide by 1/2inch thick and 1 inch shorter than chile. Stuff chiles with cheese. Secure with toothpicks if necessary.

In a medium bowl beat egg whites until stiff. In a small bowl, lightly beat egg yolks. Gently fold whites into yolks.

Roll chiles in flour mixture and then dip into egg mixture.

In a large skillet, pour oil to ¼ inch depth and heat it to 365 F. (185C). Fry chiles in hot oil until golden, turning once. Drain on paper towels. Puddle tomato sauce on plates. Top with chiles. Serve immediately.

Makes 6 servings.

I stopped making pickles and relishes because the traditional recipes required too much salt and sugar. When I started making veggie burgers, I relented and bought a small jar of hot dog relish. Nothing had changed. Too much salt and sugar. Then I experimented with an old relish recipe that called for cucumbers or zucchini. I eliminated most of the salt and sugar and was pleased when the relish turned out just fine. I skipped the boiling water bath and simply stored the 3 quart jars in the back of refrigerator.

HOT DIGGETY RELISH

10 cups peeled, chopped cucumbers
1 red bell pepper, chopped
1 green bell pepper, chopped
4 cups chopped onions
¼ cup pickling or Kosher salt
2-1/4 cups cider vinegar
½ cup sugar
1 tablespoon nutmeg
1 tablespoon turmeric
2 tablespoons celery seed
½ teaspoon black pepper

In a large non-reactive pot, stir together cucumber, peppers and onions. Stir in salt and let sit overnight. Drain. Return to pot and stir in vinegar, sugar, nutmeg, turmeric, celery seed and black pepper. Bring to a boil, lower heat and simmer 15 minutes. Ladle into hot, sterilized pint jars. Process in a boiling water bath for 5 minutes. Makes 6 pints.

FRIENDSHIP

Each year, neighbor Margritt Richter invites us for a cup of Christmas cheer because she knows how much I admire her exquisite tree sparkling with a lifetime collection of baubles. At any season, you cannot depart the Richters without an unexpected gift of friendship—fresh pears or a miniature coreopsis cutting.

When I visit Los Angeles, friend Elizabeth Thomas takes me to one of her local finds—say a new restaurant done in black marble and glass. Over mussels and pasta, we ponder the lessons of our two lives, a conversation begun 35 years ago. Elizabeth saves me her *Los Angeles Times* food sections perhaps the most lively and comprehensive of them all.

Her stack of papers—a chore for her to collect and me to lug home—is a true gift of friendship. I often decide that this whole LA Times recycling is just too trouble to continue for even one more week. Then I browse a two-month old paper and find just the research gem I need. Here in these yellowed pages, with holes where coupons once were, lies the perfect ending for an essay that has been eluding me for weeks.

Make-Ahead Meals For House Sitters

Over the years, I have had people house sit for me–for better or for worse. I also have apartment sat for others when their vacation from the big city coincided with mine from the country. I watered plants, took messages and fed parakeets–a small price for a week's lodging.

I was a small-town newspaper editor at the time. A bus ride to New York or Boston was all the vacation I could afford. Even cheap hotels were out of the question. No matter. Most of my city pleasures were free–checking the street fashion, browsing the cookware shops and visits with my stepchildren. When we ate it was student fare. In New York, I ate raisin bagels with Peter or a drugstore breakfast with Christine. In Cambridge, I shared raclette at a little Swiss place with Martin and Nancy.

There were times when the apartment sitting arrangements were made by a third party. I never met the person whose dog I walked or whose gardenia plant I misted. I did know about the projects that took them to distant places: a documentary in Santa Fe, photography school in Paris or a study of endangered Caribbean coral.

Seated in unfamiliar kitchens, I drew a picture of the absent hosts from the food clues they left behind. One New Yorker did not own a toaster or a saucepan. He did not even have what most people consider a lifeline–a coffeepot. But why should he cook? I counted six ethnic restaurants within 200 feet of his door. Now I pack a tiny percolator so I can wake up at my own pace–the jump-start of two cups of coffee.

One steamy June, I sat a Boston apartment. A cold drink–even ice water-would have been welcome refreshment. But there were no ice cubes to be had in this kitchen. Instead, ice-cream sandwiches jammed the refrigerator's tiny freezer. Someone's boyfriend had peddled them on the Boston Common until he was busted for lack of a permit. He was expected back in the fall–to pick up the sandwiches and the relationship.

In a Cambridge kitchen there were three bottles of vitamins and no food at all. Well, a couple of pouches of soy sauce from the takeout.

By contrast, we country dwellers offer our house sitters a well-stocked kitchen, and they let us know if it isn't.

"I just know there had to be Worcestershire somewhere in your kitchen," friend Elizabeth Thomas said later. There was, of course. It was stored in a glass decanter because I didn't like the looks of the original sauce bottle. That was long ago when I had the time to re-package what I considered aesthetically offensive.

Up here in New Hampshire, house sitters are often young single adults who live with parents or share close quarters with roommates.

House sitting anywhere offers space and solitude. Sitters may watch the house and pets for a week or for a season. The privileges they enjoy can vary from our austerities to the luxuries of the rich. Some sitters ride horses, drive sporty cars, bask in saunas and whirlpools, and pick and choose from the household library of movie classics.

But house sitting is not always a breeze, as one young woman found out when sitting for honeymooning friends. As the couple sunned in Cancun, the house sitter was nursing a lame horse and trying to locate a vet who made house calls. The household car broke down; the chicken feed ran out, the washing machine overflowed. Getting things fixed was complicated by the honeymooners' trail of unpaid bills. The friendship foundered, of course. The sitter learned how to choose her jobs and before long she had saved enough rent money for a down payment on a house that somebody else now sits for her.

House-sitters too can be flawed. Our sensitive country plumbing gets jammed. Irreplaceable dishes are chipped. Grease spatters dot the floor and counters. Beer cans bloom in the shrubbery. The cat won't come home for days.

Finding a house sitter resembles the trial-and-error search for a plumber or dentist. You get burned once, maybe twice, and when you finally discover a gem, you are intensely loyal and even protective.

When I sit in a friend's house, I simplify it all by making our meals ahead of time. I do not want to hunt for another's colander or curry powder. Or buy and pack staple foods. After a day at work, I would rather saunter in a post-card village than scrub sauce off the stove.

Instead, I prepare all our meals and freeze them. Some dishes I only have to refrigerate. For efficiency's sake, I double four different recipes. During our house sitting week, we have three of the dishes twice.

Admittedly, the kind of food you prepare ahead and freeze is limited, as anyone who has lived on packaged frozen entrees knows. In fact, the first meal I make when we return home is fresh, fresh, fresh: a large green salad, stir-fried ginger broccoli and lemony broiled fish.

My house sitting favorites include chili and cornbread, red lentil soup, beef and bean soup, pesto on pasta and a layered hamburger casserole. You could also try chicken curry, moussaka, lasagna or stews.

Here are some cook aheads that work for me. You can cook one half for dinner today and freeze the rest. It's always a good feeling to know there's a cook's night off waiting in the freezer.

When my step-daughter Nancy comes up from Boston, she brings us goodies from the city's natural food stores. She once brought this recipe plus all the special ingredients. This soup is a very good one with a strong curry flavor and restorative powers.

NANCY'S RED LENTIL SOUP

3 tablespoons butter
2 teaspoons cumin
1/8 teaspoon cayenne pepper
1/2 teaspoon ginger
1-1/2 teaspoon coriander
1 teaspoon mustard seeds
2 teaspoons curry powder
1-1/2 teaspoon salt
8 cups water
2 cups red lentils, rinsed
1/4 cup plus 2 tablespoons lemon juice
2 teaspoons honey

In a large pot, heat butter; stir in spices. Add water and bring to a boil. Add lentils. Cook over low heat for one hour stirring frequently. Makes 6 cups.

VARIATION: When heating the butter and spices, add 2 minced garlic cloves along with 2 cups chopped vegetables such as onions, carrots and celery. Sauté gently until onion is transparent. The vegetable mixture adds more body to soup and makes it even more nutritious

This warming soup is one of our favorites. Despite the long list of ingredients, it is quickly assembled. I make it the night before or on a weekend morning to let the flavors blend.

BEEF AND BEAN SOUP

1/2 pound ground beef or lamb
2 tablespoons vegetable oil
2 garlic cloves, minced
1/2 cup chopped onion
1/2 cup chopped celery
1/2 cup chopped green pepper
1 28-ounce can tomatoes
1 quart water
1 low-sodium beef bouillon cube
1 16-ounce can red or white kidney
beans or chick peas
2 tablespoons parsley
2 tablespoons basil
1 tablespoon oregano
1/2 teaspoon thyme
1 cup elbow macaroni

Brown beef and drain. Sauté fresh vegetables in oil until soft. In a large soup kettle, put beef, sautéed vegetables, water, bouillon cube, tomatoes, herbs and beans. Bring to a boil and simmer for 20 minutes. Add macaroni and boil gently for five minutes or until macaroni is cooked.

Makes 6 servings.

Diane Wood is one of those people with a great collection of recipes who is willing to share. This casserole is simple to fix but very hearty.

DIANE'S LAYERED HAMBURG CASSEROLE

4 ounces medium egg noodles
I pound ground beef, browned, drained
1 15-ounce can tomato sauce
1 teaspoon sugar
1 teaspoon salt1
1/4 teaspoon garlic salt

1/8 teaspoon pepper
1 8-ounce package cream cheese
½ cup sour cream
3 tablespoons milk
1 10-ounce package frozen spinach
½ cup shredded cheddar cheese

Defrost and drain spinach. Boil noodles until just chewy. Drain. Stir together noodles, beef, tomato sauce, sugar, salt, garlic salt and pepper. Stir together cream cheese, sour cream and milk.

In a greased casserole, layer beef mixture, cheese mixture and spinach. Sprinkle with shredded cheese. Bake at 350 degrees for 40 minutes.

Makes 6 servings.

This recipe doubles and triples nicely. Make one batch for today and put the others in the freezer for a busy day.

CHILI CON CARNE

1 pound lean ground beef
1/4 cup olive oil
1/2 cup chopped celery
3/4 cup chopped green pepper
1 medium onion chopped,
2 cloves garlic, chopped
1 16-ounce can red kidney beans
1 28-ounce can tomatoes, with their liquid
1 low-sodium beef bouillon cube
1 cup water
1 6-ounce can tomato paste
1 teaspoon cumin
2 teaspoons dried oregano
3 tablespoons chili powder
2 bay leaves
1 tablespoon brown sugar
1 tablespoon red wine vinegar
2 tablespoons cocoa
1 tablespoon Worcestershire sauce
1 teaspoon salt
Freshly ground pepper

In a heavy skillet, brown beef. Drain and put into a large heavy pot. Sauté celery, onion, garlic and pepper in olive oil over low heat until tender. Add to pot. Drain kidney beans and rinse under warm water. Drain again. Add beans, tomatoes, bouillon cube dissolved in the water, tomato paste, oregano, cumin, chili powder, bay leaves, brown sugar, red wine, cocoa and Worcestershire sauce.

Bring to a boil. Cover and cook over low heat for 30 minutes, stirring occasionally. Add more water as needed if the chili becomes too dry. At end of cooking, taste and correct seasoning.

Makes 4 servings.

Corn bread is simple to make and when served with chili combines to make complete protein. For a variation in color and texture, use a roasted, peeled and chopped red or green sweet pepper or a 1/2 cup fresh or rinsed frozen kernel corn. Stir gently into the batter. Or if fresh dill is available, whirl a handful in the processor and stir into the dry ingredients.

CLASSIC CORN BREAD

3/4 cup corn meal
1 cup flour
1/4 cup sugar
1 tablespoon baking powder
1 cup milk
1 egg beaten
2 tablespoons melted butter or
Margarine

Grease an 8-inch square pan. Preheat oven to 425 degrees.

Stir together corn meal, flour, sugar and baking powder. Whisk together milk, egg and melted butter. Add to corn meal mixture and stir together just until mixed. Bake 20 to 25 minutes or until a tester inserted in the center comes out clean.

Makes 4 servings.

Making The Time For Friendships

If you could take a year off from work, what would you hope to accomplish?
An acquaintance who took a year off said she was looking forward to decorating her house the way she always wanted.

I don't know whether she decorated her house or not but I do know her sabbatical produced one pleasant discovery.

"More than anything I enjoyed having the time to be with my friends. Friendships are like gardens. You must spend time cultivating them."

She is right, of course. But is there any way short of a sabbatical to find the time to work on our friendships?

Sometimes, I get the feeling I will have to wait until retirement to enjoy the luxury of leisurely friendship: a long idling tour through a museum, a two-hour lunch or a gamble on a movie that no one has reviewed.

Still, friends are important to me. I have friends who are men and friends who are couples. But it seems my friendships with women are those I attend to the least. Maybe this is a throwback to the Saturday-night movie contract we used to make with our college roommates. It was understood that if either of us had the good fortune of being asked out by a boy at the last minute, then the girls' movie date was off.

These days, most of the women I would like to spend time with have the same lifestyle I do. We are over committed to our careers, our families, our communities and our houses.

We get frantic–if not a little crazy sometimes–arriving home at night just in time to stoke the home fires between making a few more work-related calls and packing the next day's lunches.

Weekends for many women are a time to catch up with laundry and paper work that pile up during the week. Not to mention the seasonal chores and the should-attend social events with colleagues and friends: his, hers and ours.

I called a halt to all that recently and took time out for a few friends. It began when a personable young colleague told me she felt out of touch because she has so few friends in our community. "On weekends, I keep up with my friends in Boston and New York but I don't know if it's worth making friends here because I may be transferred at any time."

How sad, I thought, to be cut off from the ordinary weekday friendships. And here she is a pleasant, bright person that I, for one, would like to get to know better. Then I came up with the names of two other women at work that I would also like to know better. And the names of four other good friends I never have time to see.

In other times and other places, these are the people I would meet at the end of a day for a drink. But these days, the logistics of a spontaneous drink simply do not exist. And most people I know do not choose to get behind the wheel after a drink.

My friend Sally has to pick up her child at day care. Linda has a 5:30 computer class. It's Debbie's turn to cook. Liz's son has a science exhibit. Peggy has to get the car home because her husband's is being fixed. Lucy has a board meeting. Diane has aerobics.

So we all sigh and hustle onto the next task wondering why we don't have time to enjoy the richest resource of them all, our special friends.

What, I wondered, would happen if we all took one night off–from everything. I decided to organize a potluck supper for my women friends. I warily approached the first woman. "Great idea! Let's do it," she responded. The others were equally enthusiastic and suddenly we all were anticipating a bright spot in an otherwise duty-bound, crowded calendar.

So for the first time in my life, I actually asked people to bring a dish to dinner. But being a Superwoman when you entertain is a difficult habit to break. For one thing, the voice in your head says, "What's so difficult about tossing off a little dinner for friends? Couldn't you at least give your friends a choice of dessert?"

Not to mention the fact that I write cookbooks and always have recipes that must be tested. In fact, recipe testing is always a good excuse to entertain. But some recipes I must test sometime just do not fit into my scheme of things. For example, I have a print-out of a recipe for sesame noodles that has been on my refrigerator door for months. They just do not seem to be company fare. At least not for the main dish.

Then there is no denying the pleasure watching my guests delight in details–a novel napkin fold, a fresh flower garnish, and the hot towels after dinner. Compared to some people–although, my husband, Edward, probably will not agree–I entertain quite simply. Take my friend, Mary Campbell, who lives in the Detroit area. Once a month, she and her women friends cook the centerfold meal in "Gourmet" magazine. We are talking menus like warm shrimp and scallop salad with roasted red pepper vinaigrette;

roast goose with sausage, fennel and currant stuffing with wild mushroom gravy, sautéed potatoes and celery root; Brussels sprouts and carrots with shallot butter; Black Forest cake and eggnog ice cream. Plus three wonderful wines. These ladies-who-lunch invite their corresponding men for dinner just once a year. "It's not that we want to exclude the men it's just that having just the women makes it really special," Mary said.

Agreed, and once I organized a cooperative dinner, I was converted. All I had to do was put a self-assigned entree into the oven and set the table. Okay, I do admit I made a juicy roast loin of pork with an exquisite sauce. But the entire menu did not depend on me. Even if I burned or dropped my masterpiece, there were still seven other menu components.

I actually sat by the fire and had a cup of tea while I waiting for my guests. The usual last-minute search for a gravy boat or dessert forks seemed to evaporate.

At dinner, we laughed, visited, supported, discovered and just relaxed. How pleasant to have a free-flowing conversation without the usual tension pressing us on to the next item on our overloaded schedules. How nice not to worry about clinching the deal before the dessert cart arrived.

We enjoyed a superb and sophisticated meal and joked about how our families would manage to survive without us. Interestingly enough, we never had a pre-dinner summit conference about the menu. Several of us cooked our personal favorites. Others brought take-out. Who cared? We were just grateful for the good food and the good company.

When my guests walked out into the starlit night and back into their lives, they seemed pleased we had taken the time to water our friendship gardens. We felt refreshed and nourished for having taking time out to be with friends.

"Every time we go to dinner at somebody's house, there is always the same menu because every doctor's wife in town uses the same caterer," a local doctor once complained to me. "Rumaki–that's the only appetizer Mrs. X. knows how to make." Well, rumaki–bacon-wrapped chicken livers–is a tasty party nibble. For those of us without caterers, here is a simpler idea for an appetizer. This rumaki spread recipe was given to me by Evelyn Lambert, an energetic flight attendant who flies the international routes out of Miami.

RUMAKI SPREAD

1/2 cup butter or margarine
1/2 pound chicken livers
1 tablespoon soy sauce
1/2 teaspoon onion salt
1/2 teaspoon dry mustard
1/4 teaspoon nutmeg
1/8 teaspoon cayenne pepper
1 (6-ounce) can water chestnuts, drained and finely chopped
6 strips crisp-cooked bacon, crumbled
2 green onions, thinly sliced
Crackers

Melt butter in a frying pan over medium heat. Add chicken livers. Cook and stir until livers are firm but still a bit pink inside. Put liver mixture, soy, onion salt, mustard salt and cayenne in a food processor. Process just until smooth. Remove to serving bowl and stir in water chestnuts and bacon. Refrigerate at least 2 hours before serving to allow flavors to blend.

Bring to room temperature before serving for easy spreading. Sprinkle with green onions. Serve with crackers.

Makes about 1-1/3 cups.

When Baby Nicole Hebert was born, her mother, Medora's lets-have-lunch-buddies offered to bring lunch to her house and meet the baby, too.

We brought wine, bread, flowers, dessert and this scallop bisque. What a pleasant way to wrap up the workweek and welcome the little one to the world of intimate lunches with good friends. And brighten up a gray late winter day as well.

NICOLE'S SCALLOP BISQUE

4 tablespoons butter
1/2 cup finely chopped onion
4 tablespoons flour
2 cups milk
2 cups chicken stock
1 pound bay scallops
2 cups light cream
1 tablespoon Worcestershire sauce
2 tablespoons brandy
Chopped fresh parsley

Melt the butter in a non-reactive heavy saucepan. Add onion and cook over medium heat just until soft but not brown. Add the flour, lower heat and whisk and cook for two minutes.

Gradually add the milk and cook and stir the mixture until slightly thickened. Add the scallops and chicken stock and simmer covered for 10 minutes. Do not cook any longer or scallops will become tough. Remove from heat and puree in batches in a blender or food processor. Bisque may be prepared ahead to this point and refrigerated.

Serve with a sharp mustard, applesauce and mashed potatoes.

ROAST LOIN OF PORK

1/2 cup low-sodium soy sauce
1/2 cup bourbon
1/4 cup brown sugar
1-inch piece of fresh gingerroot, sliced thin
1 clove garlic, sliced thin
4-pound boneless top loin pork roast

Stir together soy sauce, bourbon, brown sugar, gingerroot and garlic. Place pork roast in a zipper plastic bag. Pour soy sauce mixture into bag, seal and place in a bowl. Refrigerate at least three hours, turning occasionally.

To roast, remove pork from bag and place fat side up on a rack in a shallow roasting pan. Pour soy sauce mixture into a small bowl. Roast uncovered at 325 degrees until a thermometer placed in thickest part of meat reaches 170 degrees, about 2-1/2 hours. Baste occasionally with soy sauce mixture. For ease of slicing, allow roast to rest for 15 minutes after removing from oven. Cut into thin slices.

Makes 12 servings.

When Florence Huntley managed the St. James Episcopal Church Thrift Shop in Keene, she attracted a constellation of gracious ladies as volunteers. It was always rewarding to stop in and visit whoever was on duty. Helen Doberstein was one of these special women. So was Evelyn Tilton who contributed the zucchini pickle recipe for this book.

This is Mrs. Doberstein's tomato pudding. "This dish holds up well," she noted on her recipe card. "Parts can be made early. Be sure the bread is saturated with butter. It should form a nice crust." Tomato pudding goes nicely with roast chicken, pork or ham.

TOMATO PUDDING

2 cups bread cubes or unseasoned croutons
1 28-ounce can tomato puree
A little water to rinse can
1/2 cup butter
1 cup light brown sugar

Soak bread cubes in melted butter or brown lightly in a skillet stirring frequently. Place bread cubes in the bottom of a buttered casserole dish. In a saucepan, stir together puree, water and brown sugar. Heat and add to bread cubes. Bake for 30 minutes in a 350-degree oven.

Makes 6 servings.

When I gave a talk to the Friends of the Chesterfield Library, someone asked if I had a foolproof pie crust recipe. I could not think of one off the top of my head. But my good neighbor and friend, Margritt Richter, came to my rescue and delighted the audience with this simple but effective crust recipe.

MARGRITT'S MIRACLE PIE CRUST

2 sticks margarine
2 cups flour
1 egg
1 teaspoon cider vinegar
1/2 cup water or orange juice

Slice margarine into tablespoon-size pieces. Fit a food processor bowl with metal blade. Put flour and margarine in food processor bowl. Process until mixture resembles coarse meal. Place egg in a 1-cup measure. Add vinegar and fill to 1/2-cup mark with water or orange juice. Pour into processor bowl. Pulse on and off until dough forms ball.

Makes enough crust for a single crust with a lattice top.

Herbs, The Friendship Garden

So I went to the culinary herb expert and declared my ignorance. All I wanted was the names of two easy-to-grow, easy-to-eat herbs for my plain, ordinary garden. But it was not to be.

"You must grow borage, lovage and epazote. Get some lemon thyme. But be careful because there are 400 varieties of thyme and most growers don't know the upright from creeping kind and it makes all the difference. Also, you must get some pineapple sage and opal basil. Don't forget apple mint–its real name is *mentha rotundifolia*–so that's what you should ask for. And remember no culinary herb collection is complete without oregano but not the kind with purple flowers–it's no good. The flowers have to be white . . . ."

My eyes glazed over. How did I get into this? How do I get out of here? The expert gave me a slip of thyme and mercifully sent me on my way. Whether the thyme was creeping or upright, I'll never know. It died a few days later. So did my motivation.

Intimidated and fearful that I might plant summer savory where only winter savory would grow, I continued to use the familiar dried herbs sold in little jars. My snow peas, carrots and plum tomatoes were homegrown but the herbs came from the supermarket shelf.

As a novice cook, I bought dried basil, parsley, oregano, thyme and sage. That's what ageless Betty Crocker used in her ageless meatloaf. Gradually, I added other herbs and spices to my shelf. When my mother visited my New Hampshire kitchen for the first time, she looked at my row of seasonings and said, "You must make pretty spicy food, Pat."

Mother needed only a few spices like cinnamon and nutmeg. Our family ate bland food because my dad had ulcers. Mother kept her spices for two or three decades. Years later, I was surprised when an expert told me to discard spices older than ninety days.

It turned out that friends–not experts–taught me how to grow a simple herb garden. Simple to me means seven carefree herbs introduced gradually into the garden. Each friend gave me a slip of her favorite plant and as much uncomplicated advice as I could bear. In fact, assembling an herb garden based on friendship is easier than driving from farmer to nursery to greenhouse to collect seedlings and more advice.

Much advice is not always sound advice, I learned. The voices of competence turned out to be the voices of few words. And a lot of the magic of herbs has to do with their simplicity.

Four of my herbs–sage, oregano, spearmint and chives–happen to be perennials. Each spring, I renew the annuals: I sow parsley, buy basil seedlings and the welcome the first dill volunteer that pokes up.

In the beginning, friend Fleur Weymouth gave me a clump of oregano. I stuck it in the ground. It flourished and threatened to cover the earth. Even in its first year I harvested enough oregano to perfume a winter's pizzas and hash browns. The oregano isn't the white-flowered kind preferred by the expert but Edward, the bees and I are all attracted to its cheerful purple flowers. Eventually, I moved the oregano out of the garden and onto the lawn where it grows like a proper ornamental.

Fleur's gift is the mild *Origanum vulgare*, also called wild marjoram. Some cooks say it is useless; others will not use anything else. When I come across some *heracleoticum*, the white-flowered, hardy perennial, I'll plant it and make up my own mind.

Another friend, Rebecca, introduced basil into my garden. She started the herb in a sunny window. By late spring–when the rest of us were slogging in still-muddy gardens–Rebecca was already handing pots of basil to lucky visitors.

I planted the basil next to the tomatoes. They are good companions, in the garden as well as the table. The cutworms agree. I have learned protect the stems of both seedlings. A pair of coffee stirrers planted close to and on opposite sides of the stem frustrates the encircling habit of cutworms.

When Rebecca's basil matured that August, I discovered pesto, a glorious sauce made from basil, pine nuts, garlic, Parmesan cheese and olive oil. The versatile pesto enhances many kinds of foods–hot, warm and chilled pasta, pizza, vegetables, chicken or seafood. For a tasty dip, stir pesto into mayonnaise or yogurt. Start with a tablespoon of the pesto and keep adding until it tastes right to you. The pesto itself freezes well and, in mid-January a dish of linguini fragrant with basil reminds you that no winter lasts forever.

When I first moved to New Hampshire, a neighbor gave me a clump of chives. This onion-y little perennial thrives in spite of my neglect. I have divided the original several times and each new clump takes hold wherever I plop it. Some years, I don't even think about chives until the purple flowers appear. By that time, the stems are too tough to use but the flowers make an edible garnish.

If I think of chives when they are still fresh, I sprinkle them on gazpacho, a dip or into a salad. If I take the time to slice and freeze surplus chives, I will be sprinkling them on my omelet next winter. And just this fall, my friend Diane Wood handed me a clump of garlic chives.

My sister, Joan Lindert Brod, brought me spearmint from her Connecticut garden to mine. Like chives, spearmint requires little attention until the summer heat and humidity suggest Arab menu coolers like the salad *fatoosh*, minty ice tea and *tabbouleh*, the bulgur main dish salad. A combination of mint and basil approximates the taste of a basil that Thais call "holy."

Each garden season, I ventured further. I bought a scrawny sage seedling that now yields more sage than I will ever need for turkey dressing. I have tried sage-flavored Italian dishes such as deep-fried sage leaves and two breads, *pane alla salvia* from Tuscany and *focaccia* from the south of Italy. According to herbal lore, sage is also supposed to improve memory, discourage ants and even help one to achieve immortality. My sprawling sage and I will put all this to the test.

For years I tried to start parsley indoors. Nothing happened. Frustrated, I sprinkled two whole bargain packets of seeds into my garden. Magically, they sprouted long after I had forgotten about them. I didn't know parsley requires up to four weeks to germinate. Irish legend says that parsley seeds must go to the devil and back nine times before they germinate. I don't know whether scientists have measured the speed at which a parsley seed travels.

To speed up non-Irish germination, soak the seeds overnight in warm water before sowing. But be sure to let others in your house know what you are doing. One spring, Edward inadvertently discarded my entire parsley crop. He saw a bowl of soaking seeds and concluded I had invented an effective flea trap and tossed out my "victims."

Otherwise, my parsley crop supplies enough curly and flat leaf parsley to make *tabbouleh*. When I had made enough of that refreshing salad for one season, friend Margritt Richter suggested chopping and freezing the surplus parsley.

Here's how. Rinse the parsley and let it dry. Mince it in a food processor and freeze unwrapped on a baking sheet. Then bag it. A shake of frozen parsley in January will decorate soups, stews and pasta with a welcome bit of green.

Dill is also a savory garnish. I use fresh dill sprigs to ornament sandwiches, chilled soups and salads. Traditionally, dill flavors fish, sauces and vegetables. Pickles, salad dressings and breads that demand stronger flavoring will find it in the seeds of this herb. And dill is easy to grow. Another friend, Linda Blood Hakala, pointed out that dill re-seeds itself, so I leave the stalks to winter over in the garden.

My sister, Roberta Love, can make anything grow. Lucky are the students at the high school where she is principal. Roberta has nurtured a magnificent lemon balm plant that sent me to the nursery as soon I arrived home. And for the next six springs, only a single pair of leaves emerged from the ground. That was it. The tag had suggested planting the herb in partial sun and that's what I did. Then, with nothing to lose but a couple of puny leaves, I followed friend Nancy Ancharski's advice: If an herb does not thrive in one place, move it to another. I moved the lemon balm into the vegetable garden–the last stop on the way to the compost bin–and for the first time, I had a large bouquet of lemon balm.

Despite the expostulations of the experts, the rules for cooking with herbs boil down to two.

First, remember that one measure of dry herbs equals three of fresh.

Secondly, add the herbs toward end of cooking or sprinkle on just before serving. Exception: if a recipe calls for the flavors to marry for a while, you should add the herbs in the beginning, with the other ingredients. This would apply, for instance, when marinating a leg of lamb in white wine and rosemary. Or chilling a pasta salad overnight.

Friends not only taught me to introduce herbs into my life gradually, but also rescued me from the hokum that characterizes much of herbal expertry. I have read that parsley is "the herb of life" and elsewhere that it is "the herb of death." Can oregano really cure addiction? Basil is supposed to cure both depression and infidelity. Maybe that's because, as an astrologer has actually written, this is the herb that is ruled by Mars.

Herbal advice? The best expert of all is a good friend.

When Evelyn Tilton of Keene gave me her zucchini pickle recipe she also gave me a jar of the pickles that added a bit of sunshine to our January table. Mrs. Tilton prefers to use the smaller zucchinis but adds that even large ones may be used by removing the seedy pulp and cutting the remaining firm flesh into chunks. She suggests the thriftiest way to buy mustard seed is in bulk at a natural foods store. "Sometimes I double the recipes and make it more colorful by adding sliced carrots, green beans or cauliflower florets," she said.

ZUCCHINI PICKLE

2 quarts sliced or chunked zucchini
2 cups sliced onions
1/4 cup coarse or pickling salt
1 cup water
2 cups vinegar
2 cups sugar
1 tablespoon mustard seed
1 teaspoon celery seed
1 teaspoon turmeric

Place the zucchini and onions in a large bowl and cover with the salt. Add the water. Let stand for 3 hours. Drain the vegetables and rinse with cool water. Drain again.

In a saucepan, mix vinegar, sugar, mustard seed, celery seed and turmeric and bring to a boil. Pour over the vegetables and let stand at least 2 hours or overnight.

Bring vegetable mixture to a full boil. Pack quickly into hot, sterilized jars and process in a boiling water bath for 5 minutes.

Makes 3 pints

Basil vinegar is a friendly gift from the country garden. This recipe also works well with tarragon or mint. For gifts or display, use a 10-ounce juice bottle. For a festive touch, insert a fresh basil stem in the bottle and top with a calico hat.

BASIL VINEGAR

1 quart white vinegar
1 quart Chablis
6 whole allspice
6 bay leaves
1 clove garlic, quartered
1 cup basil leaves
Basil leaves with stems

Mix vinegar, Chablis, allspice, bay, garlic and basil leaves in a large non-reactive pot. Bring to a boil and simmer for 30 minutes.

Pour into a crock or other non-reactive container and cover. Age for two weeks. Strain and bring to a boil. Pour into sterile jar.

Makes 2 quarts or six 10-ounce gift bottles

One summer, large black ants invaded my house and I became almost a full-time ant trapper. To discourage the ants, I tried many remedies including laying cucumber peels along their trails. I am not sure what finally drove the bugs away. But then what to do with all the peeled cucumbers? I made raita, a refreshing and cooling salad from India that can also be served in pocket bread. Use a slotted spoon to drain liquid and serve sandwiches immediately.

RAITA

1/2 cup yogurt
1 tablespoon honey
1 tablespoon vinegar
1/2 teaspoon mustard
1/2 teaspoon cumin
1/2 teaspoon coriander
2 cucumbers

Whisk together the yogurt, honey, vinegar, mustard, cumin and coriander. Peel cucumbers and cut lengthwise into quarters. Slice quarters crosswise into 1/3-inch pieces. Toss cucumber with yogurt sauce.
Makes 4 servings.

No matter how you pronounce pesto, you may be corrected. When I said, "PESS-toe," one evening at dinner, another guest, a psychology professor corrected me. "It's PASTE-toe," he insisted. I stood corrected until I checked the dictionary later. No matter. I concluded the best psychology was to forget the whole matter.

The splendid combination of fresh pesto tossed with hot pasta is one of the rewards of gardening. Leftover pesto may be frozen and later added by the spoonful to brighten winter tomato sauces or soups.

GARDEN PESTO WITH LINGUINE

2 cups fresh basil leaves
4 garlic cloves, peeled
1 tablespoon fresh mint
1 cup olive oil
1/2 cup walnuts or pine nuts
3/4 cups freshly grated Parmesan cheese
3/4 pound linguine

In the bowl of a food processor fitted with a steel blade, or in a blender jar, put basil, garlic, mint, oil, nuts and cheese. Process or blend until smooth.

Cook pasta in boiling salted water according package directions until tender but still firm. Drain and toss immediately with pesto.

Makes 4 servings.

This is a good impromptu lunch or light supper that uses pantry-shelf ingredients. The sauce can be prepared in advance and re-heated slowly while boiling the pasta.

Serve fettuccine with a fresh Italian bread and a lightly-dressed green salad tossed with julienned yellow bell pepper and sesame seeds. Chardonnay wine is a delicious accompaniment. For dessert, serve fresh fruit or a citrus sherbet.

SPINACH FETTUCCINE WITH CHICKPEAS

1 (15-ounce) can chickpeas
1/2 cup dry white wine
2 tablespoons olive oil
½ cup butter
2 cloves garlic, minced
½ cup finely chopped onion
9 ounces fresh spinach fettuccine
Or 8 ounces dried spinach fettuccine
1 tablespoon salt
¼ cup freshly grated Parmesan cheese
3 tablespoons fresh minced chives
9 cherry tomatoes, halved

Place chickpeas and their liquid in a saucepan. Add white wine, bring to a boil and then simmer 5 minutes. Keep warm. Melt butter in a saucepan and add onions, garlic and 1 tablespoon olive oil. Cook gently over low heat until onions are soft. Keep warm.

Bring 5 quarts of water to a boil Add 1 tablespoon olive oil and the salt.

Cook fettuccine according to package directions or until tender but still firm. Drain. Toss pasta with butter mixture. Using tongs, make a shallow bed of fettuccine on each plate. Spoon chickpeas and their liquid on top. Top with remaining fettuccine. Sprinkle with shredded cheese and top with the chives. Garnish with tomatoes. Serve immediately

Makes 3 servings.

SINCERITY

Whenever my friend Marjorie Graves declares some insincere person a "phony-baloney," I laugh. But the term does describe some food writers I have met on book promotion tours. Full of pronouncements and put-downs, these authors interrupt everyone, monopolize the microphone and blither away. On one talk show, the host asked me to describe a rice salad from my book. Before I said a word, I heard a shriek from another guest, the author of an Italian-American cookbook. "I never heard of a rice salad in Italy! In Italy, there are no rice salads!" She implied that anyone who was daft enough to make a rice salad might commit another unspeakable crime at any moment. Had I wandered into the wrong studio? Was this Geraldo's show on "Cookbook Authors Who Bash Other Cookbook Authors?" But later as I browsed the cookbook by the author who was upset by my rice salad, I had to agree with essayist M.F.K. Fisher who said," "Every cookbook no matter how crackpot, has one or two good things in it."

Just A Rumor That Won't Go Away

Whenever I see a recipe for onion marmalade, I smile. When someone earnestly describes the glass bits found by a friend in a jar of baby food, I nod. But my mind takes a hike. When an acquaintance tells me a famous chef billed her neighbor $250 for a recipe I think, "Let me out of here."

Such tales bring back the days when I was the food editor for a small newspaper. Now you might think the food beat–unlike politics, sports and religion–would not encourage any tricks from your sources. You would be wrong. Like all beginning editors, I quickly learned that a healthy skepticism is as important a tool as an unabridged dictionary.

Take for example, a simple recipe request. As I cashed my paycheck one Friday, the bank teller asked me if I could find an onion marmalade recipe for his wife.

I already had run recipes for hot pepper jelly and horseradish jelly–either is superb at cocktail time served with cream cheese on crackers. But onion marmalade was new to me. I promised the clerk I would check it out. Back at the office, I ran a classified ad asking for readers› help with the marmalade recipe hunt.

The replies trickled in. Eventually, I gathered enough information for a feature about onion marmalade. The story was no Pulitzer-Prize winner but it did the job. After the article appeared, I expected some word from the bank clerk. Nothing. Curious, I asked him if his wife found the recipes she needed.

"Oh, that. That was just a joke," the clerk explained. "My wife bet her friend she could get you to do a story about onion marmalade."

I was annoyed at the time. My boss Ken Zwicker comforted me with an old Maine saying. "You know, Pat, some people have more than their arm up their sleeve."

The marmalade may have been a joke to the bank clerk›s wife but I have since learned it is serious business to people who do indeed know their onions. This savory condiment is a brisk seller at fancy food stores. Gourmet food magazines offer onion marmalade recipes for the autumn and winter holidays.

One recipe includes Bermuda onions seasoned with rosemary, oregano and thyme. A Thanksgiving version calls for onions simmered with allspice and cloves and sprinkled with balsamic vinegar. Another autumn onion marmalade uses chestnuts and is served with roast turkey.

For a succulent roast chicken, Chinese chefs spread onion marmalade between the skin and breast of the bird. In Holland, a warm marmalade made with red onions, red wine and Tawny Port is served with venison.

The onion marmalade also appears in literature. In the mystery *Stardust*, by Robert B. Parker, detective Spenser and his girlfriend, Susan Silverman, dine on "duck breast sliced on the diagonal and served rare with onion marmalade, brown rice and brown rice and broccoli tossed with sesame tahini."

Even Betty Crocker offers her version of onion marmalade–take one ten-ounce jar apple jelly, heat until melted and add four tablespoons chopped onion. Betty, of all people, offers no serving suggestions. Even so, this marmalade would be an easy last-minute holiday gift. Just list a few serving suggestions on the gift tag: Use the marmalade to top crackers spread with cream cheese; as a garnish for lamb or combine with sour cream to glaze a pork roast.

The bank clerk's onion-marmalade joke was a bother but it was not nearly frustrating as the news tip that turned out to be a persistent rumor. Most novice editors–eager for a scoop–will chase quite a few rumors before learning how to spot one.

Take the rat tail in the birthday cake. This is how it goes: Somebody knows somebody who bought a cake at a local bakery. When the birthday cake was sliced, a rat's tail was revealed.

This rat tale arrived in the newsroom as predictably as the first robin of spring. The caller always named the same bakery–even though there were ten

different places in town that sold birthday cakes. The first time I took the call, I spent hours checking the story but I could never verify it.

It did not occur to me until later that at any birthday party, there are at least eight cameras and three videocams recording the event for posterity. Why didn't someone photograph the rat's tail? Or send the video to "American's Funniest Home Videos?" And why didn't I think to ask that at the time?

Perhaps there was a call waiting from another reader. The one who was upset with Mrs. Fields' Cookie Company. According to the caller, an elderly neighbor wrote Mrs. Fields for a copy of her chocolate chip cookie recipe. When the recipe arrived, so did a bill for $250. The caller fumed on, "This poor dear donates her cookies to the church and she gets a bill from a millionaire . . . ."

Sometimes the Fields rumor appears in a flyer that is distributed like a chain letter. One version states, "A woman who works with the American Bar Association called Mrs. Fields Cookie Company and asked for the attached recipe. She charged the requested $2.50 fee to her credit card. The charge turned out to be $250." In retaliation, the flyer explains, the recipe is being distributed free to all. Retaliation? The American Bar Association? What kind of mind dreams this stuff up?

The Fields Company has tried unsuccessfully to track the rumor's source.

Said Mr. Fields, "This is not our recipe. It isn't even close." Company officials will not reveal the trade-marked recipe–at any price. Why would they?

A similar rumor involves big city chefs. Someone's aunt dined out, ate a fabulous dinner and asked for the venison recipe. The chef handed over the formula. A few days later, a bill for $250 arrived in the mail.

I never checked that rumor because, when pressed the callers could not provide more than the name of the city: "I do know it happened at a Boston restaurant." Occasionally I heard this rumor at parties after someone discovered what I did for a living. Perhaps, I should have sent the tale-bearer a bill for $250 bill for listening. Such a gesture might have added some truth to a classic rumor.

Experts who collect and catalog such tales call them "urban myths." I never heard a single urban myth until I moved to the country and got a job in a small town. The myth experts–usually university-based sociologists–note that even when a newspaper runs a story debunking such a myth, readers remember only the rumor. And pass it on.

The experts also point out that the incident always happens to a friend of a friend–a FOAF for short. So whenever a FOAF is the source of a tale, you probably can dismiss the whole thing as rumor.

Better yet the next time someone tells you how much his friend was billed for Dolly Parton's bean dip recipe, suggest instead that if the FOAF wants a specific recipe, that she write to any fancy food magazine.

These magazines publish columns in which the correspondents gush like Old Faithful over dishes they had in certain restaurants. Just reading these treacley letters makes me gag.

For example, one reader writes, "Recently, I was in the Top of the Baobob Tree restaurant in Mombasa and had Eggs Benedict served on monkey bread napped with kiwi pesto. Could you please beg the chef to part with the recipe for this scrumptious creation?"

Or "When I ate at Pikes Pique in Seattle, I had 14-grain scones studded with Catawba raisins soaked in Swiss water-processed decaffeinated Jamaican mountain coffee steam-brewed from beans picked on the northern slopes. Can you persuade the chef to share this recipe with your readers?"

If you coat your request with enough sugar, you can get any recipe in the world–for free. Except maybe the American chop suey served at your child's cafeteria. That's only because the school lunch program doesn't have highly-paid publicists churning out phony recipe requests.

So pass the venison and the onion marmalade. For dessert let us have one of those warm chocolate chip cookies. The recipes are right here. You will not have to write away for them or have your credit card handy when you mix up a batch.

But if you must purchase a bit of cocktail party chatter, make that $250 check payable to me.

Mary's friends consider themselves fortunate to be on her Christmas gift list. A jar of her special marmalade gets the party season off to a good start. Mary suggests slightly warming the onion marmalade before serving. She spreads crackers with cream cheese or other soft, mild cheese and tops with her marmalade. Onion marmalade is also delightful on roast turkey sandwiches.

MARY B'S ONION MARMALADE

2 pounds yellow onions
1/2 cup unsalted butter
1 teaspoon salt
1/2 teaspoon freshly found pepper
1/2 cup sugar
2 tablespoons dry sherry
1/4 cup cider vinegar
1 cup robust red wine such as
zinfandel or burgundy
1/4 cup mild honey

Peel onions, halve lengthwise and cut crosswise into 1/2-inch pieces. In a large skillet over medium heat, melt butter. Stir in onions until coated with butter. Sprinkle with salt and pepper. Lower heat and cook and stir onions until golden–about 15 minutes.

Add the sugar, sherry, vinegar, wine and honey and cook until mixture is thick and dark–about 1 hour and 15 minutes. Stir occasionally and watch that mixture does not burn. Taste and correct seasoning if necessary. Store in refrigerator.

Makes 4 cups.

One year, my sister Joan, gave each of her Christmas Day guests a gift of this hot pepper jelly. I stockpiled the jelly to serve with a glass of wine or cider to drop-in holiday guests. Serve Joan's jelly with a crock of cream cheese and a basket of crackers. The cook gets to choose the color of the jelly.

HOT PEPPER JELLY

3/4 cup finely chopped green or red bell peppers
1/4 cup finely chopped red or green hot peppers
1-1/2 cups cider vinegar
6-1/2 cups sugar
2 3-ounce pouches liquid fruit pectin
2 to 3 drops red or green food coloring, if desired

Wear gloves to chop hot peppers. Put the peppers and 2 tablespoons of the vinegar in a food processor and process until liquefied. In a large saucepan, combine peppers with remaining vinegar and sugar and bring to a boil over high heat Remove from heat and stir in pectin and food coloring Bring back to a boil and skim off any foam that may form.

Pour into sterilized pint jars and seal.

Makes 5 8-ounce jars.

The following recipe is from my friend, Jane Roberts, a Chicago-based flight attendant. Jane's chocolate chip cookies are quick to mix and they make a big batch. I bake a dozen and then divide the rest of the batter into three or four batches and freeze. The cookie dough is like money in the bank when someone drops in for coffee.

For a variation, add a cup of nuts or raisins or both.

NOT-AT-ALL-THE-MALL COOKIE

1 cup margarine or butter
1 cup sugar
1 cup brown sugar
2 eggs
2 teaspoons vanilla
2-1/2 cups oatmeal
1/2 teaspoon salt
1 teaspoon baking powder
1 teaspoon baking soda
2 cups flour
1 16-ounce bag milk chocolate chips

Cream together butter, sugar and brown sugar until light and fluffy. Beat in eggs and vanilla. After measuring oatmeal, put small amounts in a blender or food processor and whirl oatmeal until it turns to powder.

Preheat oven to 375 degrees. Stir together oatmeal, salt, baking powder, baking soda and flour. Stir into butter-egg mixture. Add chocolate chips and mix in. If the dough seems too dry, add a little water, a tablespoon at a time.

Spoon golf-ball size chunks of dough onto an ungreased cookie sheet. Flatten slightly. Bake for six minutes. Remove from cookie sheet and cool on a rack. These are soft cookies that will be large and thick. Makes 4 to 5 dozen cookies.

Bill Silvester is a United Airlines captain based in Chicago. Whenever we meet, Bill recounts his latest food adventure in say, San Diego or Madrid. Once, when I mentioned to him that I could not get fish sauce in New Hampshire, I found a bottle of this pungent liquid fermenting away in my mailbox at O'Hare Airport. Another time, this recipe. Bill got it from a chef in Spain. And not a peseta changed hands. Also, if you don't have asparagus, use green peas.

CAPTAIN BILLY'S ARROZ CON POLLO

1-3-1/2 pound cut up broiler-fryer
¼ cup olive oil
1/2 cup chopped onion
2 cloves garlic, minced
1/2 cup chopped green peppers
3-1/2 cups chicken broth
1 28-ounce can chopped tomatoes
1 15-ounce can chick peas, rinsed, drained
1 4-ounce jar pimientos, chopped
10 ripe olives

1/4 cup raisins
1 teaspoon salt
¼ teaspoon fresh ground pepper
1 bay leaf
¼ teaspoon saffron, crushed
¼ cup dry sherry
2 cups raw regular long-grain rice
1 10-ounce pkg. frozen asparagus
2 hard-cooked eggs

In a 5-quart Dutch oven over medium high-heat, brown chicken a few pieces at a time in the heated oil. Remove chicken from pan and set aside.

Lower heat to medium and add onion, garlic, green pepper to drippings.

Cook and stir until onion is tender, about 4 minutes. Stir in broth, tomatoes, chick peas, pimientos, olives, raisins, salt, pepper, bay leaf, saffron and sherry. Heat to boiling.

Stir in rice and add chicken to pan. Reduce heat to low and simmer 30 minutes or until chicken is almost fork tender. Continue cooking for 15 minutes. Discard bay leaf.

Cook asparagus according to package directions. Serve the chicken and rice garnished with the peas and hard-cooked egg.

Makes 4 servings.

This is a good dip to tote to an appetizers-and-drinks potluck. It can be made the day before. To make a lighter version, use ground turkey, reduced-fat sour cream and reduced-fat cheese. For an 8-layer dip, top the bean layer with 2 cups guacamole.

SEVEN-LAYER MEXICAN DIP

1 pound ground beef, cooked, drained
1 16-ounce jar salsa
2 cups (8 ounces) shredded Cheddar cheese
1 16-ounce can refried beans
2 medium tomatoes, chopped
1 fresh jalapeno, seeded and chopped
4 green onions, sliced
1 cup sour cream
1/2 cup black olives
Tortilla chips

Mix the ground beef with 1 cup of the salsa. Spread on the bottom of a large shallow serving dish such as 8-1/2-by-11-inch, 2.5 liter or 3-quart casserole. Sprinkle 1 cup of the cheese over the meat mixture. Spoon all of the beans on top of the cheese. Pour remaining salsa on top of the beans.

In a small bowl, combine the chopped tomatoes, jalapeno and green onions. Place 1/2 cup of this mixture on the bean-salsa layer. Top this with the remaining 1 cup grated cheese. Spread sour cream on top of the cheese layer spreading to edge of dish. Sprinkle sour cream with remaining tomato mixture and black olives. Cover with plastic wrap and refrigerate. Serve with tortilla chips.

Makes 12 appetizer servings.

The Nuts Of Disillusionment

When I tasted my first macadamia nut, I did not know what a fat gram was. All I knew was that just one of these creamy, buttery nuts would never be enough. I had to eat a few more. These macadamias were salted but then so was everything else. I quenched my thirst with a sugary soda pop. What were a few hundred more calories?

I was a young flight attendant at the time and we served macadamia nuts with drinks to everybody on board–first class and whatever other classes there were back in the Sixties. Airplanes were smaller and passengers were fewer so the cost of a munchy was insignificant. The cocktails themselves were free. Salty peanuts glopped with "honey roast" and a $6 martini had not been invented.

We flight attendants nibbled the macadamias as we served the cocktails. I guess we figured that if something was free, it had no calories. We served macadamias because our airline flew the Hawaiian route–which was somewhere beyond the Milky Way as far as we were concerned. We were junior Newark, New Jersey-based flight attendants and we flew to Detroit, Pittsburgh and Philadelphia. The "older girls"—all of twenty eight years of age flew to Hawaii wearing flowered gowns.

The closest I had ever been to Honolulu was a 1940s radio show beamed every Saturday night from the Hawaiian Room of the Lexington Hotel in New York City. When my dad sat back in his chair and listened to *"Sweet Leilani,"* he dreamed about strolling those island beaches and the frigid Buffalo winter receded.

Today Hawaii is no longer just a dream for many people. If you have a credit card, you go. But you probably will have to buy your own macadamias nuts when you get there. They are just too pricey to hand out like Halloween candy on every flight.

Sometimes, the macadamia nuts reappear on first-class flights. However, the little pyramid-shaped packages may evoke a shudder–instead of a cry of delight. That's because some business travelers eat only what is unsalted, non-carbonated, non-alcoholic, de-caffeinated, artificially-sweetened and fat-free. For them, oat bran pretzels are about as decadent as it gets.

"If you eat peanuts, the fat grams take away the mental edge you need in real estate," an earnest young man told me. "Any drink with bubbles will bloat your thighs," said a consultant as she waved away a glass of sparkling water.

Don't get me wrong. Sensible eating and drinking are a good idea. But they are not a religion. You cannot go through life without an occasional treat. And I am not talking about the 9 a.m. Monday Bloody Mary on the commuter flight to from Chicago to Minneapolis. Or a Philadelphia cheese steak sandwich for lunch every day.

However, I, for one, would not have missed out on the macadamias. Even now that I know how many fat grams these little nuts contain. Of course, if I had paid attention to an alternative school of medicine called the Doctrine of Signatures, it would not have taken me so long to figure out the macadamia's fat content. According to the Signatures' Doctrine, a plant with a kidney-shaped leaf can cure a sick kidney. Whether you believe that one or not, the fact is that if you eat enough macadamia nuts, you will assume their shape: round.

In the macadamia-chomping years of my youth, I was always on some kind of diet. Like everyone else, I followed the 1960s best-selling diet books because they gave us permission to eat anything. Titles like *Calories Don't Count, The Drinking Man's Diet* and *The Air Force Diet* offered high-fat, high-sugar menus. None of these books mentioned exercise. Or macadamias. So I figured the nuts must be okay and as we all knew back then, exercise only increased your appetite. Like all the other diet hopefuls, I lost only the price of the books.

On the other hand, if I had actually planted, harvested and cracked a few macadamia nuts, I would have burned plenty of calories on the job. Which explains why macadamias are so expensive. The crops demand constant attention and even a small orchard requires a large capital investment.

The macadamia tree originated in the Australian rain forest where it was called *kindal kindal* by the local people. In the 1850s, a British botanist, Ferdinand von Mueller, who was studying Queensland flora, came across a magnificent *kindal-kindal* tree. He renamed it for his friend, scientist John Macadam. Like Denali, the local name for Mount McKinley, *kindal-kindal* feels better on the tongue. But the new name stuck and macadamia was the name exporters used in the 1880s when they shipped seedlings to warm places like California and Kenya. The macadamia tree did take root in many sub-tropical places but it flourished best in the volcanic soil of Hawaii's Big Island.

For generations, the Hawaiians were content to simply appreciate the tree's beauty. In the 1930s, a transplanted New Englander, Ernest von Tassel, who was in Hawaii for his health recognized the macadamia nut's commercial possibilities. He began the long, difficult process of breeding trees that would produce a predictable crop.

Today, each cultivated macadamia tree begins as a seedling grafted from superior nut-bearing stock. Two years later, when the sapling can stand by itself in the coarse lava, it is transplanted to an orchard. At age seven the macadamia tree will bear its first crop and about eight years later, the mature tree will produce about six crops a year. Macadamia orchards now cover about 14,000 acres on the Big Island.

When a macadamia nut is ripe, it drops to the ground. Which would be convenient–except that the tree sheds many of its leaves at the same time. Before the nuts can be collected, the leaves must be blown away.

After harvest, the nuts are husked, dried and cured. Then comes the cracking of the earth's toughest nut–the shells yield to no less than 300 pounds pressure per square inch. Personally, I think that sounds like too much trouble. I suspect that somewhere in the tropical rain forest, there is a creature that can pop open a macadamia nut in a second.

After all, here in New England, our chestnuts and hazelnuts are also tough nuts to crack. Yet every fall, the white-tailed deer and red squirrels husk and split open dozens of our chestnuts. Our dooryard regular–the tiny red-breasted nut hatch–was originally named "nut hack" for its ability to pry open a hazelnut. In Nature's grand design, the birds and beasts liberate the tough nuts to insure the next generation of trees.

But until we discover how the rain forest critters do it, the macadamia nut industry will rely on a system of counter-rotating steel rollers spaced to pound open each nut without splitting the precious kernel.

After shelling, the macadamias are color-sorted, roasted in high-grade coconut oil and sorted again. The fancy grade whole nuts are lightly salted and packed for retail sales. They cost about $15 a pound–nearly four times the price of almonds. Some fancy grade nuts are available unsalted for baking and for people who must restrict their sodium. The macadamias that do not make the grade are used for nut brittle and ice cream. My favorite–the unsalted broken pieces–are sometimes available in natural foods stores at a favorable price. These bits are just right for cooking and baking.

Now about that fifteen dollars a pound. I know what you are thinking. Why not plant your own macadamia tree and in fifteen years . . . . Well, I have already considered relocating to Hilo, Hawaii, and planting a couple of trees. Like our hill top in New Hampshire, Hilo is a congenial place to live and garden. The abundance of sushi, lush foliage and rainbows do tempt me.

On the other hand, despite my record of impractical, upcountry do-yourself-projects, I am willing to concede that macadamia nut culture is not a backyard project. Even after seventy years of breeding trials and commercial production, there are no guarantees on how any one macadamia sapling will perform. A tree grafted from high quality parents may produce inferior or bitter nuts. Or no nuts at all.

However, if you live in a warm place, and you want a splendid ornamental tree, you could not do better than a macadamia. Its shiny evergreen of the year. All you need is a single tree because the macadamia's love life requires neither a partner nor an assist from the birds and bees. In other words, each self-pollinating blossom contains both pistils and stamens.

I am willing to delegate macadamia culture to the hard-working pros and pay the price when I want to splurge. To protect my perishable investment, I store the nuts in the refrigerator or freezer. And when a midnight nut craving surfaces, I try to focus on the $1.99 jar of dry-roasted peanuts.

For cooking, you can use macadamias any way you use almonds, hazelnuts or walnuts. Consider adding the nuts to pie crust, chocolate biscotti or ordinary chocolate chip cookies. Or be inspired by the ultimate mall cookie: white chocolate chunk macadamia nut.

Macadamias also work well in savory dishes. Add finely-chopped macadamias to the breading for mild, white-fleshed fish or chicken. Chef Thomas B.H. Wong of the Royal Hawaiian on Waikiki serves Macadamia-Crusted Lamb Chops with Japanese eggplant, pickled mango ratatouille and three-cheese polenta. You can also use macadamias in salads, stuffings, pastas and pilafs.

I use a chef's knife to chop the nuts chop so I can control the outcome. You can use a food processor fitted with a metal blade but be very careful to pulse the machine on and off. Otherwise you will end up with an oily paste. To heighten flavor, toast the whole nuts or large bits in a 350-degree oven for three to four minutes or until lightly browned. Again, pay attention.

When Edward and I were touring the Big Island, we stopped at the Mauna Loa plantation where I hoped for an orchard and factory tour. I have been writing this essay in my head for more than thirty years and figured that an on-the-scene look would get my thoughts out of my head and onto paper.

Well, there was no tour available on a Saturday but we did visit the plantation's gift and snack shops. And strolled around a small but lovely meditative garden with labeled native specimens.

Unfortunately, the entire scene was overrun with frantic tourists. ("Okay, folks, you have 14-1/2 minutes to decide between milk and bittersweet chocolate-covered macadamias, use the facilities and buy an ice cream cone. Then we must leave for our next stop–a day in Australia–before heading for our night in Hong Kong.")

A convoy of tour buses with their engines running filled the island air with exhaust fumes. In the snack shop, a video about macadamia farming and processing was running at top volume. No one was watching. I am grateful the leaf-blowing machines and their operators had the day off.

We escaped south to the Hawaii Volcanoes National Park. There we walked on warm earth spouting steam. On a peaceful overlook, I took out my cache of just-purchased nuts. We savored the view and freshest, creamiest macadamia nuts I have ever tasted.

It did not matter that six of these fat little nuts contain 11.7 grams of fat. It did not even matter that the eleven grams were the good kind–unsaturated. At that moment, who cared? After all, the ever-active Kilauea might discharge a river of red hot molten lava at any moment. Roasted macadamias, indeed.

"I've been living socially on this dessert for years," says our friend Connie Wood. "It is so easy and so delicious." During the 1960s and 1970s, Connie's stately eighteenth century house, a former inn, was the beginning of the campaign trail for many Democratic candidates seeking the Presidential nomination. Of this recipe, Connie says with a grin, "This dessert is not exactly a natural food. But people always ask for the recipe."

CONNIE WOOD'S NUT BRITTLE CAKE

1 10-inch angel food cake
1 pint heavy cream
1 cup crushed macadamia or peanut brittle

Just before serving, whip cream and fold in the peanut brittle. Spread on cake and serve immediately.

Makes 8 to 10 servings.

This recipe comes from a good cook who was selling her bread at a fund-raising bake sale at Kailua (KY LOO A), Kona, on the Big Island. It is delicious made with macadamia nuts but when I don't have them, I use walnuts.

KAILUA KONA BANANA RUM BREAD

2 cups flour
2 teaspoons baking soda
1 teaspoon mace
1 cup sugar
1 cup chopped macadamia nuts
1/2 cup vegetable oil, preferably canola
2 eggs
1 cup mashed ripe bananas
1 teaspoon lemon juice
2 tablespoons rum

Grease a 9-by-5-inch loaf pan. Stir together flour, baking soda, mace, sugar and nuts. Beat together oil, eggs, bananas, lemon juice and rum. Stir oil mixture into flour mixture just long enough to mix. Batter will be lumpy. Spoon batter into prepared pan and let sit for 20 minutes.

Preheat oven to 350 degrees. Bake for 45 minutes to an hour or until a toothpick inserted in the middle of the loaf comes out clean. Cool in pan 5 minutes. Remove from pan and cool on a wire rack.

Makes 1 9-by-5-inch loaf.

In the years I wrote a newspaper food column, I published more than 3,000 recipes. When faithful readers learned about my first cookbook, *The Nine Seasons Cookbook,* they looked forward to having all their recipes in one place. Well, only 150 recipes made the final cut. Lois Hastings, a librarian at the Keene Public Library, told me she was disappointed the recipe for "The World's Best Cookies" was not in my book. So here's to Lois and all the other Cheshire County librarians who are among the world's best.

WORLD'S BEST COOKIES

1 cup butter
1 cup sugar
1 cup brown sugar
1 egg
1 cup vegetable oil
1 teaspoon pure vanilla extract
1/2 cup shredded coconut
1/2 cup chopped macadamia nuts,
3-1/2 cups sifted all-purpose flour
1 teaspoon soda
1 teaspoon salt
1 cup regular rolled oats
I cup crushed cornflakes
walnuts or pecans

Cream together the butter and sugars until fluffy. Add egg, salad oil and vanilla. Mix well. This step may be done in a food processor.

Stir together the flour, soda and salt. Add oats, cornflakes, coconut and nuts and stir well. Combine butter and flour mixture and mix well. Chill for easy handling.

Preheat oven to 325 degrees. Form cookie dough into balls the size of walnuts. Dip in sugar. Place on an ungreased cookie sheet. Flatten with a fork dipped in water. Bake for 12 minutes. Cool for 3 minutes and then remove to a wire rack.

Makes 8 dozen cookies. The dough may be mixed ahead and frozen.

This chutney goes well with grilled or broiled fish or chicken.

FRESH PEAR MACADAMIA CHUTNEY

2 cups pared, seeded chopped pears
1/2 cup brown sugar, packed in cup
1/2 cup cider vinegar
1/4 cup chopped onion
1 teaspoon minced ginger root
1 teaspoon minced garlic
½ cup chopped macadamia nuts

In a 2-quart saucepan, combine chopped pears, brown sugar, cider vinegar, onion, garlic and ginger root. Bring to a boil, lower heat and simmer uncovered, stirring occasionally, for 20 to 30 minutes or until thickened.

Stir in nuts. Makes 1 cup chutney.

"I like recipes that are quick and easy but very good," says friend Diane Wood of Albany, N.Y. Diane teaches at both the elementary and graduate school levels. She also is a very handy person who has renovated several houses and built her own furniture. Here is her favorite mousse. It will delight your guests and make entertaining easier for you.

MIRACLE BLENDER MOUSSE

1 egg
1 teaspoon vanilla extract
Dash salt
2 tablespoons sugar
1 cup semi-sweet chocolate chips
¾ cup milk
¼ cup unsalted macadamia nuts, finely chopped

Scald milk. In the following order, place in blender: the egg, vanilla, salt, sugar and chocolate chips. Pour milk over ingredients. Blend on high for 1 minute. Pour into stemmed glasses. Cover with plastic wrap and chill for at least two hours. just before serving, sprinkle with chopped nuts.

Makes 4 ½ cup servings.

What Miss Adams Knew About The Sibling Revelry

If anyone is trained in the art and science of entertaining, it is I. When I was in college, women did not study law or medicine. Instead, we were steered into nursing or teaching. And it was there, in home economics training, I learned how to give teas, luncheons and dinners.

During a six-week (24 hours a day, seven days a week) residency at an elegant house just off campus, we took a course titled, "Practicum in Home Management." During the course, each student was required to host an event, which played a big part in our final grade. Days in advance of the actual event, we submitted a detailed plan that included the menu, the recipes, a shopping list, preparation and serving timetables, a table setting diagram, a list of linens, silver, china, glassware and serving dishes, a seating chart and a sketch of the centerpiece. All the details that doctors and lawyers turn over to caterers.

Our assignment included listing three topics for table conversation. A good hostess, we were taught, provided congenial talk to aid her guests' digestion.

Acceptable subjects were the weather (our college was in Buffalo, New York) and "current events" –excluding religion and politics. Our professor, the stately Miss Lois Adams of Mattoon, Illinois, had veto power over our proposed topics.

That was in 1959. By 1969, teas and ladies› luncheons were as rare as martinis and cigarettes. No one I knew planned dinner conversations or fretted over mismatched teaspoons. Paper napkins and plastic plates were served to guests without apology.

Even I became realistic about entertaining. I recognized that the most I could do was an infrequent potluck for old friends or soup and bread for good neighbors.

However, any magazine article that insists there are easy ways to entertain can still tempt me. Say a dessert buffet or a Sunday brunch.

The dessert buffet appeals to me. I visualize double-fudge brownies, a carrot cake, a blueberry cheesecake and a raspberry torte; each perched on a footed crystal plate lined with a gold lace doily. Then, as I research the dessert wines—with names such as *etwastrinkenweisenheimer—I realize* that inviting people to dinner is easier. Especially the part about selecting companion wines and beer.

I check our schedules and select a date for a dinner party. Sometimes, I dally and the date comes and goes before I make a single phone call. One time, I did get as far as the phone calls and planned a farewell dinner for a couple who was moving away. But it turned out the guests of honor were busy that night.. Fortunately, I had not told them the event was in their honor. The other guests were available and the rest of us had a fine time–for no reason at all.

Then there is the occasional grand feast I organize when August warms the earth and the garden bursts into pink cosmos and red-ruffled lettuce. Our clearing in the forest becomes the perfect setting for the family gathering we call the "Sibling Revelry." Suddenly, the spirit of Miss Adams kicks in. No, I do not use freshly ironed, starched-to-perfection damask tablecloths rolled around mailing tubes. I do use sticky notes to remind me which salad goes into which favorite bowl.

My chore and shopping lists, menu notes and recipe printouts would surely earn an A+ from Miss Adams. On party day, I post the menu and the recipes in the kitchen to make sure I serve everything I prepared. When savvy guests arrive, they head for the bulletin board. Later, my many kitchen helpers refer to the board as we fill and garnish the platters.

It took me awhile to work out the "Sibling Revelry." My oldest sister, Joan, inspired me. Joan and I share a passion for thrift, the homemade, the bargain and fairness in the marketplace. We take our complaints to the store managers and manufacturers and take satisfaction in the results we get. We are the opposites of our other two sisters, Mary and Roberta, generously indulgent wives, mothers and daughters who shop to the tinkling of a Nordstrom's piano.

Joan lives in Connecticut and she and her husband, Geoffrey, her children and grandchildren, gather at holidays for a cooperative feast filled with delightful food and good cheer. If it had not been for Joan's celebration, Edward and I would have spent one Christmas alone listening to the drip, drip of an ice dam leaking into our kitchen.

Our immediate family–Edward's children and grandchildren–live in distant places like San Juan and Denver and their journeys require at least one overnight. Where, I wondered, would all these people sleep? They would not all fit into this six-room cottage built in 1815 by the Lincolns who farmed this reluctant stone-studded land. Then Bingo! I went to the local tourist bureau and found brochures listing accommodations from quaint and expensive inns to thrifty chains. Our guests worked out their own reservations.

The first year the revelry weather was sunny and clear. And so was the next year but we rented a tent just in case. We discovered we liked gathering outdoors in the shade surrounded by country fresh air. The year it poured, the tent was essential. We chose the yellow and white striped tent because those colors look splendid against the intense greens that compose a New England summer. I sewed tablecloths of royal blue bandanna print and served the food on yellow plates. Cosmos, zinnias, hydrangeas and black-eyed Susans spilled out of the old glass milk bottles I use for vases.

Just how do you do this, a friend asked. "Do you write it all down?" Yes, of course. In fact, I write and re-write lists on a yellow legal pad. But for me the key is doing as much as possible ahead of time. The final version of each page goes into a hanging file that also holds the rental receipt for the table, chairs and tent. Thanks to my airline schedule, I can have five consecutive days off to prepare the food. This precious chunk of time lets me cook in a thoughtful, leisurely pace. At each step, I get to savor the good feelings that come from cooking for the people I love.

My menu begins with a turkey that I roast ahead and serve chilled or a ham baked the day of the event. In either case, I roast the meat in an oven bag, a work saver suggested by my sister, Roberta. The ham requires less carving skill and its leftovers are easily dealt with and stored. Until recently, ham was too expensive for even an occasional festive meal. Thanks to the fat police, the price of ham has slipped to a reasonable level.

For one Sibling Revelry, I made a colorful pasta salad that called for green, red and yellow sweet peppers. That recipe came from a pretentious food magazine and unfortunately, the salad tasted as bland as steam-table macaroni and cheese. I redeemed the salad with red pepper sauce, fresh ground pepper and sea salt and the next year went back to my black-eyed pea ditalini salad.

Other classic make-ahead items include *tabbouleh* and baked beans. My niece, Bridget Love, introduced me to sesame noodles at a Chinese restaurant, and I added them to the revelry menu. But I only get the sesame noodles right every other time–no matter what recipe I use. One time, the noodles were gluey and dry. Another time, they were moist, chewy and fragrant with coriander and sesame. I have learned to use the freshest possible noodles. Still, even at their worst, my noodles were not as astonishingly awful as those at a Chinese restaurant near LaGuardia Airport–huge lumps of dry, choke-inducing peanut butter dumped on a pasty pile of noodles boiled a long time ago. And the white wine that accompanied the noodles is best forgotten.

For beverages I offer regular and alcohol-free beer plus California Chardonnay and Sauvignon Blanc. However, the current revelry favorite is iced tea brewed by the half gallon in the refrigerator. As the tea brews, I slip in a couple of mint stalks gathered by Edward on his morning walk along a brook that is rushing downhill toward the Connecticut River on its way to Long Island Sound.

I have experimented with several desserts. Ice cream with homemade hot fudge sauce was a delightful temperature contrast on an August night but scooping ice cream for 25 was a last-minute hassle. Next, I made a carrot cake with Irish cream liqueur frosting but that too required last-minute whipping of cream. The carrot cake was delicious but it lacked ooh-ah eye appeal One year, Peter made a superb chocolate cake for his sister, Christine's birthday. How wonderful to have a stepson who reads Rose Levy's Cake Bible as carefully as he reads the Law Journal. I discovered a recipe for blueberry lemon bars that fits into my make-ahead scheme. And every year we get a few more handfuls of berries from our own cultivated bushes.

As skilled as I have become in organizing the "Sibling Revelry," each year I learn something new. Miss Adams would be pleased that I continue to have what she called "learning experiences."

Sometimes, my teacher is only eight years old. When our invitation arrived in New Jersey one year, our granddaughter, Kim Morris, daughter of Vincent and Miriam, asked her mother if "Grandma," Edward's first wife, was going to be at the Sibling Revelry. Miriam–like me a second wife–said no, Grandma was not coming to the party. Later, Miriam told me and we smiled about it.

Then I thought, "Well, wait a minute, Nancy is the mother of these wonderful children and the grandmother to another generation of splendid children and we are all friends. So why shouldn't she be here celebrating with us?"

It turned out that Nancy was as delighted to be here as Edward and I were to have her. And thanks to Kim, our family circle is a little wider and a little more complete. Even Miss Adams would have approved.

This is a wonderful relish-like salad to make when the garden is full of bell peppers, parsley, and basil. If time is short, used drained canned corn or frozen kernels refreshed under cold running water. I quadruple the recipe for large parties. It can be made two days ahead and stored in the refrigerator.

BELL PEPPER AND CORN SALAD

4 cups corn kernels, (8 ears fresh corn)
1 red bell pepper, diced
1 green bell pepper, diced
1 yellow bell pepper, diced
1/4 cup chopped fresh parsley
1/4 cup olive oil
2 tablespoons lemon juice
2 tablespoons grated Parmesan cheese
1 garlic clove, minced
Fresh ground pepper and salt

Blanch the corn in boiling water for 3 minutes. Drain. Refresh with cold water and drain again. Blanch the diced peppers in boiling water for 1 to 2 minutes. Drain. Refresh under cold water. Drain.

In a serving bowl, gently toss the corn, bell peppers and the parsley.

Using a whisk or a food processor, combine lemon juice, Parmesan cheese and garlic. Pour over corn mixture, tossing gently to coat. Taste and add fresh ground pepper and salt to taste.

Makes 6 servings.

Microwave tip: Put three ears fresh corn in a zipper bag with two tablespoons water. Leave a three-inch opening in center of zipper for steam to escape. Microwave on high 7 to 8 minutes.

SESAME NOODLES

2 tablespoons sesame seeds
3 tablespoons cider vinegar
1/4 cup peanut butter
1 tablespoon honey mustard
2 tablespoons soy sauce
1 tablespoon hot chili oil
1/3 cup dark sesame oil
1/4 cup vegetable oil
1/4 cup freshly squeezed orange juice
Salt and freshly ground pepper
8 ounces thin spaghetti, preferably fresh
Sprigs of coriander for garnish

Place sesame seeds in hot, dry skillet and toss gently over high heat until lightly toasted. Set aside.

Combine vinegar, peanut butter, honey mustard and soy sauce. Gradually stir oils into peanut butter mixture. Add orange juice, salt and pepper. For a spicier dressing add a few more drops of chili oil.

Bring a pot of salted water to boil. Add spaghetti and boil and stir for until noodles are cooked but still have some bite. Fresh noodles cook more quickly than dried noodles. Drain immediately, shaking to remove excess moisture. Quickly rinse with cold water, drain again and transfer to a bowl.

Toss with dressing. Cover tightly. Chill for at least 30 minutes before serving. Sprinkle with sesame seeds and garnish with coriander before serving.

Makes 4 servings.

This tea is simple to make. Even better, it stays clear and does not get bitter. For easy removal of tea bags, fasten them together with a twist tie and drape tags over edge of bottle before putting on cap.

EASY ICED TEA

5 black tea or herbal tea bags
2 quarts water

Place tea bags in a 2-quart pitcher or a 1/2-gallon juice bottle. Fill with cool water. Refrigerate for a few hours or overnight. Remove tea bags. Add flavoring such as lemon, mint, sugar or honey. Makes 2 quarts.

ROTINI PASTA SALAD

Dressing
1-1/2 cups olive oil
1-1/2 cups cider vinegar
1/3 cup light soy sauce
1 tablespoon sesame oil
1 clove garlic, minced
1 tablespoon minced fresh ginger
1 teaspoon fresh ground pepper
1/2-teaspoon red pepper flakes
1/3 cup chopped cilantro or parsley

Mix dressing ingredients in a food processor or whisk together. Dressing can be prepared up to one week ahead. Store in refrigerator. Bring to room temperature before mixing with rotini.

Salad
1 teaspoon salt
1 teaspoon margarine
2 pounds rotini (spiral pasta)
2 diced green bell peppers
2 diced red bell peppers
1 diced yellow bell pepper
1 cup thinly sliced green onion
1 cup shredded carrot
Fresh ground pepper
Salt
1/3-cup sesame seeds

Prepare dressing. Preheat oven to 350. Place sesame seeds in a shallow pan and toast in oven until golden brown about 5 to 8 minutes. Check after 5 minutes and shake pan. Bring a large pot of water to a boil. Add salt and margarine. Add rotini and cook and stir until it is just al dente. Do not overcook. Drain rotini and rinse with cold water to stop cooking. Drain thoroughly.

In a large bowl, gently toss rotini with peppers and onion. Add dressing and mix gently but well. Taste and adjust seasoning. Just before serving, sprinkle sesame seeds on top.

May be made two days ahead. Store in refrigerator.

Makes 20 servings.

LEMON BLUEBERRY BARS

1 cup butter, softened
¾ cup sifted powdered sugar
2 cups all-purpose flour
4 eggs
1-1/2 cup granulated sugar
1/3 cup fresh lemon juice (2 lemons)
¼ cup all-purpose flour
1 teaspoon baking powder
1-1/2 cup fresh blueberries
Powdered sugar

Preheat oven to 350 degrees. Grease a 13-by-9-by-2 inch baking pan. Beat butter to soften. Add ¾ cup powdered sugar and beat to combine. Beat in 2 cups flour until mixed thoroughly. Press mixture into bottom of prepared pan. Bake until golden, about 20 minutes.

Meanwhile, mix eggs, granulated sugar, lemon juice. ¼ cup flour and baking powder. Beat until thoroughly mixed.

Sprinkle berries evenly on top of baked crust. Pour egg mixture over berries. Smooth with the back of a large spoon. Bake until light brown and filling is set, about 30 to 35 minutes.

Cool in pan on a rack. Cut into 30 bars. Just before serving, sift powdered sugar over bars.

To make ahead, cover cooled pan of cut bars and store in refrigerator for up to 2 days. To freeze, place cut bars in a freezer container and freeze up to 3 months. Thaw, covered, in refrigerator for 24 hours before serving.

INGENUITY

When Mother responded to my teenage demands with, "Use it up, wear it out, make it do or do without," I wanted to scream. Both Mother and I grew up in Buffalo. She survived the deprivations of the Great Depression and two world wars. I was a child of the abundant 1950s. Everyone I knew counted on a good job in a factory, a big American car, a motorboat and a summer cottage.

Eventually, I settled in New England and without noticing, I embraced the habit of Yankee ingenuity. As I learned to grow, cook and preserve our food, "Use it up" played like a mantra in my brain. It became a matter of pride to rescue, say, overripe mushrooms instead of tossing them into the compost. Some of my most memorable soups resulted from applying ingenuity to wilting vegetables.

May Mother's spirit of "Waste not, want not" challenge others as it has me and perhaps one day everyone on earth will have enough to eat.

The Magic Circle Of Juniper

The fringe of juniper that surrounds our clearing has always intrigued me. This silver-blue evergreen demands no special care and has no enemies that I know of. In the long, cold months when our world is white, grey or brown, the sprawling, close-to-the-ground juniper offers a reassuring sign of green in our dooryard. Best of all, this plant produces a berry that is prized for seasoning.

Of course, I did not know any of this until I moved to the country. As I settled in, I began to understand that conifer–not pine–was the family name for most evergreens. I learned to make fragrant balsam wreaths, planted 1,000 spruce seedlings for Christmas Future and decorated gift packages with tiny hemlock cones.

But how to use our bountiful crop of juniper berries eluded me. One cooking encyclopedia dismissed the berries in a single paragraph. "three to six berries per serving are prized for seasoning game, bean dishes and gin. One-half teaspoon of berries in a marinade or a stew is the seasoning equivalent of one- quarter cup gin."

Good cooks do season baked beans with bourbon and beef stew with red wine. But gin? Even gin drinkers disguise the spirit's taste with sweetened tonic and lime.

When I was a young Madison Avenue copywriter, I drank martinis because that is what my boss drank. When I sipped a martini from a sleek art deco glass, I felt like a sophisticated New Yorker. But the martini, the lunch staple of high-powered ad men-was too strong for me. Entire afternoons evaporated in a gin-and-vermouth fog.

When Edward proposed marriage, I quickly accepted, quit the agency, and moved to the country. The leisurely hours for martini-sipping disappeared; there were beans to plant, wood to stack, books to write, an 1815 house that drained our time and energy with it constant demands for major repairs.

By the time I discovered our juniper berries and the tip about perking up the taste of a bottle of gin with a few fresh berries, I no longer drank gin. And my former boss who came up to visit now and then, was enrolled in Alcoholics Anonymous. I yielded the juniper berries to the birds.

Meanwhile, I believed I was still a New Yorker and followed the fashions and theater. But in reality, I was becoming a waste-not, want-not New Englander. I filed away bits of juniper lore to use someday. I learned the word berry is not quite accurate in describing the fruit of *juniper communis*. The fruit is actually a tiny cone with barely visible scales. The cones, needles and branches have been used medicinally for centuries.

Cato described a juniper-berry wine that was used as a diuretic. Pliny the Elder praised a digestive tonic, *cento erbe*–one hundred herbs steeped in alcohol. The actual herbs numbered twelve and included juniper berries. That digestive tradition endures in modern Italy where festive meals are concluded with *amari*, bitter herb based potions.

In 1650, a Dutch chemist, who was searching for a cure-all combined pure alcohol and juniper berries and accidentally invented gin. Dr Franciscus de la Boe reasoned that combining two proven diuretics would flush a body of all its harmful germs. He named his tonic, *genievre,* the French word for juniper. The tonic caught on quickly and soon the Dutch considered a daily dose essential to health. When England invaded Holland, the soldiers discovered the spirit, shortened its name to gin and carried a good supply home when they left.

Dr. Nicholas Culpeper, a British physician, listed juniper berries as an appetite stimulant in his seventeenth century herbal. The English also sipped juniper tea to relieve dropsy and mild heart failure. English ladies who ventured abroad nibbled a dozen juniper berries a day to zap the germs of other lands. Even today, American herb shops sell tiny pouches of the berries–not for nibbling–but as travelers' talismans.

Many cultures valued juniper's disinfectant qualities. The Swiss, Scandinavians and Chinese used smoldering branches of the plant to disinfect schoolrooms and sickrooms.

The Native Americans used juniper to cure hiccups, snake bite, bleeding, aching joints and colds. The Hopi crushed the needles and rubbed them on the scalp to cure dandruff. Which may explain why juniper tar–also known as oil of cade–is an important ingredient in modern dandruff shampoo.

Wilderness survivors have always depended on juniper berries because they remain on the branches at all stages of ripeness and are plentiful even in winter. Eaten raw, the berries taste harsh and turpentiny, which is why most creatures ordinarily reject them. But as survival food the berries are high in sugar and Vitamin C.

I was reassured to learn that our free little berries cure snakebite, dandruff and even prevent death by starvation. But none of these were my immediate problems. Free radicals are. These recently discovered demon particles roam the body, bouncing around searching for cells to attack and cause–heavens!–aging!

Thank goodness, I discovered "Rejuvenating Blend," a tastefully-packaged handful of juniper berries, sage and chamomile available for $40 from a Texas spa. Sprinkle the herb into your bath water, and according to the spa, you will sweat out all those aging impurities. I whipped up my own blend and soaked away a few of my own free radicals. Sparingly, of course. Too much of the "Rejuvenating Blend" and I could lose my senior discount at the movies.

In any case, when the local natural foods store began advertising the berries for a bargain $5.95 a pound, I became serious about juniper's seasoning possibilities. Native Americans, I discovered, considered juniper a warming ingredient and added it to soups and stews to ward off winter chills. In the same spirit, you can use the berries to flavor cold-weather classics like chicken pot pie, red cabbage, baked beans, sauerkraut, pork chops and beef or rabbit stew. When combined with these strong flavors, juniper berries add a light, spicy note.

In Ireland, juniper wood is used for smoking the exquisite Limerick hams.

To add a taste of Limerick to your next smoked ham, insert two or three berries in the flesh near the bone. Braise or bake as usual.

French cooks use juniper to make both a wine and a liqueur. *Vin de Genievre* is made by combining one cup of crushed juniper berries, four cups of dry white wine and one-half cup sugar. Combine, bottle and let sit for a month in a cool, dark place. Strain and enjoy. The French liqueur, *ratafia*, calls for juniper berries, sugar and brandy.

The French also use the berries to flavor a terrine–a sumptuous meatloaf made with ground meats like pork, liver and eggs, cream and brandy.

Juniper berries also perfume the hearty Alsatian pork and sauerkraut dish, *choucroute garnie*. The German dish, *Schlachplatte* combines a variety of sausages with sauerkraut and has a hint of juniper.

In Italy, juniper berries and sage cut the rich, assertive flavor of *crostini* or "little toasts" topped with chicken liver. A Tuscan recipe calls for sautéing chicken livers with fresh sage and juniper berries. The livers are then mashed and spread on toasted baguette.

Angus Cameron, a sportsman and co-author of The L.L. Bean Game and Fish Cookbook (Random House), is juniper's most enthusiastic American patron. He recommends doubling the number of juniper berries in any recipe calling for them. Cameron uses juniper to season roast possum, spit-broiled fowl, and roast wild duck. He sautés grouse in butter, with shallots mushrooms, dry white wine and twenty crushed juniper berries.

A cookbook on using wild foods offers a recipe for a quick bread that calls for one cup of juniper berry flour. But what, pray tell, is so quick about collecting and pulverizing enough berries to produce one cup of flour?

Innovative chefs these days use juniper for unusual oils and butters. To make flavored olive oil, mash a few berries and add them to a small bottle of good olive oil. Or add a few mashed berries to melted butter and drizzle it over baked potatoes, steamed spaghetti squash or venison

Consider a bouquet *garni* of five juniper berries, two bay leaves, ten peppercorns, one-half teaspoon each dried savory and marjoram and one-half teaspoon each of caraway, celery and dill seed.

While chefs create new ways to use juniper, the garden catalogs also offer new versions of the shrub. How about a deep blue column of juniper that reaches for the heavens? Or a juniper with lemon-yellow foliage? Or a deep blue ground hugger that resembles a marine plant?

Over the centuries, juniper has gained a reputation for magic. The Celts believed that a juniper bush stationed by the door, drove away demons and witches.

Both the Bible and St. Francis of Assisi praised juniper's protective powers. Perhaps a spring of juniper near the telephone will protect your dinner hour from telemarketers.

Even if you never harvest a single berry for sauce, for a minimum of time and money, a juniper bush will give you years of pleasure.

And that is magic enough for me.

Crostini, a variety of rich appetizers, include chopped chicken liver spread on toast. In Italy, *crostini* are often served with drinks before dinner.

TUSCAN CROSTINI

1/2 cup chopped onion
2 tablespoons olive oil
1 pound chicken livers, drained and trimmed of fat
8 juniper berries
1 teaspoon dry sage
½ cup dry white wine
1 1-pound baguette
Salt
Freshly ground pepper

Slice baguette into 20 slices. Toast lightly and keep warm.

In a large skillet, sauté the onion in olive oil over medium low heat until soft, about 5 minutes. Add livers, sage and juniper berries. Increase heat to medium and cook and stir until livers are no longer red. Add wine and cook stirring frequently until livers are cooked through and wine is reduced, about 5 to 8 minutes.

Mash livers coarsely. Season to taste with salt and pepper. Spread liver mixture on toasted bread slices. Serve hot. Makes 10 servings.

The hunter's stew, *bigos,* originated in Poland where it was made with game meats such as deer or bear. Polish-American cooks substituted pork and beef for the game meats. *Bigos* is a hearty winter dish that can be made ahead and reheated. Like other stew, *bigos* can be varied with whatever is at hand including chicken, short ribs, lamb, turnips, parsnips, apples, dried fruits or beer. Traditionally, bigos is served with sour cream, crusty bread and potatoes

BIGOS

6 slices bacon cut in 1-inch pieces
1 cup chopped onion
1/2 pound stew beef, cut into cubes
1/2 pound boneless pork shoulder, cut into cubes
1/2 pound kielbasa, sliced
2 cups beef broth
1/2 cup dry white wine
1 cup carrot slices
1/2 cup chopped celery
1 teaspoon paprika
1 bouquet garni
12 ounces fresh mushrooms, sliced
2 pounds sauerkraut
Salt and freshly ground pepper

Bouquet Garni

6 juniper berries
2 bay leaves
1/2 teaspoon caraway seeds
1/2 teaspoon celery seeds
10 peppercorns
4 sprigs parsley
1/2 teaspoon dill seed

Tie herbs for bouquet garni in cheesecloth or put into a tea ball.

In a Dutch oven, gently sauté bacon and onion until bacon is crisp and onion is tender. Remove bacon and onion with a slotted spoon. Set aside.

Brown beef and pork in drippings. Stir in the bacon, onion, sausage, beef broth, wine, celery, carrots, sauerkraut, mushrooms, paprika and bouquet garni. Bring to a boil. Lower heat and simmer stew until meat is tender, about 1-1/2 to 2 hours. Stir occasionally. Add more liquid if necessary. Remove bouquet garni. Taste and season with salt and pepper.

Makes 10 servings.

Choucroute garnie or sauerkraut and pork originated in the Alsace region of France. This winter specialty is a hefty, savory farmer's dish full of pork, sausages, potatoes and, of course, sauerkraut. Serve with a good rye bread and a simple green salad.

CHOUCROUTE GARNIE A L'ALSACIENNE

4 slices bacon, cut in 1-inch pieces
1/2 cup chopped onion
1 pound sauerkraut, rinsed and drained
1 tablespoon brown sugar
1 clove garlic, minced
2 medium potatoes, quartered
2 tart apples, sliced
12 juniper berries
2 cloves
1 sprig parsley
1 bay leaf
4 pork chops, 1/2-inch thick
4 frankfurters, slashed diagonally
1/2 cup Riesling wine
1-1/2 cups chicken broth
Parsley

Tie berries and herbs in cheesecloth or put into a tea ball. Cook and stir bacon and onion in a non-reactive Dutch oven until bacon is crisp.

Pour off fat.

In the Dutch oven, place the sauerkraut, garlic, potatoes, apples, herbs, pork chops and frankfurters. Pour the wine and broth over the meat. Bring to a boil and then reduce to simmer. Cover and simmer until potatoes are tender, about 30 minutes. Remove herbs. Using slotted spoon, arrange meat, sauerkraut, potatoes and apples on a heated platter. Garnish with parsley. 4 servings.

If you don't have a slow cooker, place all the ingredients for this hearty soup in a Dutch oven. Bring to a boil, reduce heat, cover and simmer gently for 1 hour.

SLOW COOKER HAM AND LENTIL SOUP

1 pound lentils
1-1/2 cups chopped carrots
1 cup chopped onion
1 cup chopped celery
1/2 cup minced parsley
1 bay leaf
1/4 teaspoon dried marjoram
12 juniper berries
1 meaty ham bone, 1-1/2 pounds
7 cups water
1 tablespoon fresh lemon juice
Salt and freshly ground pepper

Pick over lentils. Rinse and place in slow cooker. Add carrots, onion, celery, parsley, bay leaf, marjoram and juniper berries. Place ham bone on top of vegetables. Add the water, cover and cook on low for 9 to 11 hours.

Remove bay leaf and ham bone from pot. Discard bone. Return meat to cooker. Season to taste. Serves 10.

You could not pick a better, more resourceful neighbor than our friend, Dan Davis. Whether the problem is a dead car battery or a stubborn chain saw, Dan is there ready to help. His vegetable garden with its raised beds is the envy of the neighborhood. His annual hunting season yields at least a 15-point buck that he butchers and adds to the winter larder. Here is a flavorful way to prepare Dan's bounty. For an elegant presentation, serve the steaks with wild rice and a julienne of buttered rutabagas, celery and parsnips.

VENISON STEAKS WITH JUNIPER BERRY BUTTER

1/2 cup softened butter
4 tablespoons juniper berries
2 tablespoons vegetable oil
4 shallots, chopped
8 ounces quartered mushrooms
1 tablespoon fresh or dried rosemary
Fresh-ground peppercorn and salt to taste
8 tender 3-ounce venison steaks, about 1/4-inch thick
1/4 cup white wine

Mash the juniper berries into 6 tablespoons of the softened butter. Set aside. Melt the remaining butter with the oil in a large non-reactive skillet. Add the shallots, mushrooms and rosemary. Gently sauté, stirring occasionally, for 4 minutes. Remove with a slotted spoon and keep warm.

Increase the heat to high and sauté the steaks for a minute on each side. Do not crowd steaks. Do in two batches if necessary. Sprinkle steaks with salt and pepper and remove to a warm platter.

Heat the wine in the skillet, scraping up all the pan juices and bits and pour over the steaks. Top each steak with a hunk of the juniper berry butter and surround each with mushrooms. Makes 4 servings.

Northern Shrimp, A Costly Bargain

How can anyone pass up shrimp on special at 79 cents a pound?

"You just can't," advised an office colleague, Carolyn Campbell, one Monday morning in January. She spread the word of the shrimp special to everyone at the small newspaper where we worked. "You better get to the store before they run out," she urged.

Some people resisted, of course. They detest shrimp, are allergic to it or watch their cholesterol.

But Carolyn knew she had me hooked. "You know that shrimp is usually $7.99 a pound at the food warehouse," she said. Well, no, I did not. Shrimp is something I eat when I dine out–garlic shrimp on angel hair pasta in New Orleans, shrimp and snow peas at a Cambridge Chinese restaurant or a shrimp-salad roll at the beach.

At any cocktail party or gallery opening, just locate the platter of jumbo shrimp and that is where I will be. There may be a blithering guest attached barnacle-fast to me. No matter. I nod and dip another shrimp into the cocktail sauce. I savor the shellfish and nod some more. "Your next book," insists the barnacle, "should be my life story. "

At a bargain 79 cents a pound, I figured I could relish several heaps of cocktail shrimp. In silence. Sitting down. At 79 cents, I could afford to make a scampi feast for two. But I was uncertain whether Edward ate shrimp. It turns out he does—minus the head, tail, shell or any other part that reminds him a shrimp is a fellow creature.

But I had never cooked it for us. I believed making shrimp was a chore one delegates—like boning a chicken breast or making puff pastry. Carolyn would have none of that. "Cooking shrimp is as easy as pie," she advised. This from a woman who makes pizzelles at Christmas for her family and anyone else who craves this anise-scented

Italian holiday cookie. She bakes the delicate thin, lacy circles one at a time in a special pizzelle iron—during the busiest weeks of the year. When you and I are wondering whether we will get any Christmas cookies baked at all.

It turned out the 79-cent shrimp special had not been advertised. Carolyn heard it about it over the weekend at the fish counter. On Monday, she called the supermarket several times to see if the shrimp boats had landed. Called the supermarket! I am impressed. At the meat counter, I have yet to summon the courage to squawk through the little microphone find a hunk of suet for our downy woodpecker family.

Anyway, all week long Carolyn issued shrimp advisories with details on delivery times and expected sell-outs. Okay, okay, I said. I will pick up a pound after work on Friday.

When I arrived at the fish counter, and asked for a pound, the clerk pointed to the sign's fine print. The shrimp was 79 cents a pound—if you bought five pounds. Otherwise, it was 99 cents per pound.

Unfair, I thought And bought five pounds. I told the clerk I thought the shrimp looked rather small. He shrugged, "It's Maine shrimp." First mention of Maine shrimp. I walked grimly to the checkout, hoping that five pounds of shrimp would produce at least one newspaper food column.

Carolyn had mentioned she spent five hours one evening cleaning her bargain shrimp. I pictured her freezer bulging with shrimp. Well, I was not going to spend five hours on a Friday night cleaning shrimp. Not me.

Instead, I spent seven hours on a cold January night cleaning shrimp. I learned the big difference between tiny northern shrimp and jumbo southern shrimp. I thought of my stepson, Andrew, who as a child, observed that if wild blueberries were the size of apples, we would fill our baskets much faster and could spend more time splashing in Spofford Lake.

Andrew's comment also applies to shrimp. If my shrimp had been the government-designated "Extra Colossal"–nine or ten shrimp to a pound–I could have raced through the following steps: Rinse the shrimp with cold water, drain, twist off the heads, peel, scrape off the eggs, cook, rinse and drain. However, I was facing five pounds of Maine shrimp with approximately 100 shrimp to the pound. At least, the "veins" in northern shrimp are tiny enough to ignore.

After 90 minutes of drudgery I had one precious cup of tiny shrimp. I also had a heap of soggy newspapers, a wet floor and a severe case of ennui.

At the one-cup mark, I went to the basement to get a work light to speed things up. I nearly lost my precious cleaned shrimp to our cabin-fever crazed cats, Madame Nhu and Lucy. I could not blame them. The cats had not hunted outdoors in weeks. The field mice were safe under hip-deep snow. The below-zero temps had taken the fun out of bird chasing. The red squirrels skated with impunity over the snow crust from the maples to the bird feeder.

Shrimp-novice that I was, I stumbled on a preferred method for cooking shrimp–in its shell. Most chefs believe that cooking shrimp in the shell improves its flavor. Some disagree.

Experts also argue about the plural of shrimp. Is it shrimp or shrimps? My dictionary says either is correct. And what about the term "scampi?" Is it the name of a shrimp dish or a Mediterranean crustacean? Actually, scampi is Italian for a small-lobster-like creature, *Nephrops norvegicus,* also known as lobsterettes, langoustine or Dublin Bay prawns. In America, scampi refers to shrimp or prawns sautéed with garlic, parsley, shallots, brandy, lemon juice and butter. If you must peel and guard five pounds of northern shrimp, it is far better to meditate on shrimp lore than dwell on the bargain that is costing you seven hours of your life.

Maine shrimp are so named because they are caught in the Gulf of Maine, which is their southernmost limit. But "Maine shrimp" is a misnomer. This circum-polar crustacean is actually a cold-water prawn called *Pandalus borealis*. Other common names for *P. borealis* include northern shrimp, pink shrimp, northern prawn and deep-water prawn. But the classification and nomenclature of the planet's 300 edible shrimp-prawns is hopelessly confusing even to scientists. Some practical experts simply divide the crustaceans by habitat–warm or coldwater shrimp.

Norwegians, who consume the largest amount of *P. borealis,* fish the deep waters where this prawn spends most of its time. The catch is hauled up, cleaned, packed and frozen aboard these huge floating fish factories.

New England fishers catch the Maine shrimp during its annual spawning season from December through March. Which explains why I had to de-egg my five pounds of shrimp.

Carolyn had good reason to celebrate the arrival of the bargain shrimp. For one thing, Maine shrimp is the only shrimp that we New Englanders can ever buy fresh. All other shrimp sold here is "previously frozen." Second, some years our local shrimp is just not available. Boom years were 1944 and 1969–30 million pounds were harvested. But then the catch fell off sharply in the 1970s alarming fishing officials. The New England states agreed to conservation measures such as net sizes and season limits and, by the mid-1980s, the shrimp catch was up to 10 million pounds. Conservationists say there still is a long way to go.

This year, northern shrimp was selling for $2.79 a pound–when it was delivered to the fish counter but apparently the 1990s were not boom years for the shrimp harvest. However, it's been nearly a decade since I peeled the five pounds of bargain shrimp and I began craving just a pound of that sweet little crustacean. The advertised special sold quickly but the man at the fish counter was expecting a delivery any day now. "They are pretty clean this year," he said. "You won't have to pick off so many eggs."

If you are lucky enough to find northern shrimp, look for a bright pink color. When fresh caught, this shrimp is bright red, a color few consumers ever see. As the shrimp ages, the color fades. Take a good sniff, too. Fresh shrimp smell sweet. If you get a whiff of ammonia, don't buy it.

To cook in the shell, bring a pot of lightly salted water to a boil. Drop in the shrimp. When the shrimp meat turns milky colored, it's done. Watch carefully, it only takes 45 seconds to one minute to cook northern shrimp.

If you don't have time to clean or cook the shrimp, freeze for a later date.

Pack the raw shrimp in a container and cover with a solution made of one tablespoon salt and I quart water. Pour over shrimp, leaving I-inch headspace. To defrost, set container in cold water.

Northern shrimp make wonderful eating. Purchased fresh and cooked correctly, they are delicate, nutty and sweet.

But most people are too lazy to spend hours preparing the shrimp, says one researcher at the Maine Division of Fisheries lab, "Too many consumers are reluctant to get their fingers dirty and take the time to clean these small spiny creatures."

Like I said, it is a job to delegate.

"Hay and straw" is the Italian way of describing the colorful blend of two kinds of fettuccine. The dish makes a nice weekend lunch or simple dinner. Serve with a simple salad of mixed greens and warm Italian bread. A tangy fruit sherbet is an effective counterpoint to pasta's richness.

HAY AND STRAW WITH SHRIMP

1/2 pound medium shrimp, peeled, split lengthwise and deveined
Salt and freshly ground pepper
4 tablespoons olive oil
1 clove garlic, gently smashed
4 tablespoons butter
1/2 cup chopped purple onion
1/2 teaspoon thyme
1 9-ounce package fresh spinach fettuccine
1 9-ounce package fresh fettuccine
1/2 cup grated Parmesan cheese
3/4 cup heavy cream
1/4 cup minced fresh parsley

Sprinkle the shrimp with a little salt and pepper and set aside. Add 1 tablespoon olive oil to a large pot of lightly salted water and bring to a boil. Meanwhile, gently sauté garlic in butter and 2 tablespoons olive oil until it is fragrant. Discard the garlic. Add the onion, thyme and shrimp and cook and stir just until the shrimp are opaque. Remove from heat but keep warm.

Add fettuccine to pot and boil just until al dente. Drain and sprinkle with 1 tablespoon olive oil. Toss with onion mixture to coat pasta. Toss again with cream. Add cheese and toss again. Divide and serve on six warmed plates. Top each serving with shrimp and sprinkle with parsley. Makes six servings.

When northern shrimp is out of season or unavailable, console yourself with the jumbos. This version of shrimp scampi wins raves for my friend Donna Chester, a flight attendant who lives in the Chicago area. Her advice: "Enjoy!" and serve with lemon rice or a rice pilaf.

SENSATIONAL SHRIMP SCAMPI

25 large or jumbo shrimp
3 lemons
2 cups dry white wine
1/2 cup butter, melted
Garlic powder
Salt
Fresh ground pepper

Peel and devein shrimp, leaving tails on if desired. Butterfly shrimp by making a deep cut along outer edge of the shrimp almost all the way to the inner edge. Open each shrimp and lay flat on a large, shallow pan such as a sheet cake pan. Sprinkle with lemon juice and wine. Drizzle liberally with butter. Sprinkle with garlic powder and salt and pepper to taste.

Place under a preheated broiler 3 to 4 inches from the flame for 5 minutes or until lightly brown. Using tongs, turn shrimp over and broil 1 to 2 minutes or until lightly browned and just firm to touch. Do not overcook or shrimp will be tough. Six to 8 minutes total cooking time should be sufficient. Makes 5 servings.

Whenever I am at home in New Hampshire and get a craving for Asian food, I make shrimp in black bean sauce. It is worth the effort to track down the beans because they are the key to this dish's characteristic flavor. Serve with rice or noodles.

SHRIMP IN BLACK BEAN SAUCE

1 tablespoon rice wine or dry sherry
2 tablespoons minced fresh ginger
1 tablespoon lower-sodium soy sauce
1/2 cup chopped green pepper
2 cloves garlic, minced
2 tablespoons fermented black beans, rinsed and finely chopped
1 cup sliced green onions
1/4 teaspoon freshly ground pepper
1 pound raw shrimp, shelled and deveined
1/4 cup peanut or corn oil
1 10-ounce package frozen peas, rinsed under cold water and drained
2 teaspoons cornstarch dissolved in 1/4-cup cold water

Combine sherry, ginger, soy sauce and pepper. Pour over shrimp and marinate for 15 minutes. Drain. Heat 2 tablespoons oil in a non-reactive heavy skillet or wok and stir-fry peas and green pepper for 2 minutes. Remove with a slotted spoon and set aside. Add remaining 2 tablespoons oil to skillet or wok and stir-fry garlic and black beans for 10 seconds. Add drained shrimp and stir-fry until shrimp turn pink.

Return vegetables to skillet. Stir in green onions. Whisk in cornstarch mixture. Stir well and cook and stir just until sauce thickens. Makes 4 servings.

When I was a young bride, I was convinced that my versions of shrimp Creole, shrimp jambalaya and Brunswick stew–all from Fannie Farmer—made me an expert on the cooking of the American South. After all, I dined once in a New Orleans hotel. And, of course, I had read all of Tennessee Williams. Well, that was before Paul   Prudomme. I know better now but this shrimp Creole is still one of my favorites.

SHRIMP CREOLE

2 tablespoons oil
1/2 cup chopped onion
1/2 cup chopped green pepper
1/4 cup chopped celery
2 cloves garlic, minced
2 cups chopped fresh tomatoes or
1 16-ounce can chopped tomatoes
1 bay leaf
1/4 teaspoon thyme
1/4 teaspoon red pepper sauce or to taste
Sugar
Salt and freshly-ground pepper
1-1/2 pounds shrimp, shelled and deveined
Hot cooked rice tossed with 2 tablespoons chopped parsley

Sauté onion, green pepper, celery and garlic in heated oil over medium heat until onions are translucent. Stir in tomatoes, bay leaf, thyme, red pepper sauce and sugar. Bring to a boil, reduce heat to low and simmer uncovered for 20 minutes or until mixture is slightly thickened, stirring occasionally. Taste and add salt and freshly ground pepper to taste.

Stir in shrimp. Simmer for 5 minutes or just until shrimp turn pink. Discard bay leaf and serve with rice.

Makes 4 servings.

For a hearty lunch, serve with a warm loaf of herb or garlic bread.

MAINE SHRIMP CHOWDER

1/2 cup chopped onion
2 tablespoons butter
2 tablespoons flour
4 cups milk
1 pound Maine shrimp, cooked, cleaned and deveined
1 cup cooked fresh or frozen tiny peas
12 tiny cooked new potatoes
1 cup cream
Salt and freshly ground pepper

Sauté onion in butter until soft. Stir in flour and cook and stir for 2 minutes. Add milk to onion mixture and stir and cook over low heat until mixture is heated. Do not boil. Add shrimp, peas, potatoes and cream and cook and stir until mixture is heated through. Taste and season with salt and freshly ground pepper to taste.

You may prepare this a day ahead to let flavors mellow. Heat gently but do not boil. Makes 4 to 5 servings.

Road Food

To many people, a picnic cooler means summer fun. To me a picnic cooler loaded with sensible food is a matter of survival in any season. Whenever I leave home by car for a few hours or a few days, my food cooler is as essential as a spare tire. When I travel by air, I stuff food into the corners of my carry-on bag –a tiny tin of tuna, a little box of raisins, a navel orange, cereal bars and a few biscotti to sweeten the morning coffee. Sometimes, we are diverted to Canada and I must willingly discard the fresh fruit and little carton of milk. I am a gardener, after all.

Not that I am not a compulsive eater, a health food nut or a penny-pincher. It's just that I do not think food away from home must be as bad as the usual roadside fare.

Like many Americans I work hard to stay in shape. Why should I blimp out on food that I would not eat on my own turf? Is it too much to ask that food away from home be tasty, healthy and ready when I am?

Road food. I take it with me all the time. Experience has shown time and again that without road food–or the reliable prospect of a good meal–it is a jungle out there. I have already had all of the plastic burgers, sludge salads and incompetent service I will ever deserve. Travel is tiring enough without the drag of poor food.

Packing road food does not mean a lot of work. It does mean collecting a standby supply of non-perishables. My stock includes dry-roasted nuts, fruit and vegetable juices and good crackers varied with pate, cheese spreads, smoked oysters, bottled water, mixed dried fruits and raisins. Who needs the unpredictable?

My road food rations are strictly reserved from any domestic use. They are also stored out of reach of munchies raiders. The day before a trip I add fresh items from the refrigerator or deli: vegetable sticks, soup in a thermos, hard-cooked eggs, fresh fruit, rolls, cheese, bar cookies or slices of fruit-nut bread.

On cold days I fill an insulated jug with orange-flavored herbal tea or hot cranberry juice laced with cinnamon and cloves. For warmer days: lemon squeezed into ice water.

Special occasions or special friends may inspire delights that are as fancy as they are mobile. How about chilled chicken pieces roasted with tarragon or, say, a couscous salad?

Does toting travel food mean you forgo serendipitous dining discoveries?

Not at all. It just means saving serendipity for holidays and vacations when there is more time for potluck and its hazards.

I began stowing road food when commuting between New Hampshire and New York City. Turnpike restaurants were already in decline. Off-pike restaurants were serving sugar, salt and fat combinations at highwaymen's prices.

And I noticed other people packing portable food. A friend who travels to weekend antique shows said she does it all the time. "There you are surrounded by all that sparkling crystal and old Spode and the only purchasable food is hot dogs, doughnuts and soda." She and her antiquing buddy pack gourmet picnic fare and after a long day of haggling and counter-haggling in the fields of Brimfield, Massachusetts, the two women kick back and enjoy a feast complete with wine and candles.

Packing road food is not limited to car travel. From my corner of New Hampshire, a meeting in Boston means rushing out the door at dawn for the early bus. I take in the scenery while breakfasting from a carry-on bag. A tip: do not fill beverage cups to more than half–a protection from the slosh as the bus tha-wumps over the road heaves.

And air travel Food aloft-such as it is–you already know about, but think about food on the ground where air travelers actually spend most of their time. With raisins, nuts., cheese and fresh fruit in your shoulder bag, you will never be victimized by airport coffee shops as a flight delay creeps from minutes to hours.

Speaking of serendipity be sure to check airport shops for local specialties like cheeses or, in California, sourdough bagels, good chocolate and wines. Pack a corkscrew. Portland, Oregon's airport bursting with local specialties such as smoked salmon and pear wine is a shopper's dream

For overnight trips, pack three-ounce pop-top cans of tuna or applesauce, one-serving boxes of cereal and a plastic spoon. You'll be grateful the night you arrive at a hotel exhausted and hungry hours after room service has shut down. Consider packing a few teabags, bouillon, a lightweight plastic mug and an immersion heater. I carry a tiny percolator and coffee so I don't have to wait for my first cup of morning brew. Some hotels are catching on and furnishing their rooms with 4-cup coffee makers and coffee packets. However, I really question the hospitality extended by a hotelier who sells a coffee packet for $4 from a locked "mini bar." There are times–ask any woman who travels solo–when a $4 mini bar beer is worth the price of solitude but a coffee packet?

A Denver hotel gets the award for the most mean-spirited gesture of them all. On the night table, was a basket heaped with vending-machine packages of Oreos, chips and pretzels. At the bottom of the basket was the fine print: a card telling you had just consumed 4 packs of goodies at $2 a pack.

Perhaps that is what drove an airline pilot I know to pack his homemade oat cereal, which contains much less cholesterol and fat than the ordinary hotel omelet. He said that six weeks of his own blend helped lower his cholesterol count–and probably increased his bank account.

In any case, I learned early that the road food idea does not work if you think you can get away with eating and driving at the same time. It is almost as foolhardy as drinking-and-driving.

As with all other land mammals, food to work at all must be taken from a position of rest. Find a scenic spot. Pull over. Relax. You are actually saving net time.

Whenever I lapse and leave survival food at home, I am corrected by the inevitable karma. After a day of cruising on Lake Winnipesaukee, we foraged as far as Concord, New Hampshire, where the only restaurant at one end of our state capital drove us away by the stench of its rancid fat, and the big chain restaurant at the other end had already shut down its grill–at 8:30 p.m. We settled for packaged cold cereal, which of course I could have brought from home. How I wished we had made a supermarket stop for crackers, cheese, cider and grapes.

I am not a purist. If the opportunity for an exciting meal comes over the horizon, I am ready to bypass my pantry-on-wheels. Who would ignore fresh caught lobster at dockside in South Harps well, Maine, or a succulent clam chowder at Menemsha, Massachusetts, or poached salmon at a restaurant poised over the Connecticut River, or chicken barbecue at any of the Old Home Days in upcountry New England?

But if such delights are not available in the next town I drive through, I still know where my next meal is coming from. Wishing you the same, here is a list of road food tools. Plus some favorite recipes for traveling foods that will help liberate you from the highway blahs.

When selecting a cooler, look for a one that is sturdy but lightweight. A 32-quart cooler is a good all-round size. And why did it take so long to invent the new 32-quart size with a pullout handle and little wheels? For shorter trips the handy 16- inch cooler is just the right size. Look for one with a shoulder strap that will save a few trips to the car.

- Ice packs for each cooler
- Plastic tumblers with lids
- Heavy plastic mugs
- Plastic cutlery
- Bottle-and-can opener
- Corkscrew

- Square plastic containers
- Dinner-size paper napkins
- Compact pepper mill
- Breadknife
- Paring knife
- Plastic grocery bag for trash
- 48-inch square fabric tablecloth (nice but optional)

CAPTAIN TOM'S CEREAL

2 cups uncooked oats
2 cups grape nuts
1 (2-1/2-ounce package) slivered almonds
1/2 cup raisins

Mix and bag. Use ½ cup per serving. To serve, add milk.

This salad is best when made with fresh herbs. White kidney beans may also be labeled, *cannellini*, as they are called in Italy.

WHITE BEAN SALAD TONNATO

2 cups cooked white kidney beans
1 6-ounce can tuna, rinsed and drained
1/3 cup finely chopped red onion
1/2 cup black olives, sliced
6 tablespoons olive oil
6 tablespoons cider vinegar
1/2 cup chopped fresh parsley
2 tablespoons chopped fresh mint
1 tablespoon fresh basil
2 medium tomatoes, chopped
Lettuce

If using canned beans, refresh under cold running water and drain. Lightly mix the beans, tuna, onion and olives. Gently stir in the oil, vinegar, parsley and mint. Cover and refrigerate. Mix the tomatoes and basil. Cover and refrigerate. To serve, line glass plates with lettuce. Spoon in salad. Top with chopped tomatoes.

Makes 4 servings.

Couscous is a wheat product. Buy it in bulk at Middle Eastern or natural food stores. Avoid the over-salted packaged couscous mixes. Here, a refreshing but satisfying salad.

COUSCOUS SALAD

1 cup couscous
1-1/2 cups low-sodium chicken broth
1/4 cup whole almonds
1 cup peeled, diced cucumber
1/4 cup grated Parmesan cheese
1/2 cup pitted black olives
1/4 cup chopped purple onion
1/4 cup sliced radish slices
1/2 cup chopped green pepper
1/4 cup olive oil
2 garlic cloves, peeled, minced
1 tablespoon lemon juice
Dill sprigs
Boston lettuce

Bring chicken broth to a simmer. In a large bowl, combine broth and couscous. Let stand 10 minutes. Fluff with a fork.

Blanch almonds by boiling 5 minutes. Drain and when cool enough to handle slip off skins. Toast for five minutes in a preheated 350-degree oven. When cool, chop coarsely.

To the couscous add the almonds, cucumber, cheese, olives, onion, radishes, pepper, olive oil and lemon juice. Serve on Boston lettuce leaves and top with dill sprigs.

Makes 6 servings.

This chicken is so simple to make and yet so delicious. It may be served hot or cold. Serve hot with rice pilaf, cold with marinated vegetables.

TARRAGON PICNIC CHICKEN

1 3-1/2 pound cut-up chicken
2 tablespoons corn oil margarine
2 tablespoons tarragon

Preheat oven to 375 degrees. Place margarine in a pan large enough to hold chicken in a single layer. Place pan in oven until margarine melts.

Place chicken skin side down and sprinkle with tarragon. Bake for 25 minutes. Turn chicken over. Check to see if breast pieces are done. Chicken is done when pierced with a fork, juices run clear. When done, remove breast pieces. Cool slightly and refrigerate.

Continue cooking remaining pieces until done, about 20 to 25 additional minutes. Cool slightly and refrigerate. If desired, skin chicken before serving.

Makes 4 servings.

Sara Victora grew up in Los Angeles and settled in Atlantic, Iowa, where her husband set up his veterinary practice and "where our kids can walk to school." Sara commutes from Omaha to her flight attendant base in Chicago. She shared her best Heartland-style recipes with me including a meat loaf from her mother. Sara says the meat loaf is "very moist and very flavorful." Leftover meat loaf on a bulky roll makes a hearty lunch-to-go.

MRS. DONNELLY'S MEAT LOAF

2 eggs
2 pounds lean ground beef
1/3 cup chopped green bell pepper
1/2 cup chopped onion
1 carrot, finely shredded
1 5-ouncecan evaporated milk
1 8-ounce can tomato sauce
1 cup crushed saltine crackers
1 teaspoon salt
1/8 teaspoon pepper

Mix eggs, beef, pepper, onion, carrot, milk, tomato sauce, crackers, salt and pepper. Spread mixture in an ungreased loaf pan or place meat mixture in an ungreased 13 by 9 by 2 inch pan, and shape into a loaf. Bake uncovered at 350 degrees until done–about 1 to 1-1/4 hours or until an instant-read thermometer reads at least 160 degrees. Let rest 15 minutes before slicing.

Makes 8 servings.

HEALING

It always surprises me that traditional medicine is more about pharmaceuticals than nutrition. Nutrition is also a science that incorporates, among others, anatomy, biology and chemistry. Good food can also heal. A friend who brings a steaming kettle of chicken soup relieves your suffering and warms your spirit.

Specific cause-effect data appear daily: vitamin E protects the heart, calcium strengthens bones, fiber prevents colon cancer. Too much salt, fat, sugar or alcohol cause serious disease. If you pay attention to what you eat, you probably will live a long, healthy life.

Even as you are dying, you ought to be able to savor a bit of good food. That is James Haller's point. An author and a founding chef of the glorious Blue Strawbery (sic) restaurant in Portsmouth, New Hampshire, Haller teaches Hospice volunteers to nurture with, say, fresh apricot sherbet.

"I brought a dying man a fresh peach custard. His attitude improved right away. He regained some sense of control. It was wonderful for the family."

What a splendid way to think about the last suppers for someone you love.

Mother Was Sometimes Right

D o you remember when the dinner table was the bargaining table?
Deals were made–not over–but about vegetables and dessert. My mother, for one, made this offer: Just eat a few peas or two spoonfuls of spinach and you qualify for apple pie or ice cream.

We now know that mother's heart was in the right place. Today each vegetable has its own scientist eager to explain how a carrot, for example, builds a lot more than character.

But in those days no one including my mother knew precisely why vegetables were good for you. They just were. Like everyone else, Mother bought most of her vegetables by the can. That was the way the harvest was preserved, shipped and stored.

Of course, canning processed away the taste, texture and color of most vegetables. Peas shriveled; spinach resembled unhealthy marine life. Out went the flavor. In went the sugar and salt.

But talk about convenience–no peeling, paring, chopping or cooking. All mother had do was open a can and heat. The cans carried no expiration dates because they were not expected to expire. Ever.

For women like mother, canned vegetables were a rare luxury in the work week. Washing clothes, for example, required one full day–if the weather was good. Ironing required most of the next day. On ironing day, cooking included three meals plus a pot of starch for dad's shirts and our Sunday dresses. And those two major chores were just the week's openers. Today's necessities–automatic, cordless, instant, and microwave–were unknown.

Frozen vegetables did not exist. Neither did frozen juices, TV dinners or ice cream by the carton. Most people stored their eggs, milk and fresh vegetables in an ice box, a large wooden chest cooled by a block of ice. As the ice melted, water flowed into a drip pan accessible by getting down on all fours and testing the water's depth with a finger. No blinking lights or electronic beeps warned you about an overflowing pan. Instead, cold water sloshed over your bare feet at breakfast or the neighbor in the apartment below let out an angry howl.

We were more modern and had graduated to an electric refrigerator. It was two feet wide and four feet high and sat on shapely little legs. A tiny freezer held an ice cube tray. Like all 1930s appliances, the refrigerator came with a recipe booklet written by a home economist. Caroline Coldspot, our refrigerator brand's home economist, enthused about homemade ice cream made with canned evaporated milk. Trixie, our cocker spaniel, was the only family member who finished a bowl of Ms. Coldspot's favorite dessert. Trixie also parked under the dinner table where she helped us children clean our plates and become eligible for dessert.

With the exception of fresh oranges for Christmas treats, no market sold out-of-season produce from other climates and countries. Even if we had known that Dutch growers harvested sweet red peppers in December or California farmers picked asparagus in January, well, that had nothing do with us.

We simply waited for two glorious weeks in August when fresh corn and tomatoes arrived at the farm stands. In autumn, my dad drove us out to the country where we bought vegetables from a farmer and stored them for the winter in a basement corner. Sent down to the cellar to collect potatoes for dinner, we inhaled the musky perfume of apples, onions and winter squash. "Fill the apron," my mother said. Slipping her apron over my head and carrying the vegetables made me feel very grown, very responsible. That feeling evaporated when I had to peel ten potatoes with ten times that many "eyes." To pass mother's inspection, the eyes had to be dug out completely.

Peeling potatoes seems easy to me now. When did those pesky eyes disappear? Did some geneticist fling them on a scrap heap next to the grape seeds and cucumber burps?

At our house, the winter vegetables were treated with reverence. We were city people and there was something magical about buying food from the man who had planted the seeds. During those long drives to the country dad tried to teach us that there were many people who did not have enough to eat. At Sunday dinner, mother heaped the squash or mashed potatoes in special dishes decorated with tiny pink flowers and gold rims.

Mother's cookbooks advised careful cooking to save a vegetable's nutrients. The 1949 version of "The American Woman's Cookbook," noted, "Deep fat frying is a satisfactory way to retain most food values. The vegetable is sliced, dipped in egg and crumbs or batter and immersed in enough hot fat to cover well, permitting cooking with little loss of vitamins."

Mother knew that cookbook writers do not know everything and rejected that advice. She boiled the carrots and baked the squash and skipped frying's fat, cholesterol, fuel consumption, cleanup and persistent odor. Not to mention the safety hazards of deep frying anything in a kitchen where six rambunctious schoolchildren played "go fetch" with a leaping cocker spaniel.

The 1940s cookbooks also ignored two simple, classic ways to cook vegetables–steaming and stir-frying. It took another two decades before cookbooks recognized these quick, fuel-efficient, and healthful cooking methods.

Mother fed us vegetables because she thought it was a good idea–not because some expert said so. She never mentioned the "Basic Seven Food Groups," created in the 1940s by the U.S. Department of Agriculture to help people choose a balanced diet. In grade school, I learned to recite the Seven Sacraments, the Seven Deadly Sins, and the Seven Gifts of the Holy Ghost, but I did not discover the "Basic Seven Food Groups" until college, 20 years after the USDA introduced them.

That may have been a blessing. The "Basic Seven" diet was heavy on foods that could cause health problems. For example, meat, milk, eggs and fats each made up one of the seven required groups.

A healthy breakfast, according to the Basic Seven, included ham, eggs and buttered toast. Mother fed us fruit, cereal and toast with margarine. Her choice was a simple, thrifty 1940s breakfast. Besides, this was World War II and meat, butter and eggs were rationed. Mother's menu turns out to be the healthiest choice for the 1990s.

The margarine of the 1940s was cheaper than butter. However, it was an unappealing white. To color the margarine, you beat a separately packaged orange powder into the margarine–a messy job even when you remembered to bring the spread to room temperature first. Then some manufacturer came up with a little red bead of dye that was inserted in a pillow of plastic-wrapped margarine. You popped the bead and then kneaded the package of margarine until the color was evenly distributed. Eventually, the butter lobby permitted the sale of yellow margarine. Today, I depend mainly on olive oil for a daily spread and for cooking (baking being another matter) because the butter-versus-margarine issue gets more complex with every reading of the newspaper.

That was the problem with the Basic Seven. It was too complicated for most people. So the USDA boiled it down to the Basic Four Food Groups. Judging from the contents of today's grocery carts, most people still do not know what to eat. Or they think the four basic foods are fat, sugar, salt and preservatives. That is the what you might conclude from watching an hour of television.

Well, today the USDA still thinks that most people in this richest of countries still do not have a clue about what to eat. Thus the agency spent one million dollars developing the "Eating Right Pyramid."

The resulting pyramid graphic, designed to be an easy-to-understand illustration, was sent to an approval committee. As a result, an additional $106,000 was spent to determine whether the pyramid shape was clearer than an alternate, a bowl. The pyramid won. Then the meat industry objected to the "Eating Right Pyramid." The USDA spent another $855,000 for more research. After 33 minor changes, the two-million-dollar Food Pyramid was released.

The graphic shows five kinds of foods with recommended servings. The nutritional message is this: cut down on fats and added sugars and eat a variety of foods from the five recommended groups with emphasis on the bread, cereal, rice and pasta group. The other groups are fruits; vegetables; meat, poultry, fish and eggs; and milk, yogurt, cheese and eggs. A pyramid information kit was sent out to schools, Indian reservations and feeding programs for the poor and elderly.

The government could have saved a lot of time and thousands of dollars. They simply could have asked my mother what she fed her family.

Carrot-raisin slaw used to be a standard offering at school cafeteria counters. I became nostalgic one day for this combination of carrots and raisins and created a modern version of a childhood favorite. A food processor shredding disk quickly prepares the carrots.

CARROT-RAISIN SLAW

4 medium carrots, shredded
3 tablespoons raisins
1/4 cup orange juice
2 tablespoons non-fat yogurt
1 tablespoon olive oil
Pinch each: cinnamon, coriander,
cumin

Combine ingredients in a medium bowl. Refrigerate until serving. Makes 4 servings.

I like to make this soup the night before or early in the day to let the flavors blend.

MUSHROOM BROCCOLI SOUP

1 12-ounce package mushrooms
2 tablespoons olive oil
1 pound broccoli, chopped
1 medium onion, sliced
2 cloves garlic, minced
1/2 to 1 teaspoon tarragon
Salt and freshly ground pepper to taste
1/2 cup dry white wine
6 cups chicken broth
3 tablespoons butter
3 tablespoons flour

Reserve 4 mushrooms for a garnish. Slice the remainder. In a large non-reactive saucepan, sauté broccoli, onion and garlic in olive oil until soft. Do not brown. Stir in mushrooms and sauté mixture for three minutes.

Add chicken broth, white wine and seasonings. Cover, bring to a boil, lower heat and simmer 30 minutes.

Puree soup in a blender. Return to large saucepan. In a small non-reactive saucepan, melt butter and blend in the flour. Add 1 cup of soup to small saucepan and cook and stir until blended. Pour soup-flour mixture back into large saucepan. Cook and stir a few minutes until soup is slightly thickened. Makes 10 servings.

AUNT CORA'S VEGETABLE SOUP

1 pound ground beef
1 cup chopped onions
2 tablespoons butter
4 cups hot water
1 low-sodium beef bouillon cube
1 16-ounce can tomatoes
1 cup sliced celery
1 bay leaf
1/2 teaspoon Worcestershire sauce
1/8 teaspoon pepper
1/2 teaspoon thyme
1 cup egg noodles

Brown ground beef. Drain. Put into a large non-reactive pot. Cook onions in butter until soft. Add onions, water, bouillon and tomatoes to the pot. Simmer 30 minutes Add seasonings and egg noodles and simmer 15 minutes.

Makes 9-1/2 cups or 8 to 10 servings.

A friend gave me this wonderful recipe for these veggie burgers. Garnished with tomato slices and cucumber relish, these burgers have become the burgers of choice at our house. I use a food processor to prepare the vegetables and mix everything the night before.

In the winter, I sauté the vegetables and cook the grains on top of the wood stove. I broil the burgers in two or three batches and store the surplus burgers in the freezer. When I am flying, my husband microwaves a couple of burgers for a quick meal.

SUSIE'S HIGH-GRAIN VEGGIE BURGERS

3 cups water
2/3 cups barley
2/3 cup lentils
2/3 cups brown rice
2 cups shredded carrots
1 cup chopped onion
1 cup chopped celery
1/4 cup sunflower kernels
2/3 cup lentils
2/3 cup brown rice
4 cloves garlic, minced
3 tablespoons Italian seasoning (Basil, oregano, thyme)
Salt
Freshly ground pepper
4 large eggs, beaten or equivalent liquid egg substitute
3/4 cup whole wheat flour
Cooking spray
English muffins or burger buns

In a large, heavy pot bring 3 cups of water to boil. Stir in the barley, lentils and brown rice. Reduce heat to low, cover and cook until grains are tender–about 40 minutes.

Line a colander with a tea towel. Transfer grains to colander to cool and drain thoroughly. This step is important to burger texture.

Heat olive oil over medium low heat in a large skillet. Add carrots, onion, celery, sunflower seeds and garlic. Cover and cook until vegetables are just tender–about 10 minutes. Stir in Italian seasoning. Taste and add salt and fresh ground pepper to taste.

Cool vegetables and transfer to a large bowl. Stir in grains, beaten eggs and flour. Mix lightly but thoroughly.

Lightly spray a cookie sheet or broiler pan with cooking spray. Using a ½ -cup measure, form grain mixture into patties and place on cookie sheet. Spray top of each patty.

Broil three inches from heat until golden brown and heated through–about 7 minutes on each side, depending on your broiler. Place each patty on a toasted bun and add your choice of garnish.

Makes about 15 burgers.

A long time ago many non-traveling people dined at airport restaurants because that is where the best restaurants were. Chef Albert Stockli created Chicken Divan at the Newarker airport restaurant in New Jersey. Chicken Divan was the most popular dish on his menu. Even in a lighter version, chicken divan is a still a comforting entree.

LIGHT CHICKEN DIVAN

1 pound broccoli
3 whole chicken breasts, halved, boned and skinned
1/4 teaspoon ground white pepper
1 teaspoon dried tarragon
1/3 cup all-purpose flour
2 tablespoons olive oil
1 cup non-fat sour cream
1 cup (4 ounces) shredded reduced-fat Cheddar cheese
1/4 cup dry sherry
Dill sprigs

Break broccoli into flowerets and steam about 5 minutes, until crisp-tender. Meanwhile, place chicken between 2 pieces of wax paper. Pound with meat mallet until 1/4-inch thick.

Mix pepper, tarragon and flour. Dredge chicken with flour. In a skillet, heat oil over medium heat. Add chicken and sauté about 3 minutes on each side. Add wine, turn chicken and cook 1 minute. Remove chicken and keep warm.

Turn heat to medium low. Using a whisk, stir sour cream into drippings in skillet. Add cheese and sherry. Stir and cook just until cheese is melted. Arrange chicken breasts on a platter. Surround with broccoli. Spoon sauce over chicken and broccoli. Garnish with dill sprigs.

Makes 6 servings.

Is Homemade Chicken Soup A Miracle Drug?

So you have a cold. Throat raw. Nose red. Head like a stuffed cabbage. You will try anything–drugstore remedies, herbs, Vitamin C, cod liver oil, sweating in the sauna, hot toddies, even going to the doctor–but you will probably end up with steaming, homemade chicken soup.

At some expense, the doctor will call it an upper respiratory infection, one of two hundred varieties of rhinoviruses. *Rhino* is Greek for nose.

The doctor will order rest, warmth and plenty of liquids and, in six or seven days, your cold will be gone or well on its way. The only known cure for the common cold, the doctor will say, is time.

But you cannot afford time. You want relief now. So you decide to take charge.

First, you turn to the All-American cure for anything at all–money. You will buy instant health with over-the-counter medicine. You are not alone. Every year Americans will sniffle away two billion dollars for fever relievers, bronchial relaxers, cough suppressors, nasal decongestants, antihistamines and sore-throat gargles.

In all, the Food and Drug Administration lists 50,000 different products sold to relieve cold symptoms. And "relief of symptoms" is the only claim the FDA allows. No manufacturer may call its product a "cure" or even a "cold medicine."

Even natural food purists won't let a cold run its course. Herb manuals offer long lists of do-it-yourself cold remedies: garlic, elder, ginseng. boneset, eucalyptus, horehound, palmetto fruit, borage, thyme, lobelia, goldenrod, linden, slippery elm and hundreds more. But by time you locate your slippery elm and make the prescribed infusion, tisane, tonic, decoction, or compress, I predict your cold will be long gone.

What about cod liver oil? The folk wisdom is that anything that tastes that bad should kill any germ, but my mother fed it to us broadside every winter morning and we still snuffled through the same four childhood colds every season.

But it is now turning out that childhood colds can be healthy. Yes, a new study indicates each childhood cold sets up immunity to one of those 200 rhinoviruses and, by the time we are 60, we could actually resist them all.

Then there is vitamin C. C as in cold. C as in controversy. We do know that vitamin C prevents scurvy but there is no evidence that it does anything to prevent the common cold. One study did conclude that vitamin C does reduce the severity of cold symptoms in some people. Nobel laureate Linus Pauling says he takes 1,000 milligrams of vitamin C hourly until his cold symptoms disappear. Other scientists caution that such large amounts may cause kidney stones or even scurvy–when the high dose is withdrawn.

If I am soggy and depressed by a cold, my right brain suggests a week on a toasty beach in Eleuthera. Then my left brain–which balances my checkbook–argues that flying with a cold in a pressurized aircraft can ruin your ears. But sweating out a cold is probably a healthy instinct; it thaws body fluids–like chicken soup.

Back in college, we believed hot toddies cured a cold. (We also believed cigarettes made us thin and sexy.) The toddy formula included brandy, lemon juice, honey and hot water. After a couple of mugs of toddy, you crawled under a mountain of blankets. While you slept, the germs were sweated out; when you woke, you were cured.

Well, not quite. The brandy put you to sleep and that felt good until a few hours later. When you awoke with a thundering hangover and an unquenchable thirst.

That's because when you have a cold, you perspire more body fluids than usual. Alcohol and the caffeine in coffee, tea, colas or chocolate can dehydrate you further. If you replace the fluids–say a half pint of plain water every two hours–you will feel better.

And that's what chicken soup does for you; it restores your hydraulics. This is why science–always skeptical of folk remedies–now smiles with approval on the chicken soup tradition. In the Middle Ages, stewing an old hen produced a cure-all not only for the common cold but also leprosy and impotence.

As the Age of Miracle Drugs arrived, the chicken soup cure was at first denigrated as too simple, too cheap, too unprofitable an idea. Advertising budgets for patent medicines become second only to booze–the other leading self-medication.

But cooks guided by their nurturing instinct kept making the magic broth anyway. Their snuffling children felt loved and recovered. Maybe it was the love that did the trick.

Scientists are now trying to find out if there is any material basis for the chicken soup cure.

A landmark study by Dr. Marvin Sacker at Mount Sinai Hospital in Miami concluded that chicken soup opens up stuffed nasal passages. The researchers compared the blocked noses of cold victims sipping chicken soup with victims sipping plain hot water. The soup sippers were relieved sooner.

As the soup cleared the mucus from the nasal passages, it also got rid of a lot of the virus. The hot chicken broth also increased the amount of mucus secreted by the bronchial tubes thus easing the cough and tightness in the chest.

The Miami hospital is capitalizing on its research. You can now buy Mount Sinai Brand chicken soup in the hospital's gift shop.

The Mayo Clinic's newsletter also recommends a bowl of steaming chicken soup for cold relief: "Although the pharmaceutical companies make huge profits from many different cold remedies, aspirin and hot beverages seem most effective in reducing symptoms."

"Among hot beverages, we know of nothing better than leisurely sipping a bowl of steaming chicken soup," advises Dr. Joseph Kiely, the newsletter's medical director. The Mayo Clinic specifically recommends "the homemade variety with chicken parts, vegetables, herbs, spices and noodles.

Recipes for the universal chicken soup vary by geography and budget.

In a pricey Beverly Hills restaurant, rich chicken stock is flavored with parsley, sage, thick carrot slices and a light, tasty matzo ball. In the center of each bowl is a neatly-sliced chicken breast. Best of all, soothing beads of schmaltz (chicken fat) float on the surface.

Saffron, a precious spice, flavors one Pennsylvania Dutch version. Egg noodles and kernel corn–both fresh–are added to the pot. Popcorn garnishes each serving.

Another Pennsylvania Dutch chicken soup includes rivels–bits of homemade pasta. The rivels are added to the soup along with crumbled hard-cooked eggs.

In France, the chicken soup restorative includes carrots, parsley, turnips, leeks and a handful of vermicelli. A get-well wish–*Un bon bouillon vous regapera* (A nice broth will get you back in shape)–accompanies each bowl served.

In Hungary, a richer, golden chicken soup is achieved by carefully browning carrots and onions in chicken fat. It took me most of an afternoon to make *pho ga*, a Vietnamese chicken and rice noodle soup. But it was well worth the time and trouble. It was full of good flavors like ginger root, fish sauce, star anise, cloves and Asian basil, saw leaf herb, Serrano chilies and lime wedges. The version I prepared was inspired by Mai Pham, chef-owner of the Lemon Grass restaurant in Sacramento, author of *The Best of Vietnamese and Thai Cooking.*

An American authority on pulmonary drugs now adds a hot and spicy twist to the chicken soup magic. Dr. Irwin Ziment, of the University of California at Los Angeles School of Medicine, had observed that many ancient and modern cultures used hot foods–mustard, garlic, hot peppers and horseradish, fresh ginger–to treat pulmonary diseases. He concluded that both the folk remedies and the modern drugs set off a similar response. Simply speaking, the hot, spicy foods cause an internal burst of tears.

That flood cleanses the system, breaks up the nose and lung congestion, flushes out the sinuses and washes away the irritants.

Thus the Ziment recipe for chicken soup calls for 15 cloves of garlic, five herbs, curry powder and a hefty dash of red or black pepper. He says his soup is the standard against which all other therapeutic cold remedies should be judged. "It's probably the best there is."

But science or no science, many a grandma is likely to challenge that claim. They have a household word for the healing power of their chicken soup: *bubbamycin.* 'Mycin' has come to be slang for anything that cures; 'bubba' is Yiddish for grandmother.

CLASSIC CHICKEN SOUP

1 6-pound stewing hen
3 large onions, sliced thinly
2 cloves garlic, minced
1 bulb celery root or two parsnips, chopped
4 carrots, sliced
5 sprigs fresh parsley or dill or 1 tablespoon each dried
12 peppercorns
Water to cover
Salt and freshly ground pepper
1 pound noodles
Minced fresh parsley

Place hen, onions, garlic, celery root or parsnips, carrots, dill or parsley and pepper-corns in a large pot. Cover with cold water, bring to a boil and reduce heat to a simmer. Cover and cook gently for 5 to 6 hours.

Remove chicken. Bone and chop meat and return to soup.

Add salt and freshly ground pepper to taste. Add noodles and cook according to package directions. Sprinkle each serving with parsley.

Makes 8 servings.

CHICKEN SOUP DELUXE

1 3-pound chicken, cut up
Cold water
1-1/2 teaspoons salt
1 teaspoon chopped parsley
1/2 teaspoon chopped tarragon
1/2 teaspoon basil
1 tablespoon chopped celery leaves
1/2 teaspoon pepper
2 tablespoons olive oil
3/4 cup chopped celery
3/4 cup chopped green onions, tops included
3/4 cup chopped green pepper
1 16-ounce can tomatoes
1 tablespoon vinegar
1 bay leaf

Place the chicken, salt, parsley, tarragon, basil, celery leaves and pepper in a Dutch oven. Add water to cover. Bring to a boil, lower heat, cover and cook for about 1 hour or until meat falls readily from the bones. Remove chicken. Cool both chicken and broth briefly and refrigerate.

The next day, remove fat from top of broth and discard. Remove chicken meat from bones and chop into bite-size pieces.

In a large pot, gently heat olive oil. Add celery, onions, green pepper and sauté just until onion is translucent. Add tomatoes, vinegar, bay leaf and chicken broth. Bring to a boil, lower heat and simmer covered for 10 minutes. Add cooked chicken pieces and heat just to boiling.

Makes 6 servings.

PENNSYLVANIA DUTCH CHICKEN AND CORN SOUP

1 3-pound broiler-fryer, cut up
2 quarts water
1 cup chopped onion
1/2 cup chopped celery
3 teaspoons salt
1/2 teaspoon pepper
1 10-ounce package frozen corn, thawed
1/4 cup chopped fresh parsley
1 recipe rivels

Combine chicken, water, celery, 3 teaspoons salt and pepper in a large pot. Bring to a boil, reduce heat, cover and simmer 1 hour.

Meanwhile prepare rivels. When chicken is cooked, remove from pot. When cool enough to handle, cut chicken into bite size pieces. Discard skin and bones.

Add chicken, corn and parsley to broth. Bring to a boil and sprinkle rivels into soup. Cook 15 minutes. Taste and correct seasoning if necessary.

Makes 10 cups soup.

RIVELS

1 cup flour
1/4 teaspoon salt
1 egg, beaten
2 teaspoons milk

Combine flour, salt, and egg and stir until mixture resembles small peas. Add up to 2 teaspoons milk to get a crumbly texture.

In Greek, this classic soup is called *avgolemono*. I discovered *avgolemeno* in a New York restaurant in the West Forties that was described as "Persian." I ordered this tasty lemon soup and a glorious dish of baked onions stuffed with breadcrumbs, ground lamb and pine nuts. A few weeks later, I brought a friend to share my find. But the "Persian" restaurant had disappeared and a seafood restaurant hung with fishing nets and floats was in its place.

GREEK LEMON CHICKEN SOUP

2 quarts chicken stock
1/2 cup raw rice
1 cup diced cooked chicken
4 egg yolks
Juice of 3 lemons
Salt to taste
Chopped parsley

Bring the stock to a boil in a large pot over medium heat. Add the rice, lower the heat and simmer for about 10 minutes or until the rice is cooked. Stir in the chicken and keep stock simmering. In a small bowl, beat the eggs and stir in the lemon juice. Just before serving, slowly add a little of the hot stock into the lemon juice-egg yolk mixture. Then slowly pour 1 cup of the simmering stock into the egg mixture, stirring constantly until blended. Stir the egg mixture into the remaining stock and continue to stir over low heat until slightly thickened. Season to taste with salt. Increase heat and stir until steaming but do not boil.

Ladle into soup bowls and sprinkle with parsley.

Makes 8 servings.

This is one hearty soup I make for Edward when I am about to fly off to work. I make a big pot, refrigerate it and he dips into it and micros a dish for himself. The soup keeps well in both refrigerator and freezer. When we have large projects underway, this soup serves for a few nights as "dinner in the bank." Served with good bread, it's satisfying meal.

LEEK AND BARLEY SOUP

1/2 cup barley
2 quarts chicken stock
1 onion, chopped
1 cup chopped celery
1 cup diced carrots
5 cups chopped leeks
4 cups sliced potatoes
1/4 cup olive oil
Salt and freshly ground black pepper
Minced fresh parsley

Blanch barley in 1 quart boiling water for five minutes; drain. Bring 1 quart of chicken stock to boil. Add barley, cover and simmer until barley is cooked, about 1 to 1-1/4 hours.

Sauté onion, celery, carrots and leeks in olive oil over low heat until the vegetables are soft. Add the potatoes and remaining chicken stock and simmer covered until the potatoes are cooked, about 15 to 30 minutes. Combine barley and vegetable mixture. If soup is too thick for your taste, thin with stock or water. Adjust the seasonings to taste. Sprinkle fresh parsley on each serving. For smooth soup, puree the vegetables in a food processor before adding the barley. For richer soup, add 1 cup heated milk or cream. Makes 6 to 8 servings.

Powerful Medicine At The Produce Counter

When I heard the awful news that my annual Pap test revealed abnormal cells, I turned to vegetables. What else could I do? I mean, me personally. Me, instantly.

The-doctor-in-a-hurry brushed off my questions and ordered me to make yet another billable office appointment. This one to sign surgery consent forms. First mention of surgery. What kind of surgery, I asked. "Well, it will either be a big or a little procedure," the doctor said as she and her nurse swept out of the room.

The bottom dropped out of my world. Did I have cancer? Did I have options? How big is a big procedure? Does it have a name? How could I begin to deal with any of this without a shred of information?

I started at the public library. I needed enough background to draw up a list of questions. I checked out half a shelf of books on women's health.

Then on to the supermarket where a knowledge of nutrition can help us make healthy choices. When we are paying attention. Or like me, scared. I bought two heads of broccoli and a couple bunches of carrots.

Munching on the vegetables made me feel a little better–a little more in control. Still, my thoughts swung from updating my will to wondering if it was normal to feel healthy if you have–well, I did not even know what I was supposed to have.

I submitted to one more unsettling office visit. Naively, I assumed I would finally get the facts–about my health, my body, the proposed surgery. However, even my considerable interview skills could not pry any such details out of the doctor.

Edward insisted that I find another doctor. So did my father. "It's your life, Pat," advised my dad, who is a healthy 81. Through friends, fax and phone I located a skilled local doctor, who patiently answered all my question, repeated the series of tests and then declared me healthy.

I am thankful I did not have to deal with imminent cervical cancer. Those abnormal, possibly cancerous cells belonged to someone else. However, my impulse to devour gold, green, and red vegetables was no mistake.

The National Cancer Institute and the National Academy of Sciences had already declared that a nutritional diet could reduce the risk of developing three kinds of cancers: breast, lung, and colon.

The scientists recommended high-fiber foods, vegetables and fruits high in vitamin A, and vegetables and fruits high in vitamin C. Especially recommended were vegetables in the cabbage family–broccoli, Brussels sprouts, cauliflower, collards, kale, kohlrabi, turnips and water cress. Impressive evidence indicates these vegetables strengthen the immune system.

During my desperate ninety days of medical fumbling, I learned even more about plant substances–called phytochemicals–which have exhibited strong anti-cancer properties in laboratory and human tests.

The big news focused on three nutrients called antioxidants: beta-carotene, vitamin C and vitamin E. The current research strongly suggests that beta-carotene and vitamins C and E are major factors in protection against serious disease including many common cancers. These nutrients were familiar to people like me who already take vitamin E and C supplements just in case Linus Pauling and Robert Rodale were right after all. They were, but it took the scientific establishment two decades to stop pooh-poohing and actually test the theories of Nobel Laureate Pauling and *Prevention* magazine publisher Rodale.

Simply put, here is how antioxidants work: They neutralize the effects of bad guys called free radicals. Unchecked, the free radicals race around the body searching for healthy cells to invade and destroy. These powerful particles are products of ordinary metabolism. We also pick up free radicals from environmental sources like air pollution and other people's tobacco smoke.

Beta-carotene's power at the cellular level has been demonstrated in widely diverse settings. In the lab, beta-carotene proved toxic to lung cancer cells. For centuries, Native American women sipped carrot tea, to prevent conception. Both cancer and conception depend on cell division.

Rich sources of beta-carotene include cantaloupe, carrots, kale, spinach, Swiss chard, watercress and winter squash.

The strongest evidence of vitamin C's protection is against stomach cancer, possibly due to the vitamin's role in preventing nitrates and nitrites in foods from being converted into carcinogens. Studies also link vitamin C or vitamin C-rich foods to decrease of such cancers as esophagus, mouth, lung, pancreas, bowel, breast and cervix.

"The evidence is extremely strong and extremely consistent," says Gladys Block, a professor of public health nutrition at the University of California at Berkeley. "I am thoroughly convinced there are thousands of people out there dying for lack of antioxidants in their diets."

Strong words about everyday foods. But that is just the beginning. We are just now discovering many other helpful phytochemicals. Take the antioxidant lycopene, the red pigment in tomatoes, red peppers, pink grapefruit and watermelon. People with high levels of lycopene in their blood are at a lower risk for certain cancers, mainly cervical and pancreatic

University of Illinois researchers studied 102 women with a pre-cancerous inflammation called CIN (cervical intra-epithelial neoplasia) and the same number of disease-free women. Analysis showed that women with the lowest blood levels of lycopene had five times the risk of developing CIN than those with the highest levels. The 102 disease-free women consistently ate more servings of tomatoes, the richest lycopene source.

Folic acid, a lesser-known B vitamin, may also help prevent cervical cancer–even if you already are infected with the human *papilloma* virus (HPV), a common virus implicated in 80 percent of cervical cancer.

Dr. Charles Butterworth Jr. of the University of Alabama at Birmingham, studied 464 women infected with HPV. He found that when women with low levels of folic acid were exposed to HPV, they were five times as likely to develop cell changes leading to cervical cancer than women with higher red cell levels of folic acid.

Dr. Butterworth suggests the combination of a poor diet and the virus may cause cervical cancer. "It's kind of a double whammy," he says. Good sources of folic acid include barley, chickpeas, endive, lentils, green leafy vegetables, liver and orange juice.

Folic acid can also prevent spinal deformities in newborns. The Food and Drug Administration recommends that all women of childbearing age take a multivitamin containing folic acid, so that in the event of pregnancy, the fetus will be protected during the first weeks of pregnancy, the most critical time in the development of congenital defects.

D-limonene is another promising phytochemical. It occurs in orange peels and has been shown to prevent breast cancer in animals. Michael Gould of the University of Wisconsin Comprehensive Cancer Center in Madison fed D-limonene to rats with tumors. More than 80 percent of tumors disappeared. Gould is working on a more potent synthetic form, which could be used to fight cancer.

Flavenoids, compounds found in most fruits and vegetables, also have anticancer potential. Oncology professor Ajit Vermaof of the University of Wisconsin, found that one flavenoid, quercetin, inhibited colon cancer, prevented skin cancer and inhibited breast cancer–all in lab animals. Quercetin occurs in citrus fruits, berries, roots, tubers, herbs and spices, legumes, grains, tea and cocoa.

Carbinol, a substance available from broccoli, Brussels sprouts, cabbage and cauliflower, reduces levels of estrogen in the body, according to researchers at the Foundation for Preventive Oncology and the Institute for Hormone Research in New York. Many scientists believe there is a link between estrogen levels and breast cancer. Controlling the amount of estrogen in the body may prevent breast cancer.

All of which make you want to gobble vegetables. Or sip a whole bowl of them. James Duke, a United States Department of Agriculture researcher who has assembled a vast database on medicinal phytochemicals holds that "vegetable soup is a more potent anti-carcinogen than any present or future medicine."

Epidemiological experts estimate that 70 percent of modem diseases have a dietary link. Says Dr. Herb Pierson, former chief of NCI'S designer foods project, "The fastest way to make real public-health changes is to reach the food supply. And the idea that everyday foods could prevent major diseases–you couldn't come up with a hotter way to change the whole damn world."

Another expert holds that actual food–rather than vitamin supplements–is the way to protect ourselves from serious disease. "Our evidence more clearly demonstrates the protective role of fruits and vegetables than that of micro-nutrients," said Regina Ziegler, a nutritional epidemiologist at the National Cancer Institute. "We want people to focus more on fruits and vegetables. We aren't sure which ones so we want them to eat use a variety. It may also be prudent to take a one-a-day-vitamin. What is dumb is mega doses of vitamins, which interfere with absorption of other nutrients."

Most experts recommend that we eat five one-half cup servings of fruit and vegetables each day. That sounds easy enough until you realize that only one in ten Americans actually gets around to having five servings a day.

And there is more to come. The National Cancer Institute is sponsoring a $20.5 million study on certain phytochemicals that are thought to inhibit cancer. The subjects include flax, the garlic group, citrus, parsley and licorice root.

Meanwhile, the next time you crave a banana or a Brussels sprout, don't dismiss the idea as mere whimsy. Instead, listen to a scientist who has catalogued 900 phytochemicals that have demonstrated they can prevent certain diseases.

"The correlation between folk medicine and phytochemicals is astounding," says Dr. Chris Beecher, an assistant professor of medicinal chemistry at University of Illinois at Chicago. "It convinces me that people's tastes are shaped at least in part by the subliminal knowledge of what keeps them alive."

BUTTONS AND BOWS PASTA SALAD

3 tablespoons red wine vinegar
1 tablespoon dried basil
1/4 cup chopped fresh parsley
2 cloves garlic
1/3 cup Parmesan cheese
1/2 cup olive oil
Freshly ground pepper to taste
6 carrots, sliced in 1/4" rounds
8 ounces pasta bows (farfalle)

In a food processor or blender, combine the vinegar, basil, parsley, garlic, Parmesan cheese and pepper. Process until smooth.

Cook the carrots in a small amount of boiling water until crisp tender, about 5 minutes. Drain and rinse with cold water.

Cook the pasta until al dente. Drain and toss lightly with dressing. Fold in carrots. Cover and refrigerate at least 1 hour before serving. Serve at room temperature or slightly chilled.

Makes 4 to 6 servings.

When the doctor prescribed three months of bed rest for a friend with a problem pregnancy, we took turns bringing the mom-to-be special dishes. Once, she mentioned she loved cauliflower but that it was too expensive for most cooks. The next treat I brought her was this salad accompanied by a loaf of cheddar-caraway-whole wheat bread.

CAULIFLOWER SALAD WITH WHITE WINE DRESSING

1 head cauliflower
1/2 cup finely chopped onion
1 green pepper, finely chopped
1/2 cup olive oil
1/2 cup cider vinegar
1/4 cup dry white wine
1 sweet red pepper, cut into 1/4-inch strips
1/2 cup ripe olives
Salt and pepper to taste

Rinse cauliflower and cut into florets. Drop into boiling water and cook for 8 minutes over medium-low heat. Drain, rinse with cold water and drain again. Sauté the onion and green pepper in 2 tablespoons olive oil cooking until the onion is soft. Stir in the remaining olive oil, vinegar and white wine. Bring to a boil and remove from heat. Pour over the cauliflower and toss gently. Chill at least 2 hours.

Before serving, add red pepper strips and ripe olives. Taste and correct seasoning if necessary.

Makes 8 salad servings or 4 main-dish servings.

We love this dish because it is a celebration of the fullness of the earth. All the vegetables and herbs come from our garden. One summer evening, I served the zucchini parmesan with pickled beets, pickled Szechwan vegetables, red oak leaf salad vinaigrette, corn on the cob, tomatoes sprinkled with basil and a little olive oil and some round Italian bread. Dinner was on the deck in the Middle Eastern mezze style: a variety of flavors to be lightly sampled.

ZUCCHINI CASSEROLE PARMESAN

3 cups shredded zucchini
1 large onion, minced
4 cloves garlic minced
4 eggs, beaten
1/2 cup olive oil
1/2 cup grated Parmesan cheese
1 cup flour
1 tablespoon baking powder
1/4 teaspoon baking soda
1/cup chopped parsley
1 teaspoon each fresh basil,
  Rosemary, oregano
Salt, pepper to taste
Additional grated Parmesan cheese

Preheat oven to 350 degrees. If desired , use food processor to shred zucchini, chop onion and garlic. In a large bowl, mix zucchini, onion. garlic, eggs, oil, Parmesan cheese, flour, baking powder, baking soda, parsley, basil, rosemary and oregano. Season to taste with salt and pepper.

Spray a shallow ovenproof pan with non-stick coating. (I use a Corning Ware French White 2.5 liter pan.) Spoon zucchini mixture into pan. Lightly sprinkle top with more cheese.

Bake 30 to 40 minutes until golden brown on top. Let sit 10 minutes before serving. Serve warm or at room temperature. Makes 6 to 8 servings.

When Melanie Carey brought this festive dish to a Thanksgiving dinner party, everyone asked her for the recipe. That was all I needed to hear. And Melanie, a flight attendant who lives in Chicago, generously passed her recipe on to me.

SWEET POTATO RING MOLD

8 large sweet potatoes
1/2 cup butter
1/2 cup light brown sugar
5.3 ounces evaporated milk
1 teaspoon nutmeg
1 egg lightly beaten
3/4 cup raisins
4 tablespoons butter
3/4 cup dark brown sugar
1 cup pecan halves

Cook potatoes in boiling salted water until soft–about 20 minutes. Peel and mash. Add 1/2 cup butter, light brown sugar, evaporated milk, nutmeg and egg. Mix well. Fold in raisins

Grease a 6-1/2 cup ring mold with 4 tablespoons butter. Sprinkle dark brown sugar into mold, patting sugar into butter. Press pecan halves flat side up into sugar. Spoon potato mixture into mold.

Bake in a preheated 350-degree oven for 45 minutes. Invert on to a round serving plate.

Makes 6 to 8 servings.

I have to agree with Dorothy Kingsbury on the baking of winter squash and pumpkin. Miss Kingsbury is the former chairman of the Home Economics Department at nearby Keene State College. She holds that baking is the best way to cook squash and pumpkin. Baking develops the vegetable's special sweetness and keeps the flesh from getting soggy. If you have no fresh squash, use a 10-ounce package of frozen.

WINTER SQUASH WITH CHESTNUTS

2-1/2 pounds winter squash such as butternut
Salt and pepper to taste
6 teaspoons butter, melted
1/2 cup cooked, peeled, chopped chestnuts
Tarragon and chives to taste

Peel squash and cut into 1-1/2-inch chunks. Steam, microwave or bake until tender. Mash or puree in a food processor until smooth. Add butter, salt and pepper. Sprinkle with tarragon, chives and chestnuts. Serve at once.
Makes 4 servings.

FUN

In college, I spent hours in food laboratories baking bread, braising beef, canning tomatoes and steaming turnips. None of this involved any particular pleasure–just a lot of anxiety about getting a good grade. To that end, one evening at my parents' house, I made a pie shell that promptly curled up into a ball as it baked. I did not know I was supposed to prick the shell before baking. As I burst into tears at this disaster, my father gently suggested that if I got so upset over a pie shell, perhaps I should consider another vocation.

A few months later, I discovered something about myself in a pass/fail course teaching at a nursery school. The supervising teacher capitalized on my enthusiasm for seasonal decorations and food. I decked her halls with corn stalks and pine boughs. The children and I patted orange dough into pumpkins and twisted pink and white dough into candy canes. While the cookies baked, I read the children ghost or reindeer stories. Those satisfying moments–free of letter grades–revealed that I needed to have fun in the kitchen or I would curl up into a little ball.

Summer In A Bottle

Canning is a noble and time-honored way to put by the season's final harvest of vegetables and fruits. But if you prefer to preserve the fresh flavors of summer without turning your kitchen into a steam bath, consider making your own homemade cordials.

Call a fresh fruit or berry concoction whatever you like–a liqueur, balm, *digestif* or *creme*. By any name, cordials are fun to make and to serve, or give away at Christmas, New Year's or whenever the spirit moves you.

Compared to commercial cordials or liqueurs, homemade cordials are remarkably cheap to produce. All you need to concoct your own memorable label are ordinary vodka and fresh fruits or berries.

If you hesitate to make your own cordials because "bought is best," you should know that even French chefs make their own. Television chef Jacques Pepin, for one, mixes up his own version of Grand Marnier, a pricey cognac-based liqueur that is flavored with bitter oranges.

Or perhaps you buy cordials because a legend comes with each bottle.

Take Drambuie, for example. The story goes that Bonnie Prince Charlie gave a Scottish chief the Drambuie formula in gratitude for sheltering the defeated royal party back in 1746.

Amaretto, according to its legend, was invented by a young widow to signal her affection to her new suitor. Another legend holds that one of the Emperor's mistresses inspired the citrus-flavored *Mandarine Napoleon*. Parfait Amour is a relic of the age when love potions were popular in Europe. This very sweet liqueur is flavored with citrus and violet and is appropriately colored deep red or purple. And Strega–Italian for witch–is named after a legendary coven of witches who used the herbal brew as a love potion.

Of course, such legends do not come cheap. But if you are willing to create your own legend and your own liqueur, you can save money on both.

You will need some lead time, however. At least for the cordials. They require several weeks of aging before reaching their fullest bloom in the bottle. I prepare my favorite wild-blackberry cordial in late August but it takes until December for it to turn the color of rubies.

As for technique, making cordials is as easy as making a pot of tea. You simply mix alcohol-vodka, gin or brandy–with the fruit or berry of choice and allow the mixture to steep for a time in a dark place. For beginners, I suggest using domestic vodka because it has no flavor or color. Choose a smooth brand because even the strongest fruit flavors will not mask a harsh taste. Sweetening, such as sugar or honey, is added before or after steeping.

For steeping, I put my concoctions in a wide-mouth Mason jar. Most cordial recipes call for stirring the mixture periodically, and Mason jars allow easy access to the brew. Since you do not have to seal the jars as you do in canning, consider covering the jar with a peanut butter or mayonnaise lid that fits. That way, you won't have to juggle a two-piece Mason jar lid when you stir or taste.

You can also use fruit juice bottles for steeping. Just make sure your container is made of glass or crockery. Other materials like metal or plastic will react with the ingredients and produce an off taste.

If you plan to give away your cordials, collect empty glass bottles while the mixture is steeping. This is a good way to recycle interesting wine, whiskey and sparkling water bottles. Collect corks for stoppers if you need them

One handy bottle is the ten-ounce size used for single servings of fruit juices. This bottle is also good for experimenting with small amounts of different kinds of fruits. You will find that neighbors, friends and office lunch mates are happy to recycle these bottles in your direction.

For gift giving, you can decorate the bottles with sparkly stickers. If you have time and fabric scraps, make a little bonnet to decorate the bottle cap. Using pinking shears cut a round of fabric two inches larger in diameter than your bottle top. Attach the bonnet to the lid with a ring of tape–sticky side out–under the fabric. Secure with a rubber band and add a decorative ribbon, lace or cord.

When the cordial has finished steeping, line a funnel or strainer with cheesecloth or a paper coffee filter, strain and bottle. Be patient as you pour and make sure your straining setup is sturdy.

If you like a thicker cordial-say for a dessert topping-this is the time to stir in glycerin, which is available from a pharmacy. Use one-quarter teaspoon of glycerin for each cup of liquid.

Pour your cordial into a glass bottle allowing a little air space. This will protect the flavor. Cap or cork tightly. Store your cordial in a cool, dark place to preserve the color. And remember the life of a homemade cordial is about eight months.

I wish I had a recipe for a legend to accompany your liqueurs. I wish I could say that when I go to my blackberry patch on an August evening, I am wearing a gauzy pale yellow dress of hand-embroidered organdy and a floppy straw hat with yellow silk streamers. And that I carry a linen-lined wicker basket to hold my berries and that a handsome prince seeking a hideout . . . .

Well, actually, survival in our blackberry patch on a steamy summer eve does require a special costume: sturdy shoes, heavy socks, long pants, a sweatshirt, gloves and a coat of nasty-smelling bug repellent. You see, the berries are protected by barbed bramble, a network of subterranean mole holes and ground bee nests and swarms of deer flies and mosquitoes lusting for a taste of sweaty flesh. My outfit gets the berries picked but it will never appear on the cover of *Cosmopolitan* magazine.

If you have no berry patch, try the local farmers' market or a pick-your-own-berry farm. If you miss the berry season, you can try pear or apple cordial a little later. Or use fruits like lemons or oranges or beans like coffee. By the time you have bottled those flavors to your satisfaction, the fresh ones in the orchards or meadows will be on their way to ripening in time for your next batch of homemade cordials.

Most of the fun in cordial making is varying the recipes. Since a little cordial goes a long way, it is simple to experiment with one-cup batches using smaller jars. To keep a record of each cordial formula used, make a note and tape it to the jar.

For variety, try gin or unflavored brandy instead of vodka. If you prefer your cordials less sweet, gradually decrease the amount of sugar used. If blueberries were fine one year, try cherries the next. Drop in a few whole cloves, an orange or lemon peel, and a bit of stick cinnamon or a vanilla bean. Consider the kinds of flavors you like to combine in other foods and be adventurous. Throughout the year, there are scores of fruit and berry candidates available for cordial brewing.

Herbs are another source of cordial flavors. I have collected recipes using mint, lemon balm, anise, sweet cicely and lovage. The proportions are usually one cup crushed fresh herb, eight ounces vodka and one-quarter cup–more or less to taste–warmed honey. Mix and let stand for one month shaking gently once a week. Some herb liqueur recipes call for the addition of green food coloring.

I do not have much experience in herb potions because my crops of suitable herbs have been sparse. My sister, Roberta Love, has a large lush lemon balm bush that inspired me to plant one, too. Every spring when my lemon balm reappears, I take heart. Only to be disappointed when it produces a single eight-inch stalk and then quits for the season.

As for sweet cicely, my sister-in-law, Pat Comerford Haley, gave me a handful of sweet cicely seed that refused to germinate in this New Hampshire soil. But I savor the memory of Pat's arrival one spring evening at my parents' house in Buffalo with an armful of sweet cicely that filled the house with the scent of licorice and anise. My niece, Nora, just harvested another crop of cicely seeds and I will try again.

Perhaps there is something in the western New York State soil that encourages lemon balm and sweet cicely. Of course, some herbs do perform for me-parsley, basil and oregano. But elegant entertaining does not include the phrase, "Would you care for a Courvoisier, a Bailey's or some of my very own parsley liqueur?"

If you make more cordials than you can use or share, try them in cooking, adding a drop at a time. Try orange liqueur in winter squash or sweet potatoes. Flavor a fruit tart glaze with cranberry liqueur. A bit of coffee liqueur adds a certain tang to a chocolate frosting or brownies.

The most appealing aspect of cordial making may be its simplicity.

Perhaps that is why someone designed an expensive gadget to complicate things and discourage the novice. So now we can buy an eighty-dollar electric cordial maker that reduces steeping from weeks or months to eight hours. Why plan ahead when you can make amaretto on Christmas Eve in your spare moments?

You can also buy a liqueur-making kit: for a mere $39. Here's what you get: six flavorings, six labels, a bottle of anti-ruff (anti-what?), an instruction guide and imagine this, free recipes. Each kit yields six quarts of cordials with you supplying the vodka. You don't need a calculator to figure out that it might be cheaper to buy a few bottles of the superb Fra Angelico in the first place.

But if you are pleased with the results of the recipes included here, you may be ready for advanced cordial making. For ideas, do a little research at the liqueur counter. There you will find a honeydew liqueur from Japan, a passion fruit liqueur from Hawaii, a fig cordial from Italy. You'll find imported *digestifs* based on anise or mint, and perhaps even the unusual Finnish blend of brambleberries, cloudberries, and lignonberries harvested by Laplanders up near the Arctic Circle.

Which proves no growing season is ever too short to make a fresh fruit cordial.

BLUEBERRY LIQUEUR

4 cups blueberries
3 cups vodka or gin
1 cup water
8 whole cloves
1/2 teaspoon coriander seeds
2 cups sugar

Rinse and drain berries. Crush the berries in a bowl and scrape into a 2-quart glass jar. Add vodka or gin, water, cloves and coriander. Stir to mix. Cover container and let stand for 10 days in a dark place. Stir every other day. Cordial will turn a deep blue-black color.

Strain mixture through a fine sieve, cheesecloth or paper coffee filter. Add sugar and stir until dissolved. Pour into a glass bottle, cap or cork and store in a cool, dark place. Let mature for 4 weeks. Makes 1 quart.

WILD BLACKBERRY CORDIAL

2 cups fresh blackberries
1 cup sugar
2 cups vodka

Rinse and mash blackberries. Place in a 1-1/2 quart jar. Add the sugar and vodka. Stir gently until the sugar is dissolved. Cover and store in a cool, dark place for 8 weeks.

When steeping is completed, strain the mixture through a cheesecloth or paper coffee filter. Pour into a bottle and cap or cork. Store in a cool, dark place.

Makes 1-1/2 pints.

ORANGE CORDIAL

4 large oranges
2 cups vodka
1 cup brandy
1 cup sugar
1 cup water

Using a swivel-bladed peeler, remove the zest from the oranges. The zest is the orange part of the peel. Avoid using the any of the white part because it is bitter.

Place the zest into a 1-1/2 quart jar. Add the vodka and brandy. Cover and store in a cool, dark place for 2 weeks turning the jar every few days.

When steeping is complete, strain cordial through a fine sieve, cheesecloth or a paper coffee filter. Mix water and sugar in a small, heavy saucepan and bring to a boil over medium heat. Lower heat and cook and stir until sugar is dissolved–about 5 minutes. Cool thoroughly. Stir sugar syrup into cordial, mix and pour into a bottle. Cap or cork. Store in a cool, dark place. Let mature for 3 to 4 weeks.

Makes 1 quart.

CRANBERRY CORDIAL

1 pound fresh cranberries
3 cups sugar
2 cups gin

Coarsely chop cranberries using a food processor if available. Place berries in a 2-quart jar. Add sugar and gin. Cover jar tightly. Store in a cool, dark place turning daily for 3 weeks. Strain and bottle. Cover and refrigerate berries. Serve over ice cream if desired.

Makes 1 quart.

CHERRY BRANDY

1 cup sugar
2 cups brandy or vodka
1-1/4 pounds (2-3/4 cups) sweet cherries such as Bing

    Choose cherries individually. Look for cherries that are glossy, firm and dark with stems attached. Rinse and drain on a towel. Stem cherries. Using a darning needle, pierce each berry once to the pit. This will release the pit's flavor.

    Place the cherries in a 1-quart glass jar. Cover with the sugar. Put the lid on the jar. Gently shake the jar a few times to coat the cherries with sugar. Add the brandy, top with lid and gently shake a few more times. Store in a cool dark place for at least four weeks.

    Strain the mixture through a strainer fitted with a coffee filter. Bottle. The brandy should be ready to drink and has a shelf life of 2 to 3 months.

    Makes 2 cups.

Pumpkin Heads And Pumpkin Bread

Every autumn, strange creatures appear on New England lawns. These life-sized dolls have pumpkins for heads and bodies fashioned from old clothes like jeans and sweats stuffed with pillows and rags.

The dolls slouch on lawn chairs and add a bright touch to the landscape now carpeted with crackling brown leaves.

Although some people call these lawn critters dolls, it's more likely they are "guys." We may never know for sure, because like many other seasonal rites, the dolls' origins have been forgotten. We do know the English colonists celebrated Guy Fawkes' Day November 5 instead of the Catholic feast of Halloween.

Guy Fawkes was a member of the "Gunpowder Plot," a 1605 scheme to blow up King James I and the Parliament in retaliation for the monarchy's anti-Catholic decrees. Fawkes and company were discovered hours before they lit the fuse on that November 5 and were arrested and executed. Ever since, on that day, English children carry dolls through the streets begging "pennies for the guy." The guys may also be burned in village bonfires.

Writer Alice Morse Earle described an American version of Guy Fawkes Day in her "Customs and Fashions in Old New England," published in 1895. "Throughout New England for many years, the day was observed with much noise, the burning of bonfires, and parades of young men and boys dressed in fantastic costumes and carrying 'guys' or 'popes' of straw."

Halloween itself is a late entry in the American calendar. When the Irish immigrants arrived in the mid-19th century, they brought their custom of observing All Hallow's Eve on October 31. The Eve refers to the night before the Catholic feast of All Saints.

The Irish observance of the Eve included Druid and Celtic rites marking the beginning of winter–bonfires, mischief and masquerades.

The Irish immigrants to America were also the first to put a face on the pumpkin. They discovered that the big orange berry was much easier to carve than rutabagas or potatoes, the traditional jack-o-lanterns. The Jack of the lantern was a mean-spirited, heavy-drinking Celt who was condemned to wander the earth searching for a final resting place. He lit his path with a hollowed-out rutabaga holding a glowing coal straight from the fires of Hell. The devil himself, according to the legend, equipped Jack with his vegetable lantern.

Our own Connecticut River Valley is the setting for the New England legend of the "racer pumpkins." According to that tale, huge pumpkins grown by a Northfield, Massachusetts, farmer escaped from his field and raced up the valley like a litter of pigs.

Every few days, the giant pumpkins put down roots in towns like Vernon, Vermont and Hinsdale, New Hampshire and then resumed their race northward eventually reaching the Canadian border for reasons and a fate that are still unknown.

Centuries before the European settlers arrived, Cherokee and Seneca farmers cultivated a great variety of squashes including the pumpkin, *Cucurbita Pepo*. The Native Americans introduced these fruits to the settlers and taught them how to cook and preserve them. Thin pumpkin griddlecakes were a favorite dish of the times.

Mashed cooked pumpkin combined with pastry, eggs, milk, molasses and spices added up to pumpkin pie, a main dish the settlers ate for breakfast or dinner. The first written recipe for pumpkin pie appeared in "American Cookery" by Amelia Simmons published in 1796. The first published "receipts" for cranberry sauce, watermelon rind pickles and dishes using corn also appeared in the Simmons book.

Eventually, the very pumpkin that offered subsistence to the hungry settlers became an object of ridicule. New England author Edward Johnson scolded those who joked about the pumpkin. "Let no man make jest of the pumpkin," he wrote in "Wonder-Working Providence" (1854). "For with this fruit, the Lord was pleased to feed his people to their content until corn and cattle were increased."

Colonial Governor Roger Williams called pumpkins by their local name, "askutasquash," which means cooked by the sun. The word "pumpkin" began with the Greek word for a large melon, *pepon*. Pepon became *pompion* in French. In his "Herbal of 1597," Englishman John Gerard used pompion to include pumpkins, melons and squash.

And yes, there were really "pumpkin heads" in Colonial times. The term was used to describe Connecticut males, whose hair length and shape were regulated by law. A barber placed a hardened pumpkin shell on his customer's head to guide his scissors to the legal locks.

My grandmother, Elizabeth Beardsley, was a Connecticut native. I never knew her because she died when her son, my father, was a child. My dad, who grew up an orphan, worked hard at civilizing his own six rambunctious children. Dad tried to set a good example for us and avoided four-letter words. When another driver cut him off, my exasperated dad, exclaimed, "Would you look at that pumpkin head!" Did he learn that expression at his mother's knee?

Nearby Keene, New Hampshire, is the setting for a Harvest Festival featuring 10,000-plus carved and illuminated pumpkins displayed on three huge scaffolds. The carved pumpkins range from primitive to exquisite. Strolling Main Street to inspect the flickering pumpkins is a memorable way to salute the harvest.

At the Hopkinton State Fair in New Hampshire, roundness counts. Judge David Seavey of the University of New Hampshire Cooperative Extension Service, says the ultimate pumpkin should be turned while it grows to avoid flat spots and maintain an even color. A prize-winning pumpkin, Seavey adds, will sit straight rather than crooked and will have a nice handle.

Circleville, Ohio, hosts a four-day Pumpkin Show that includes the crowning of Miss Pumpkin who rides on a float resembling Cinderella's carriage. If you want to enter your biggest pumpkin in the Circleville competition, your entry must be a true pumpkin with a five-sided stem. If you count three, four or six sides on your pumpkin stem, you have grown a pumpkin that was cross-bred with a squash somewhere along the line and you are ineligible for the Circleville competition.

The squash crosses are eligible for a contest sponsored by the World Pumpkin Federation of Collins, New York, because all that matters in this event is size. The federation's 2,000 members from 30 nations compete to grow the largest pumpkin. One recent season, Howard Dill of Nova Scotia hauled his 616-pound pumpkin around his country and ours for to collect prizes totaling $14,500. Dill's champion pumpkin, the size of a washing machine, aroused the suspicion of the U.S. customs officers who, called in their drug squad to inspect the big berry. The pumpkin only contained 500 seeds for the next generation–albeit stud seeds that Dill sells for $5 each. Despite their price, the stud seeds carry no guarantee because the giant pumpkins are extremely sensitive and can be done in overnight by a fungus, or variation in moisture and temperature. Even before you have a chance to count the number of sides on the stem of a promising candidate.

Unfortunately, the monster pumpkins are not good eating–they are stringy, watery and bland. The best pumpkins for cooking are the small sugar pumpkin variety. To cook a sugar pumpkin, cut it into chunks and bake, boil, steam, microwave or pressure cook. I think baking produces the best flavor and texture. When we have the wood-stove going, I cut the pumpkin into wedges, wrap them in foil and roast slowly in a pan on top of the stove. Then I puree the flesh in the food processor and use it then or freeze it. I also toast the seeds for 5 to 10 minutes at 350 degrees in a standard oven.

Separating the seeds from the flesh is a messy job. Anticipating the delicious crunch of the fresh, toasted seeds is the only thing that keeps me from dumping the whole bowlful of glop into the compost heap. But then I would also be tossing out the pumpkin seeds' antidepressant effect. Ethno biologist Jim Duke of the U.S. Department of Agriculture, calls pumpkin seeds, a "happy food," because they contain the natural mood enhancer, tryptophan.

The pumpkin flesh, of course, will do much more than fill a pie. Viennese cooks oven-braise the beef-and-beer stew, *Carbonade* in a pumpkin shell. In Italy, pumpkin-filled ravioli are tossed with brown butter and sautéed in fresh sage. In Mexico, pumpkin flan includes the roasted and salted pumpkin seeds as does the special treat, a brittle studded with the seeds.

Here some autumn favorites for those who regard the pumpkin as more than just an empty shell.

MUSHROOM PUMPKIN SOUP

1 cup finely chopped onion
4 tablespoons butter
4 tablespoons all-purpose flour
1/2 teaspoon ginger
1/2 teaspoon nutmeg
1 quart chicken broth
4 cups pumpkin puree
Salt and freshly ground pepper to taste
2 cups half-and-half
1 cup sliced fresh mushrooms

Sauté the onion in butter until soft. Stir in the flour, ginger and nutmeg and cook until bubbly. Stir in the chicken broth and pumpkin. Cook for 15 minutes over medium-low heat. If smooth soup is desired, puree pumpkin-chicken broth mixture in a blender. Taste and correct seasoning if necessary.

Return to pot and add mushrooms. Cook just until mushrooms are soft. Stir in half-and-half and heat. Do not boil.

Makes 12 servings.

I like this recipe because the same amount of effort produces two loaves of bread–one to eat and one to give away or bank in the freezer until needed

PUMPKIN SPICE BREAD

1-1/2 cups sugar
1 cup vegetable oil
3 eggs, lightly beaten
2 cups pumpkin puree
3 cups sifted unbleached all-purpose flour
1 teaspoon baking soda
3/4 teaspoon baking powder
2 teaspoons cinnamon
1 teaspoon ground cloves
1 teaspoon nutmeg
1/2 teaspoon mace

Preheat the oven to 325 degrees. Generously grease and flour 2 9-by-5-inch loaf pans. Mix the sugar and the oil. Beat in the eggs. Add the pumpkin and mix well.

Stir together the flour, baking soda, baking powder, cinnamon, cloves, nutmeg and mace. Add the dry ingredients to the pumpkin mixture. Stir just until mixed. Pour the batter into prepared pans. Bake for one hour or until top of bread is lightly browned. Cool in pans on a rack for 15 minutes. Then remove bread from pans and finish cooling on a rack.

Makes 2 loaves.

PUMPKIN DATE MUFFINS

1-1/2 cups unbleached all-purpose flour
1-1/2 teaspoons baking powder
1/4 teaspoon baking soda
1/4 cup sugar
3/4 teaspoon cinnamon
1/2 teaspoon nutmeg
1/2 cup finely chopped dates
1/3 cup melted butter or margarine
1 egg, slightly beaten
1/2 cup milk
1/2 cup pumpkin puree

Line muffin cups with paper liners. Sift together the flour, baking powder, baking soda, sugar, cinnamon and nutmeg. Stir in the dates. Set aside.

Mix the butter, egg, milk and pumpkin. Add pumpkin mixture to dry ingredients, stirring just to mix. Do not beat. Fill muffin cups 2/3 full. Bake in a preheated 400-degree oven for 15 to 20 minutes or until a toothpick inserted in center of muffin comes out clean.

Makes 12 muffins.

Here is a great way to use up the sugar pumpkin centerpiece. I like to package small jars of this butter for gifts.

MAPLE PUMPKIN BUTTER

3/4 cup sugar
1/4 cup pure maple syrup
1/2 cup water
1 teaspoon allspice
1/2 teaspoon cinnamon
2-1/2 cups mashed, cooked pumpkin

In a heavy saucepan, combine the sugar, maple syrup, water, allspice and cinnamon. Bring to a boil, lower heat and cook and stir for 3 minutes.

Stir in the pumpkin and stir and simmer for 10 minutes or put in a slow cooker and cook uncovered on low for 1 hour.

Cool and spoon into jars. Store in the refrigerator. Makes 3 8-ounce jars.

Winifred Watts Cray is a painter and poet who has contributed much to our little town of Chesterfield, New Hampshire. Her husband, Winston, served on our board of selectmen for many years. Resolving neighborhood complaints was a large part of his work. One dispute involved a rooster that crowed too early and too late for a nearby neighbor. "I had to laugh at that one," said Winnie. "After all, this is the country and that is where most roosters live." These pumpkin cookies are named after Winnie's nephew who served in Vietnam. "I first made them for him and they were always well received," she said.

GARY'S PUMPKIN COOKIES

1/2 cup margarine or butter
1 cup brown sugar
1 egg
1 cup mashed cooked or canned pumpkin
1-3/4 cup flour
½ teaspoon salt
½ teaspoon nutmeg
1 teaspoon cinnamon
½ teaspoon cloves
1 teaspoon baking soda
1 cup bran cereal
½ cup raisins
½ cup nuts

Cream margarine and sugar. Add egg and pumpkin and beat well. Sift together flour, salt, nutmeg, cinnamon, cloves and baking soda. Add to margarine-pumpkin mixture. Stir in bran, nuts and raisins.

Drop by teaspoonfuls onto a greased baking sheet and bake in a preheated 375 oven for 12 to 15 minutes until lightly browned. Cool on a wire rack. Makes about 48 cookies.

My Love Affair With Lobster

When the summer crowds abandon our beaches in September, Edward and I drive to the seacoast to walk by the ocean, do some serious shopping and eat seafood. To me, food at sea level means lobster dripping with broth, lemon juice and butter.

We used to eat our shore dinners in harbor side restaurants where we took a number and waited until it was shouted at us. Balancing paper cups and plates, we tripped over high chairs and pocketbooks searching for a place to eat sit somewhere in the cigarette haze. Lobster lovers will put up with anything.

Eventually I realized I could cook three lobsters at home for the price of one harbor side special, even without the sugary coleslaw and soggy French fries. I can toast my lobster with a glass of good white wine—often unavailable in family restaurants. As for lobster bibs, mine are reusable: I buy fabric placemats and stitch ties on the short ends. And I consume my lobster in an atmosphere that reveres the world's second most expensive food.

Lobster was not always a delicacy. "Let 'em eat lobster," was the way New England fed its poor people in the 17th century. Poorhouse inmates at Plymouth, Massachusetts, complained about eating lobster morning, noon and night.

But who could fault the town officials? *Homarus Americanus,* our native lobster, washed up on the beach in piles two feet high after every storm. Since talk radio had not yet been invented, no one whined over the airwaves, "Do you know what welfare people are eating down at the almshouse?"

Fishermen used lobster as bait for the more valuable striped bass. Farmers used it to fertilize their fields.

There was more than enough lobster for everyone for the next hundred years–with one interruption. During the Revolutionary War, the six-foot-long lobsters of embattled New York harbor fled to more peaceful waters.

The American lobster crawled along its unpopular and unendangered course until the mid-nineteenth century when it was discovered as a delicacy equal to its smaller European cousin. Celebrities like Diamond Jim Brady and courtesan Lillie Langtry elevated the lobster to their trend-setting tables. The new railroads could rush ocean-fresh lobsters to Chicago in a speedy 30 hours. "Lobster palaces" sprang up in major American cities. Downing a dozen lobsters made news. The lobster beds were over-fished and, by 1918, the yield sank to an all-time low. Conservation efforts now permit American lobstermen to take 70 million pounds a year–still below demand.

Conservationists and marketers eagerly study lobster breeding. Here's how it goes: when the lady lobster is ready for her springtime mating, she sprays a sex attractant into a gentleman's burrow. He invites her in. "Well, hello there. Come on in and slip out of that hard shell," could be his line. She molts and the pair gently mates. She usually stays around for a few days, until her new shell hardens, though some lobster couples share a rocky cave for months.

Lobsters use their powerful claws to catch their dinner: mussels, crab, and other lobsters. That's why their claws are pegged when you buy them. Imagine a fishmonger whose 25 lobster order turns out to be one fat lobster burping on the last of his traveling companions. That is also why lobsters have not yet been successfully farmed—bred for their meat—but the high stakes are stimulating widespread experimentation.

If the lobster's dark blue or deep green carapace is not your favorite shade, just wait. A Long Island scientist is working on such designer colors as tangerine, gold and light blue–though they too will turn red when boiled. The natural blue lobster, a mutant that occurs once in every 30 million, matures to market size in a mere 20 months–one-fourth the usual time.

Lobster tastes best eaten seaside, of course. It also helps to cook it in the Native American style– in a large pot of ocean water covered with seaweed over a wood fire. Fill the pot with salted water, bring to a boil and add the lobster. To steam, pour salted water two inches deep into the pot. Bring to a boil; place the lobster on a rack above the water and cover. Boil or steam the lobster about 12 minutes or until the shell turns bright red. Overcooking drives out the sweet tenderness that lobster is all about.

Is it humane to throw a live lobster into boiling water? Some scientists say it is. Others urge swiftly cutting the spinal cord before cooking by thrusting the tip of a knife downward into the breach between the head and forward abdomen.

Lobster, of course, is an acquired taste. Like most youngsters, I had little appreciation for seafood. I never gave much thought to the great difference between the yellow bass my dad patiently hauled out of Lake Erie or the fish sticks my mother served on Lenten Fridays. I was reminded of that recently when I had dinner with my youngest brother, Tom, and his wife, Pat. While we three feasted on fresh-caught brook trout that Tom caught, Michael and Nora, brought equal gusto to fish sticks. "That's what they like," said Pat with a shrug and a smile.

The sweetest, juiciest lobster I have tasted was served at a picnic on an uninhabited island in Maine. Edward and I were cruising Penobscot Bay on the schooner *Heritage*.

Captains Doug and Linda Lee hailed a passing lobster boat and negotiated for the morning's catch. Later we anchored off Wreck Island and rowed to the beach where the crew boiled lobsters in a galvanized wash tub. Half an hour later, we lined up for a plate of lobster awash in lemon butter.

Our chatter ebbed to a silence. The only sound in that pink-gold evening was the crunch of lobster shells and an occasional groan of pleasure. The lobster I ate that night was the freshest I had ever eaten–straight out of the sea. It was glorious. But not everyone thought so.

"So what's the big deal?" a young man wondered. "I like crab better," said a California woman.

"I got half of one down," said a plump woman as she discarded a meaty pair of lobster claws into the waste bucket.

Not me. When I am sitting on a beach in Maine with fresh-caught lobster and lemon-butter dribbling down my chin, I know life does not get much better than this. In respectful silence, Joy Tranquilly of Simsbury, Connecticut, and I slurped up our second lobster of the evening. We had already spent lots of time together in the *Heritage* galley chopping, peeling and even better, talking. But out here on Wreck Island, we sat in magnificent satiety and for once Joy's hearty cove-bouncing laugh was silenced.

As unlikely as it may seem, there were actually leftovers. After 34 people dined at Wreck Island there were still 14 leftover lobsters. The next day they reappeared in chowder and a cocktail dip.

And if you are very thrifty, consider this use-it-up recipe from Lillian Beckwith in her "Hebridean Cookbook." Pound the empty shells into small pieces and simmer for 2 hours in a quart of water seasoned to taste with salt and pepper and a pinch of fresh basil. Strain using a fine sieve or cloth. Then melt 2 tablespoons butter. Stir in 1 tablespoon flour until mixture begins to froth. Slowly add the lobster stock, stirring constantly. Simmer for 10 minutes. Remove from heat and stir in 1 /2 cup cream. And there you have it—lobster-flavored soup.

And if lobster is the world's second most expensive food, what can be the first?

Well, it takes a Los Angeles restaurant to put them together, of course.

The menu reads: "Warm Lobster Salad garnished with White Truffles flown this morning from the South of France."

The price is not mentioned. Meaning, if you have to ask, you can't afford it.

A delightful make-ahead salad that offers a pleasing contrast of refreshing, cool salad served on a bed of just-cooked, warm pasta.

CARIBBEAN LOBSTER SALAD

1 pound cooked fresh lobster meat
1/2 cup fresh lime juice (2 to 3 limes)
1/2 teaspoon salt
2 cucumbers, peeled, quartered lengthwise, seeded, sliced
4 green onions, sliced
1 sweet red pepper, seeded, cut lengthwise into thin strips
1 cup chopped, roasted, unsalted cashews
1/2 cup unsweetened, reduced-fat coconut milk
1 teaspoon red pepper sauce
1/4 cup chutney
1/4 cup chopped fresh cilantro
8 ounces linguine
2 tablespoons peanut oil

Combine lobster, lime juice and salt in a medium bowl. Refrigerate at least 30 minutes.

Place sliced cucumber in a sieve. Drain 15 minutes. In a medium bowl, combine cucumbers, onions, sweet red peppers and cashews. Stir together coconut milk, red pepper sauce and chutney. Pour over cucumber mixture. Stir in lobster, lime marinade and cilantro. Refrigerate until ready to serve.

Bring salad mixture to room temperature. Cook the linguine in boiling, salted water until tender but still firm. Drain and toss with 2 tablespoons peanut oil to prevent clumping. Arrange the pasta on four plates. Top with the lobster salad. Makes 4 servings.

Generally, a 1-1/4 pound lobster will yield 1 cup meat. If you are in a hurry, check the fish counter where cooked shelled lobster chunks may be offered. The cooked lobster needs only to be heated briefly. Otherwise, it will become tough.

FUSILLI WITH LOBSTER

6 tablespoons olive oil
2 cloves garlic split in half lengthwise
1/2 cup chopped onion
1 pound Italian tomatoes, peeled and chopped
6 basil leaves
1 teaspoon sugar
Salt and freshly ground pepper
2 cups cooked lobster meat, cut into 1/2-inch pieces
1 tablespoon parsley, minced
1 pound fusilli, corkscrew-shaped pasta
Large pot boiling salted water
1/2 cup thinly sliced scallions including green tops

Heat 4 tablespoons olive oil in a large skillet, add the onion and 1 clove garlic and sauté over medium-low heat until vegetables are softened. Discard garlic. Add tomatoes, basil and sugar. Cook and stir over low heat for 1 minute. Taste and season with salt and pepper. Remove from heat, cool slightly and puree mixture in blender or food processor.

Heat 1 tablespoon olive oil in a large skillet.Add 1 clove garlic and heat gently until fragrant. Remove garlic. Add lobster and cook and stir over medium-high heat for 2 minutes. Add pureed tomato mixture and cook and stir for 2 minutes. Keep warm.

Add 1 tablespoon olive oil to the boiling pot of water. Add fusilli, return to a boil and cook the pasta, stirring occasionally, for 10 minutes or until it is *al dente*. Drain the pasta; transfer to a heated serving bowl. Add the sauce and the scallions to the pasta and toss well to combine ingredients.

Makes 4 servings.

Fresh sage can flavor more just than the Thanksgiving turkey dressing. This version of lemon-butter makes a great dipping sauce for a lobster feast.

LEMON BUTTER WITH SAGE AND GARLIC

1/2 cup butter
1 large garlic clove, finely chopped
1 tablespoon chopped fresh sage
1 tablespoon fresh lemon juice

Melt butter. Stir in garlic, sage and lemon juice.
Makes 1/2 cup dipping butter.

This outrageously rich lobster dish must be the affluent cousin of everything else we label a stew. Serve with a loaf of fresh-baked bread, a mostly-green salad, a bottle of sauvignon blanc and a peach sorbet and you will have a simple but sublime feast. This recipe is so named because ingredients like the lobster, butter and cream can easily be overcooked–or worse–if you do not pay full attention.

PAY-ATTENTION LOBSTER STEW

3 small boiled lobsters or 3/4 pound cooked lobster meat
1/2 cup butter
3 cups clam juice
2 cups heavy cream
2 tablespoons dry sherry
Salt and freshly ground pepper

Melt butter in a non-reactive 3-quart saucepan. Lower heat, add lobster and cook and stir for 3 minutes. Slowly add cream. Stir in clam juice and sherry. Continue to stir and heat almost to a boil but do not boil. Remove from heat. Taste and season with salt and pepper.

Refrigerate several hours before serving to allow flavors to blend. To serve, heat slowly and carefully to just below boiling. Ladle into heated bowls.

Makes 6 servings.

LOVE

When I was a child, the birthday girl got to pick the menu. My choice: spaghetti followed by cherry Jell-O with real whipped cream.

Occasionally, when I think of it, I repeat Mother's custom. One birthday, I decided to cook my favorite menu for the two of us. On the way home I bought oysters for bisque, filet mignon for steak au *poivre,* some decent burgundy, sour cream to top the baked potatoes, artichoke hearts for the salad, fresh California asparagus, chocolate and heavy cream for mousse.

As I stood in line at the checkout, I spotted the hospital dietician in front of me. As she X-rayed my cart's contents, she said loudly, "I wish I could afford to eat like a newspaper editor." (No one, not even dieticians counted fat grams back then.) I sighed but did not bother to explain. Edward and I savored my birthday feast. And drank a toast to each other.

Over Kona coffee and Cognac, I finally agreed to let Edward do the weekly grocery shopping. It is his way of saying, "I love you." So far no one ever editorialized over the groceries in his cart.

Lovers Still Want To Believe In Aphrodisiacs

There you are burning with romance while your love object is decidedly cool. Is it possible to concoct a menu that will create a fever in your favor?

Suppose you serve a dinner of oysters, caviar, Champagne, truffles, ripe olives and chocolate. Would you create a grand passion? Or dyspepsia and all its disheartening consequences?

Whatever happens, tradition says your heart is in the right place. These foods have all been considered aphrodisiacs by one culture or another.

The word, aphrodisiac, (say afro DIZ ee ack) comes from Aphrodite, the ancient Greek goddess of love. It has been that long since lovers have been trying to find a food that will do their seducing for them.

No matter what nutritionists say—science has yet to isolate a true aphrodisiac—the lovelorn still want to believe. The search goes on.

The Greeks began with carrots. Yes, carrots. Maybe they noticed what the carrots did for rabbits. In any case, carrot cake—delicious on its own merits–is nowadays a favored wedding cake.

The Roman, Petronius, in charge of evening entertainment at Nero's court, never failed to put shellfish on the menu—along with pomegranate pitch, mushrooms, snails, onions and even fava beans. With a boss like Nero, Petronius had to try anything.

Asparagus did it for Sheik Abu Nafzawi. In *The Perfumed Garden for the Soul's Delectation,* this Arab prince revealed "He who boils asparagus, then fries them in fat and then pours upon them the yolks of eggs with pounded condiments, and then eats every day of this dish, finds in it a stimulant for his amorous desires."

According to legend, the Aztec emperor Montezuma drank 50 goblets of chocolate before entering his bedchamber, but he could have saved all those calories and many pesos by simply falling in love. Chemists today say that phenyl ethylamine—PEA for short—is supposed to be released into the bloodstream when anyone falls in love or eats chocolate, whichever is first.

To that end, I suppose, one out of two men gives boxed chocolates for Valentine's Day, according to the American Boxed Chocolate Survey conducted by the Baltimore Research Agency. Further, five percent of Americans believe giving boxed chocolates improves their chances of getting sex. And then there is the mystery of why one quarter of the American population admits of hiding boxed chocolates from other household members.

As every New Englander knows, the all-time sure-fire aphrodisiac is shellfish in any of its forms. If New Englanders are lustier than inlanders, it is clearly because they live next to a cold-water shelf teeming with clams, mussels, lobsters and shrimp.

Back in 17th century France, Dr. Nicholas Venette noted in his *Tableau de l'Amour* that those who live almost entirely on fish "are more ardent in love than others. In fact," he confessed, "we ourselves feel most amorously inclined during Lent."

In any century, rare and expensive ingredients have become sought-after aphrodisiacs. Pliny's list of love foods included pine nuts or pignoli—now $10 a pound. In love as in war, expense has never been a hesitation. Today you can order 5-1/4 pounds of Godiva chocolates for your Montezuma in a ribboned and lace box for a trifling $295.

Speaking of rare essentials, you won't find truffles on special at the supermarket either. But this subterranean fungus is a legendary equal-opportunity aphrodisiac. Anthelme Brillat-Savarin says right here in *The Physiology of Taste* (1825) that truffles "make women more tender and men more apt."

Apt was the word for my own most memorable Valentine turn-on. At the time I was a flight attendant under orders to lose five pounds or my job. My daily ration of cottage cheese and grapefruit set off raging fantasies of satin-covered boxes filled with dark chocolate creams with coconut centers. Then, on Valentine's Day, he appeared at my door with a red, heart-shaped box—filled with saccharin tablets. Well, dear reader, I married him.

Why the abiding hunger for aphrodisiacs? Why do we persist in this amorous alchemy? Probably because we are human. We want our cures to be magic. We want our solutions to be easy. If something is exotic, romantic or expensive, we think it will do the job.

Consider this explanation for the magic we ascribe to the bubbly. "Although Champagne is a noted ingredient in seduction scenes, whatever effectiveness it may have is probably due to the flattery of being offered an expensive commodity—as well as possibly the titillation produced by the ejaculative pop of as the bottle is opened."

So say Peter Farb and George Armelagos, authors of *Consuming Passions: The Anthropology of Eating* (Houghton Mifflin).

Then are love potions mere notions? Only lovers really know. If you so qualify, you will need the Valentine's menu below. Each entry is supposed to be an effective aphrodisiac—just how effective, I am not sure. Try them and see. You are on your own.

COCKTAIL OLIVES

1 pint ripe olives (about 14 ounces)
1/4 cup olive oil
2 cloves garlic, minced

Drain the olives and discard liquid. Add the oil and the garlic to olives. Stir. Cover and let season at least 4 hours. Store in refrigerator. Bring to room temperature before serving.

Makes 1 pint appetizer olives.

OYSTER STEW

1 cup milk
1 cup half-and-half
3 tablespoons butter
8 ounces shucked oysters with liquid
1/2 teaspoon white pepper
Salt to taste
1 tablespoon dry sherry
Snipped chives

Gently heat the milk and half-and-half over medium heat until tiny bubbles form around edge. Keep warm over low heat.

Melt the butter in a saucepan. Add the oysters and their liquid. Simmer over low heat for about 2 minutes or until the edges of the oysters begin to curl. Do not overcook. Add the warmed milk mixture, pepper, salt and sherry. Serve in warmed bowls. Sprinkle each serving with chives.

Makes 2 servings.

ROMAINE SALAD WITH SESAME DRESSING

6 ounces romaine
2 tablespoons apple cider vinegar
2 tablespoons sesame or olive oil
1 teaspoons Dijon mustard
Salt and freshly ground pepper to taste
2 tablespoons sesame seeds

Wash and drain the romaine. Wrap in a towel to dry. Refrigerate until serving time. Whisk together the vinegar, oil, mustard, salt and pepper. Tear the romaine into bite-size pieces. Toss dressing lightly with romaine. Sprinkle with sesame seeds.

Makes 2 servings.

This fillet of sole goes nicely with rice prepared with 1 tablespoon fresh lemon juice and 2 tablespoons chopped fresh parsley. To serve, top rice with 2 tablespoons toasted slivered almonds or pine nuts.

DIANE'S FILLET OF SOLE CHAMPAGNE

1/4 cup chopped onion
1 tablespoons minced parsley
1/2 cup sliced mushrooms
 1/4 cup dry bread crumbs
1/2 pound fillet of sole
¼ teaspoon white pepper
½ cup dry Champagne
¼ cup freshly-grated Parmesan cheese

Heat oven to 375 degrees. Grease a shallow baking dish. Mix the onion, parsley and mushrooms. Scatter 1/2 of the mushroom mixture in the bottom of the baking dish. Sprinkle with 2 tablespoons bread crumbs. Place the fillets on bread crumbs in the dish. Top with remaining mushroom mixture. Sprinkle with pepper. Add Champagne. Bake in preheated oven for 10 minutes.

Mix the remaining bread crumbs and cheese. Sprinkle over fish and bake 10 more minutes. Makes 2 servings.

The combination of sweetened and unsweetened chocolate titillates the palate. Serve on a plate lined with a heart-shaped doily.

CHOCOLATE TRUFFLES

¼ cup unsalted butter
2-1/2 ounces semi-sweet chocolate
2 tablespoons dark rum
½ cup grated unsweetened chocolate
or unsweetened cocoa
Fluted foil or paper candy cups

Melt butter and chocolate in top of a double boiler. Remove from heat, add rum and stir to mix. Refrigerate 30 to 40 minutes or until firm.

Using 1 teaspoon of chocolate mixture, shape into small balls. Roll each ball into grated chocolate or cocoa. Place in a fluted foil candy cup. Refrigerate until served.

Makes 24 truffles.

Ecstasy By The Cup

I do not understand why some people fidget about their cable TV. Or crave over-priced ice cream mixed with bits of junk candies. Or require exercise machines that beep and chime.

But when it comes to coffee, I too can fidget and crave and beep and chime. Maybe it is because coffee is the last of my vices. Cigarettes went out of my life years ago. Saccharine-laced soft drinks are a fading memory. A pepper mill has replaced my salt shaker. No more two-martini lunches. Just sprout salads and herbal tea.

And coffee.

I have cut down on my coffee, of course. At one time I drank it all day and into the night. Coffee was my warm and friendly companion during youthful all-nighters like cramming for exams or sewing my bridesmaid's dress on the very eve.

Eventually I decided moderation could do no harm. I came down to three cups a day. I still do not know whether coffee is good or bad for me. One study says coffee causes ulcers, panic attacks and high blood pressure. The next says coffee improves mental performance, staves off depression, relieves asthma and prevents cavities. Who knows? As long as I still have to get up in the morning, I will start my day with the bean that stimulates.

It all began with a climb onto my mother's lap toward her coffee. Mother dipped buttered bread into her coffee for me. It was warm, soggy, sweet and fatty–all the things infants crave long before they discover coffee.

Before anyone yells "unfit mother," let me say we are talking about World War II. It was difficult to abuse anything then because, like everything else, coffee was rationed.

I soon learned to dip donuts into warm milk or cocoa. But when I began school, I was astonished to learn that dunking a donut into one's coffee was as evil as red lipstick, Atheistic Communism and non-Catholics.

I did not tell Mother what the nuns said about dunking.

When it came to the universal coffee-and, my mother excelled with the "ands"–her own bread, sweet rolls and coffee cakes. She entertained one-on-one, cup-to-cup. I wonder what shake of the gene pool inspires me to the festive dinner party?

Despite my half-century love affair with coffee, I am relatively new to brewing my own. Like everyone else in the 1950s, my parents drank instant coffee. Madison Avenue convinced us all that instant was best. Never mind the taste.

In college home economics, we brewed real coffee in different kinds of equipment. As soon as the exams were graded, sure enough I forgot the difference between Drip and Vacuum.

In graduate school, I learned this: if you pour boiling water from a height into a cup holding instant coffee powder, the result is supposed to taste almost as good as brewed coffee. The professor did not address the hazards of climbing on a stool–in the heels and skirts of the Fifties–aiming a kettle of boiling water at a tea cup.

For years, I drank instant coffee with "lightener" and saccharine. It was not until I quit smoking that I actually tasted this stuff. I switched to instant freeze-dried coffee flavored with whole milk and honey.

Then a house guest pointed out that boiling our 40-degree well water for instant coffee took as long as perking a pot of fresh, real coffee. She predicted coffee brewed with our own well water would be delectable. So I hauled out the electric percolator we had received as a wedding gift.

I began prepping the coffee at night, plugging it into an electric timer. The coffee pot was supposed to wake up and perk before I did. Most of the time, it did not. And I never did figure out why.

When *The Wall Street Journal* reported a new coffee maker with a built-in timer, the experts said the market was not ready for a $55 coffee maker. But I was. The automatic dripper set off a morning aroma that jump-started my days.

The $55 coffee maker had its drawbacks–disposable filters that you had to remember to buy, a fragile glass carafe that cracked when you looked at it and a too-hot plate that cooked fresh coffee down to sludge. On windy nights here in the country, the digital timer flashed 00:00 whenever a branch brushed a power line, issuing a pot of fresh coffee at, say, 2:30 a.m.

In the end, I replaced my luxury coffee maker with a later, cheaper model, with a low-tech timer. When the power goes out, the clock hands simply stop. No honk, no flash, no midnight coffee.

My no-nonsense coffee maker was just the beginning of a new generation. Next came the sleek European imports with cord storage, his-and-her carafes, space-saving compacts and built-in coffee mills. Not to mention a $500 espresso machine from Italy.

Then we coffee lovers thought we discovered fresh-ground beans–like Java, Kenya and the $32-per-pound Jamaican Blue Mountain. But that's what Mother ground for herself at the corner A & P back in the 1940's. However the rediscovered beans also came in decaffeinated versions and flavorings like hazelnut, chocolate raspberry, cookies and cream, snicker doodles and German chocolate cake.

If you would rather not grind your beans at the store–and spill them on the floor like everyone else–you can now grind them at home in your own coffee mill. This also means you can refrigerate the freshness until you are ready to release it.

A home-style coffee mill can cost anywhere from $15 to $75, but who cares? The aroma alone is worth it. At this level of technology, coffee became so delicious I abandoned milk, honey and all other condiments.

I had already learned to take my coffee straight when I lived in the Middle East. Turks, Greeks and Arabs wonder why westerners spoil good coffee with milk. Orientals revere coffee so much they boil it three times to bring it to the consistency of light syrup. It is a heady brew, inducing a respectable caffeine buzz, so it is sipped–not gulped–from tiny cups. In that non-booze culture, coffee is the drink of friendship and hospitality, and the corner coffee house displaces the corner bar. Business cannot be negotiated until coffee is brought. It even has ritual applications; Sufi mystics of Yemen use the magical bean to help transport them to enchantment.

Here in the Occident, coffee consumption is now in decline. We are drinking it less, if enjoying it more. Market analysts note that many of us are getting our caffeine from cola drinks–even at breakfast. But parents who forbid coffee to their young can still wonder why Johnny and Jane are so hyper.

To recover market share, coffee manufacturers are fighting back with sex. In one commercial, a luscious young couple fresh out of bed strolls to a Parisian cafe where they sip an American brand of coffee. In another ad, a sensual female voice suggests celebrating "your special moments" with an artificially-sweetened, chemically-flavored instant java cosmeticized with a svelte European name. Coffee marketers are driven to such extremes because their usual supermarket blends are so boring.

But specialty coffee shops like Gloria Jean's and Starbucks have discovered there is a real demand for a decent cup of coffee–even at $2 per cup. And two new magazines celebrate the joys of java: *Cafe Ole* and *Coffee Journal*. Articles include travel pieces on such coffee-flavored destinations as Kenya and a glossary of coffee selections at your favorite coffee bar.

As for me, just lead me to a barrel of fresh Kona beans and let me inhale. This is ecstasy. It evokes in me the memory of a mother's love. And the progressive excitements

of high tech hardware bringing on quicker, better brews.   And the right-at-home per-
fumes of beans I can grind myself. And the first sip of French roast warming the dark of
a winter morn. And the fragrance of decaf after dinner with friends. And Sufis dancing
in their enchantment. I know the feeling.

CLASSIC SOUR CREAM COFFEE CAKE

½ cup soft butter
2 cup sugar
2 eggs, well beaten
1 teaspoon vanilla
1-3/4 cups flour
2 teaspoons baking powder
½ teaspoon salt
1 cup sour cream
1 teaspoon baking soda
1/3 cup brown sugar
½ teaspoon cinnamon
¼ cup chopped walnuts or pecans

Cream butter and sugar. Beat in eggs and vanilla. Stir together flour baking powder and salt. Add dry ingredients. Combine sour cream and soda and stir into butter flour mixture.

Combine brown sugar, cinnamon and chopped nuts. Spread half the batter in a greased Bundt or angel food cake pan. Sprinkle with half the brown sugar-cinnamon mixture. Spread remaining batter on top. Sprinkle rest of topping onto cake. Bake at 350 degrees for 40-50 minutes or until a toothpick inserted in the center comes out clean. Cool in pan. Makes 10 to 12 servings.

This delightful brownie recipe is the way I say thanks to the all the people who make our life in the country a lot easier–the ticket agents at our regional airport, the cat sitter, our trusted mechanic and the helpful staff at our recycling center. The cookies go together in record time but still say "I appreciate you." I recently handed this recipe down to the next generation at a cookie-recipe shower for a bride-to-be.

QUICK AND EASY DOUBLE CHOCOLATE CHIP BROWNIES

1 12-ounce package semi-sweet
chocolate chip morsels, divided
½ cup (1 stick) butter
3 eggs
1-1/4 cups all-purpose flour
1 cup granulated sugar
1/4 teaspoon baking powder
1 teaspoon vanilla extract
½ cup finely chopped nuts

Grease a 13-by-9-inch baking pan. Melt 1 cup of morsels and butter in a large heavy saucepan over low heat. Stir until smooth. Remove from heat. Cool slightly. Add eggs and stir well.

Add flour, sugar, baking soda and vanilla. Stir well to mix. Stir in remaining morsels. Spread into prepared pan. Sprinkle chopped nuts on top.

Bake in a preheated 350-degree oven for 18 to 22 minutes or until a wooden pick inserted in center comes out just slightly sticky. Do not over bake. Cool completely. Cut into 2-inch squares.

Makes 2 dozen brownies.

Chocolate flavored with coffee and amaretto makes this mousse a fitting ending to a special meal.

AMARETTO CHOCOLATE MOUSSE

6 ounces semisweet chocolate, cut into small pieces
2 tablespoon strong hot coffee
4 eggs, separated
1/4 cup sugar
2 tablespoons amaretto
1 cup heavy cream
1 ounce semisweet or bitter sweet chocolate for shaving

Melt the chocolate in the top of a double boiler over simmering water. Stir in the coffee. Cool.

With an electric mixer, beat the egg yolks and the sugar about 3 minutes or until mixture is thick and light yellow. Stir in the chocolate mixture.

Beat the egg whites until they hold a stiff peak. Whip the cream with the amaretto. Into the chocolate mixture, gently fold in the beaten egg whites alternately with the whipped cream.

Spoon the mousse into a chilled serving bowl or dessert glasses. Chill 1 hour. Use a swivel-bladed vegetable peeler to make chocolate shavings. To serve, top mousse with shavings. Makes 6 servings.

In Vienna, the coffee break is elevated to an art. The coffee shops offer exquisite displays of pastries such as *dobostorte, linzertorte* and almond crescent cookies. This simplified version of *linzertorte* is easy on the cook but the result can still transport me back to time I visited this great city.

LINZERTORTE SIMPLIFIED

1 cup whole almonds
1-1/2 cup flour, sifted
1/4 teaspoon cloves
1/2 teaspoon cinnamon
1 teaspoon grated lemon peel
1-1/2 cups raspberry jam
1 cup butter, at room temperature
1/2 cup sugar
2 egg yolks
Confectioners' sugar

Blanch almonds by dropping in boiling water and simmering for five minutes. Drain and cool until safe to handle. Slip off skins and dry almonds on paper toweling. Finely chop almonds. Use a food processor if desired.

Cream butter and sugar until light and fluffy. Stir together almonds, flour, lemon peel and spices. Add to butter and sugar mixture and mix until crumbly. Set aside one-quarter of this mixture. Add the egg yolks to the remaining mixture and mix well. Shape into a ball. Wrap each of the doughs in plastic wrap and refrigerate one hour.

Preheat the oven to 350 degrees. Butter a nine-inch square baking pan. Pat the larger portion of chilled dough into the pan. Spread the raspberry jam over the dough. Crumble the remaining dough on top of the jam.

Bake for about 40 minutes or until just golden. Do not over bake. Cool on a rack. Lightly sift confectioners' sugar over top of pastry. Cut into 16 squares.

When I was a newspaper food editor, this recipe for coffee liqueur was one of the most requested by my readers. This is a Kahlua type liqueur. For an imitation Tia Maria, use rum instead of vodka.

COFFEE LIQUEUR

2 vanilla beans
1 cup strong black coffee
1 cup honey
1 bottle (25.6 ounces) vodka

Mix the vanilla beans, coffee, honey and vodka. Let stand one month. Remove vanilla beans and strain cordial. Bottle, cap or cork and store in a cool, dark place.
Makes 40 ounces.

My Man In The Supermarket

My husband likes to do the food shopping.

He does it efficiently and well. In fact, he admits to liking it.

I do not. To me there is nothing pleasant about pushing an oversized cart with sticky wheels over a quarter of an acre to collect a week's supply of broccoli, shredded wheat and plastic wrap.

There are exceptions. Shopping can be a pleasure for me when I am planning a special dish. I browse among the chocolate–unsweetened, bittersweet, semisweet, Dutch process–to find just the right one for a decadent torte. Or how about a serendipitous search among the snails and balsamic vinegar for a showy appetizer?

Too, shopping can be redeemed for me if it becomes a social event. Traditionally, a marketplace has always been a meeting place. When I am rummaging through the cheese case, a fellow rummager is likely to be friend Carmela Azzaro. She too has a bumper basil crop and needs a hunk of Parmesan for a summer night's pesto on pasta.

Looking back, I regret I did not surrender the grocery shopping sooner and more graciously. Edward had to convince me (1) he really wanted to do it and (2) he was capable.

He came up against the ancient tradition of food gathering by females. Besides, I have a home economics degree, earned by writing 20-page tracts on comparison shopping for powdered milk.

Men who shop have always been a target for women's jokes. They still tell the one about the fellow who bought washing soda instead of baking soda and used it to bake a cake. And the man who thickened the sauce with laundry starch. We female chauvinists roll our eyes about somebody's husband blowing the food budget on impulse items like artichoke hearts and crabmeat. Or at the races or the corner tavern. Men are not to be trusted. Our mothers warned us.

However, it is turning out that men are educable. In today's multi-career households, men are doing more of the food shopping and it shows. Marketers are introducing technologies that speed check-outs, obviate those intimidating and time-consuming "Price Checks!" and reduce the number of times an item is handled–up to seven times per can of kidney beans when mere women did the shopping.

But grocery shopping is also being made more boring, for me anyway. Shopping carts are heavier though households are smaller. People of any gender, age and stamina can lose their balance reaching into some of these box cars to retrieve a carton of yogurt or a little bottle of extra virgin olive oil. My solution? I put a store-provided hand basket in the bottom of the cart for the tiny cans of cat food for finicky cats and the tiny jars of capers.

Worse is the barbaric exact-change-only-cart-lock-up system installed in supermarket parking lots. In bad weather, don't ask me to dig deep for change that only jumps out of my numbed fingers and disappears into a pile of snow or under a car. People who design such systems do not understand that a shopper's hands are always full–of baby, list, purse, gloves, coupons, flyers, deposit bottles, two kinds of bags to recycle–sometimes all of these.

Every so often, I do the marketing. It feels like I have joined a surreal scavenger hunt. Where, I wonder, is the coriander? The corn meal? The barley? The molasses?

"I have no idea. I don't work here," says the person stocking the soda pop. And just last week, I came across a poor soul who was perched on top of a battery-operated cart which was blocking the aisle much to the annoyance of the crowds of 5 PM Friday shoppers. She told me the battery had run down right there in the middle of the aisle and her husband had said he would be right back after he fetched the bananas. I hurried over to the "service desk," asked for help and hopefully the woman was rescued soon after.

Some supermarkets have installed information telephones throughout the store. That is step in the right direction. Unless, you have to search for them, too. The telephones need to be well marked. And the info line operator needs to be informed every time the round toothpicks are moved from party goods to cake decorating to dental products.

Perhaps my impatience with today's shopping goes back to childhood, when my parents shopped the cavernous Washington Street and Broadway markets in Buffalo. Here every Saturday, bakers, butchers, farmers, green grocers and fishmongers offered their wares. Entering the market from the bright sunshine of a winter morning, my first impression was darkness relieved by dim bare bulbs strung overhead. Shoppers strolled from stall to stall checking for the pinkest lamb, the flakiest *kimmelweck* roll, the brightest flowers, the sweetest oranges. "Stan has the best meat," my father used to say.

We tagged behind our parents and were relatively well behaved. Otherwise, there would be no market outing the next week. Instead mother would take us to the new, shiny, predictable A&P.

The Washington Street and Broadway vendors knew how to handle children. When Mother bought a ham or a loaf of bread, there was always the free slice of the world's most scrumptious bologna or a warm sugar cookie for us. There was even a free package of bones for the dog that had stayed home.

Perhaps there because there was no such market in Manchester, New Hampshire, Edward is more patient with the supermarket experience. By the time I track down the leeks, Romano cheese and lentils, I have reached my canned music threshold and must escape—without the romaine and milk I need for dinner. I have had more fun haggling for groceries in the souks of Jerusalem. Or strolling the cool, cavernous market in St. John, New Brunswick where cooked, chilled lobster chunks are sold for snacking. Or on Granville Island, British Columbia, where the noshing tourists must decide between steamed Vietnamese dumplings or fragrant *foccacia* that comes in eight varieties. When I discover some lush lemon grass seedlings in the Granville Island market, I regret I cannot bring them back into the States. In San Francisco's Chinatown, I buy hot sauce by the quart, some dim sum to bring home and a wonderfully smelly bottle of fish sauce. Well, it certainly smells like fish sauce, although I cannot read the label. Closer by there is the Food Co-op in Brattleboro, Vermont, and a Whole Foods in Hadley, Mass. where grocery shopping can be more interesting.

But in the ordinary supermarket, my man has the patience to read the labels for fat, sugar and salt content. He takes the time to calculate the unit price and searches out the store brands that save money. He has learned which generic garbage bags are just that and which house brand plastic wrap actually works. Edward is even beginning to understand the difference between a cut-up fryer and chicken quarters—an accomplishment for a man who refuses to eat any identifiable animal.

Back when we ate more beef I made special runs because I was confused by all the different cuts of meat. How could I explain labels that read "heel of round" or "short plate" or "bracciola steak" to a man who pales at the sight of a dismembered animal? Another good man, brother-in-law Ray Lindert, was less squeamish and more useful in the meat department. He could look at a meat case and say, "Well, that eye of round looks very good." Or "That sirloin is nicely marbled." But Ray was from Wisconsin and people from the Heartland just know these things.

Edward organizes his shopping with a running list from the kitchen bulletin board. Once I have written lemons on the list, they appear the next time I need them. When Edward's daughter, Nancy, summered here as a child, she re-wrote our list in her careful printing. Her version was neater than our flour-smudged one. But it was not until we ran out of coffee or foil that we realized Nancy was editing out items she felt were unnecessary. Today, Nancy has a successful career with an international foods conglomerate and I am certain she is no longer eliminating items from the company's list of products. At least not on a whim.

What about all that impulse buying the male is famous for? Actually, men are innocent of that canard, according to a Boston survey. It showed men are more likely to stick to a list than other shoppers. Of course, Edward may bring home a surprise–Vermont cheddar studded with caraway or the season's first asparagus. It's his way of getting me to unload the car.

Someday, they say, we will shop for our food by computer or by satellite–anything to make it even more boring. Will it surprise me with a great cheddar or an unscheduled nosegay? It could certainly put an end to that sort of impulse.

I would rather unload the car.

I have no idea who gave me the following recipe. But apparently he or she used it often enough to have it committed to memory. I scribbled it on a paper napkin.

EASY SPINACH APPETIZERS

1 10-ounce package frozen spinach, cooked and well-drained
1 4-ounce can mushroom pieces
1 cup cooked rice
4 ounces shredded jack cheese
1/3 cup milk
2 tablespoons chopped onion
1 teaspoon soy sauce
1 teaspoon Worcestershire sauce
2 eggs, well beaten

Preheat the oven to 350 degrees. Mix the spinach, mushrooms, rice, cheese, milk, onion, soy sauce, Worcestershire sauce and eggs. Spoon into a well-greased 13-by-9-inch pan. Bake 20 to 25 minutes or until set.

Cool 5 minutes. Cut into 1-1/2-inch squares. Serve warm or cool.

Makes 50 appetizers.

Here is a simple recipe that Edward uses when it is his night to cook. If you partially freeze the chicken breast, it is easier to slice into strips.

QUICK CHICKEN WITH RICE

1 cup raw rice
2 cups water
3 large sweet green peppers cut into 1/2" strips
1 medium onion, sliced into rings
2 cloves garlic, finely chopped
3 tablespoons vegetable oil
1 whole boneless chicken breast cut into 1/2" by 2" strips
1 8-ounce can of tomato sauce
3 tablespoons sesame seeds

Put rice and water into a saucepan and bring to a boil. Cover and lower heat to medium low. Cook 18 to 20 minutes until water is absorbed.

Meanwhile, in a large frying pan, cook peppers, onions and garlic in oil over medium low heat until peppers are soft, about 5 minutes.

Add chicken, increase heat to medium and cook and stir until chicken is no longer pink, about 5 minutes. Add tomato sauce, cover and cook 5 minutes.

Serve chicken over rice. Sprinkle with sesame seeds.

Makes 2 to 3 servings.

Our Fitzpatrick-Sullivan grandchildren, Laura and Joe, call this salad, succotash. No matter what you call it, this salad is a delicious addition to the picnic buffet table. Leftovers may be stuffed into pita for a quick lunch.

SOUTHWESTERN BEAN SALAD

1 pound dried pinto beans
1/4 cup catsup
1/4 cup cider vinegar
1/3 cup olive oil
1 tablespoon Worcestershire sauce
1/4 cup brown sugar
1 tablespoon chili powder
2 teaspoons cumin
1 teaspoon salt
1/4 teaspoon pepper
1/4 teaspoon Tabasco sauce
2 tablespoons Dijon mustard
1/2 cup sweet red pepper, diced
1/2 cup sweet green pepper, diced
1/2 cup purple onion, diced
1 15-ounce can whole kernel corn, drained

Pick over beans and cover beans with water by at least 4 inches and soak overnight. Drain beans. Return to pot and add fresh water to cover beans by at least 2 inches. Bring to a boil. Reduce and simmer for 1 to 1-1/2 hours or until beans are tender but not falling apart. The beans may also be cooked for 5 to 7 minutes at 15 pounds pressure in a pressure cooker.

When beans are cooked, drain and rinse under cold running water. Drain again thoroughly.

In a non-reactive saucepan, whisk catsup, vinegar, olive oil, Worcestershire sauce, brown sugar, chili powder, cumin, salt, pepper, Tabasco sauce and mustard. Bring to a boil, lower heat and simmer 10 minutes. Cool catsup mixture slightly and gently mix with beans. Refrigerate.

Just before serving, toss beans with sweet peppers, onion and corn.

Makes 14 servings.

When the plum tomatoes finally ripen up here at 41 degrees latitude, there is reason to celebrate. This fresh tomato sauce is one way I like to savor the first tomato harvest.

PASTA WITH FRESH TOMATOES

8 ounces uncooked pasta
1 green bell pepper, chopped
1 small onion, chopped
2 tablespoons olive oil
1 medium zucchini, slices
3 tablespoons capers
¼ teaspoon dried thyme
2 pounds plum tomatoes, peeled seeded and chopped
Shredded fresh basil to taste
Dash or two of red pepper sauce
Salt and pepper to taste

Sautee green pepper, onion and garlic in oil until garlic is fragrant. Stir in zucchini and mushrooms and sauté one minute. Stir in tomatoes, thyme and capers and sauté for 4 to 5 minutes. Add basil, red pepper sauce, salt and pepper. Serve over pasta.
Makes 4 servings.

Whenever I serve this dessert, no one can believe this rich creamy stuff contains only 2 healthy ingredients. The first time you make it, process half the recipe at a time to get the feel of it and avoid a spattering mess. This dessert is also a good way to use up those overripe bananas. The ripest bananas make the sweetest dessert.

BANANA ICE CREAM

2 ripe bananas
1/2 cup non-fat milk

Peel and slice bananas into 1/2-inch pieces. Freeze on a tray until firm– about 1 hour. Bag and store in freezer.

When ready to serve, put frozen bananas and milk in food processor. Process until thick and smooth. Serve immediately. Makes 2 generous servings.

CONTENTMENT

Contentment follows dessert. I can feel it settling over our friends and family as we sip our coffee. The chocolate-raspberry torte has been reduced to a few crumbs on the white plates. We hardly talk. As the candles melt down, my mind wanders and I fret I have yet to get the lighting right in this room with its massive hand-hewn beams.

Was Mrs. Levi Lincoln, the first woman of this house, content with the lighting of this room? She probably depended on light from the candles and fire. In this high-tech era, I suppose we could spend every spare minute fixing our house so it would work better. Say, at least like a house built in 1975.

But our writing has always come first. We backed away from total restoration and let this old farmhouse teach us contentment, acceptance. We have put up with some peculiar inconveniences and when we remedy them, we say, "How did we every put up with a well that ran dry every July?"

Some day the solution to lighting might occur to us. Meanwhile, I scan the faces of our friends in the lights and shadows from an ancient brass candlestick, a gift from Aunt Esther Sullivan. I am content.

Fresh Chestnuts, A Labor Of Love

When our twin chestnut trees produced a mere handful of nuts every autumn, it was a simple matter to deal with the crop. I surrendered it to the squirrels. But even trees reach puberty and when our chestnuts did, we were confronted with a record two-pound harvest.

Now two unaccounted pounds of Chinese chestnuts are not going to rumble the commodities market, but the trees are beginning to shed the makings of a cash crop. In my town, fresh chestnuts are selling anywhere from $1.89 a pound (the natural foods store) to $2.89 a pound (the upscale supermarket).

How can any baker ignore a $6 windfall? I decided it was time to deal with the chestnuts because, like zucchini, they won't go away. In fact, according to my husband, the tree planter, our chestnuts will produce as many as 200 pounds annually in their mature years.

Americans now grow hardy Chinese chestnuts because the native variety *Castanea dentata*, common from Maine to Florida in colonial times, has been nearly extinguished by blight. These Chinese nuts *Castanea mollissima*, announced by white star-burst blossoms in summer, should not be confused with the Oriental water chestnuts–no relation.

My first lesson about chestnuts was a lesson in economics. Removing the (1) porcupine-prickly husk, (2) the tough outer shell and (3) the clinging inner skin turned out to be a labor-intensive, time-consuming chore. At $1.98 for a 15.5-ounce can, chestnut puree was beginning to look like a bargain.

I now understand why shelled, roasted chestnuts imported from France cost $6.50 a pound from a stateside mail-order specialty shop. And why the ultimate dessert topping–chestnuts preserved in vanilla syrup–is worth its weight in francs.

Fresh chestnuts like fresh apples have high water content. Chestnuts are not as imperishable as they look; they rapidly lose moisture through their porous shells. The nuts deteriorate quickly at room temperature in dry winter heat. Store them in a plastic bag in the refrigerator or freezer.

If you need a pound of shelled chestnuts (2 cups), begin with a pound and a half of fresh chestnuts. Allow at least 45 minutes to shell and peel a pound. Fresh chestnuts are in no sense a fast food.

I experimented with several ways of shelling and skinning and concluded they all work. And they are all work.

First, the blanching method. Score the flat side of the chestnut with an X or score along the narrow outer edge. Place chestnuts in a saucepan, cover with cold water, add two teaspoons of salt, bring to a boil, cover and boil five minutes. The salt seems to help loosen the shells. Remove nuts with a slotted spoon. Cool chestnuts until they can be handled. Keep water hot in the event you need to re-dip a chestnut to loosen a resisting shell or skin.

Use a nutpick or a small fork to pry out the meat. The inner skin may be removed using a paring knife or a swivel-blade vegetable peeler or by working the skin with your fingers. If the shell or skin won't yield, try dropping back into hot water for a few minutes.

At this point, you can refrigerate or freeze the nut meats or simmer the chestnuts for 20 minutes until tender. I shelled and skinned my crop and froze it to use later.

Weeks later, I simmered the nuts in milk and whirled them in the food processor adding just enough warm milk and butter to make a puree the consistency of freshly made peanut butter–just right for making a decadent holiday torte.

You can also roast chestnuts–like the New York and Italian street vendors do. If you don't have a charcoal brazier-equipped wagon, roast the nuts in a 400-degree oven for 20 minutes or until the shell curls. Use a shallow pan and before roasting sprinkle the nuts with a little oil or vegetable oil spray.

When roasting, scoring the nuts with an X is even more essential. Otherwise, the steam will build up inside the nut and it may explode. Scraping chestnut meat off the insides of an oven–unlike chestnuts roasting on an open fire–is not one of the joys of Christmas.

If you are serving roasted chestnuts as a snack, just pass the nut picks and let family and friends get to the meat of them.

The microwave can also share peeling duty. Place two cups scored chestnuts in a 1-quart microwave-safe dish. Add one cup water, cover with plastic wrap turning back one section to vent. Microwave on high until water boils–between three and four minutes. Let stand five minutes and then peel.

Another recommended microwave method not only peels the chestnuts but cooks them as well. But the results are uneven. This method calls for placing one cup scored chestnuts in a microwave-safe pie plate and microwaving on high for a recommended time of four to eight minutes.

However, I have discovered that in about one minute and 50 seconds, two things may happen. At least three chestnuts explode into bits that cling to the microwave's ceiling and walls. One chestnut out of the whole bunch shed both its outer shell and inner skin leaving a beautifully intact, ready-to-use chestnut. If only I could find the secret to peeling and entire pound with this perfect result.

Microwave cooking is not yet an exact science but with time and patience, you can probably work out an efficient chestnut peeling method for your microwave. I spent an afternoon with friend Katherine Cox, experimenting with her microwave.

"This is a lot of work," said Kathy as we shelled and scraped. But any tedious job becomes a good visit when shared with a friend.

And Kathy discovered a labor-saving clue: do not be timid with the knife. She noticed that the deeper you score the nut, the easier the shelling. Exposing the interior to the heat seems to loosen both the shell and the inner skin. Deep cuts also prevent those messy oven explosions. I have learned to use a sharp knife and score the nuts at least one-third inch deep.

When baking, chestnut and chocolate go hand in hand. Orange, rum, Cognac, vanilla, almond or pine nut can be a third flavor in the chocolate-chestnut combination.

Traditional European Christmas feasts include a variety of chestnut sweets. How about Finnish chestnut fingers? Or a Hungarian rum-flavored chestnut bon bon? Or Italian chocolate chestnut fritters? Or a Maltese chestnut pudding flavored with tangerine and chocolate?

In the United States, a celebrated chestnut dessert has been Nesselrode pie. It originated in Europe, named for Count Nesselrode, the Nineteenth Century diplomat. The count's chef combined a custard cream with chestnut puree, currants, white raisins and whipped cream. American cooks later omitted the chestnuts and added instant pudding, candied cherries–in bright red and green–and rum. By the 1950s, Nesselrode was a popular, if sugary, Christmas ice cream flavor.

Chestnuts of course flavor dishes other than desserts. The rich nut meat makes a scrumptious cream soup from chicken broth flavored with onions and pureed and thinned with a little cream or buttermilk. The braised chestnut goes well with such vegetables as Brussels sprouts, cabbage, sweet potatoes, small onions, leeks or mushrooms. For some, Christmas would not be Christmas without a chestnut dressing for the roast turkey or goose.

If you want to use chestnuts off-season, consider the shelled, skinned and dried chestnuts used in Italian and Chinese cooking. In the natural foods store, four ounces of China Bowl Brand cost $1.89. Despite the brand name, the fine print reveals the chestnuts are a product of Italy. Cookbook author Giuliano Bugialli, calls his homeland a "great land for chestnuts."

Like many fine foods, chestnuts have inspired the invention of special equipment.

A chestnut knife has a one-inch stainless steel hooked blade designed to score chestnuts like nothing else can. The traditional chestnut roasting pan looks like a frying pan with holes in the bottom and is used over a charcoal or gas flame. The cook is supposed to hold and shake the pan over the flame for about 40 minutes. Like I said, we are not talking fast food.

So I don't think I will invest in special chestnut equipment until I hear the sound of 200 pounds of chestnuts drumming the earth in an autumn wind.

Meanwhile, here are some of my holiday favorites.

CREAM OF CHESTNUT SOUP

1 pound chestnuts, shelled and skinned
4 cups chicken broth
2 tablespoons butter
1 carrot, diced
1 stalk celery, sliced
1/3 cup finely chopped onion
1/2 teaspoon mace
Dash white pepper
2 cups light cream
1/2 cup blanched, toasted whole almonds

Cover the chestnuts with broth and simmer covered for 30 minutes or until chestnuts are fork-tender. Meanwhile, sauté the carrot, celery and onion in butter over low heat until soft.

Combine the chestnuts, broth and vegetables. Puree 1/3 of the mixture at a time in a food processor or blender. Pour the puree into saucepan. Stir in the cream, mace and pepper. Taste and adjust seasonings if necessary. Heat just to boiling. Watch carefully and do not boil. Top each serving with a few almonds.

Yield: 12 servings or 7 cups soup.

CHESTNUT STUFFING WITH CALVADOS

½   cup butter
½ cup chopped onion
12 cups slightly dry bread cubes
1 cup chicken stock
½ cup Calvados
2 cups peeled, cored and chopped McIntosh apples
1 cup chopped roasted or boiled chestnuts
1/2 teaspoon dried ginger
Salt and pepper to taste

Sauté onion in butter until soft. Toss bread cubes with butter and onion. Add remaining ingredients and toss gently. Stuff turkey just before roasting. Or bake in a greased, 2-quart covered casserole in a pre-heated 325 degree oven for 25 to 30 minutes or until stuffing is heated through.

Yield: Stuffing for a 12-pound turkey or 5 cups of stuffing.

ELENA'S CHESTNUTS IN TWO-WINE SYRUP

1 pound chestnuts, shelled and skinned
1-1/2 cups Marsala wine
1/2 cup Port wine
3 tablespoons sugar
1/2 cup heavy cream

Place chestnuts in a heavy saucepan and cover with the wines and sugar. Stir to mix. Bring to a boil, lower heat, and simmer gently for 20 to 30 minutes until chestnuts are tender and wine is syrup-like. Serve warm or at room temperature with whipped cream.
Makes 4 servings.

I made this torte for our book group one holiday season. Just one taste and groans of pleasure filled the room Even so, it is so rich that a very thin slice is just the right size serving.

CHOCOLATE CHESTNUT TORTE WITH CHOCOLATE ICING

3/4 cup sugar
8 eggs, separated
1/4 cup flour
1 cup unseasoned unsweetened
3-1/2 ounces unsweetened chocolate, grated
¼ cup flour
1 cup unsweetened chestnut puree

Separate the eggs while they are still cold from the refrigerator. Then bring all ingredients to room temperature. Grease and flour a 9-inch spring form pan. Preheat oven to 325 degrees. In a large bowl, beat egg yolks and sugar until thick and lemon colored. Beat in chocolate, flour and puree. This step may be done in a food processor. Pour yolk mixture into a large bowl.

With a whisk or an electric mixer, beat egg whites in a large bowl until soft peaks are formed. Blend a tablespoon of the egg-whites into the yolk mixture to lighten it. Using a rubber spatula, gently fold the rest of the egg whites into the yolk mixture. Pour into prepared pan and bake for 45 minutes to 1 hour or until the point of a knife comes out clean when inserted in the center. Cool in pan on a rack. Carefully unmold cake and frost.

To keep things tidy while icing the cake, place the unfrosted cake on a plate lined with a paper-doily. Carefully tuck four 4-inch wide strips of wax paper under the edges of the cake. Then frost with abandon. As soon as the frosting is set, carefully remove the wax paper.

FROSTING

1/4 cup butter at room temperature
2-1/2 cups sifted confectioners' sugar
2 tablespoons unsweetened cocoa powder
1 tablespoon rum or brandy
2 tablespoons hot strong coffee
16 shelled almonds

Drop almonds into boiling water. Simmer 5 minutes. When almonds are cool enough to handle, remove skins. Toast on a baking sheet in a 300 degree oven for 10 to 15 minutes until lightly toasted. Stir occasionally. Cream butter. Gradually beat in powdered sugar, cocoa, rum, and coffee until smooth.

Frost sides and top of cake. Make a border of whole toasted almonds placing them perpendicularo the edge of the cake.

Yield: 12 to 16 servings.

This is the classic French dessert sauce, *coupe aux marrons*, chestnut pieces in syrup. It requires a lot of time and work and is delightful served warm over vanilla ice cream. Is it worth the effort? I think so.

CHESTNUT ICE CREAM TOPPING

2 cups chestnuts, shelled and skinned
3 cups water
1 cup sugar
1/2 cup light corn syrup
Rind of two oranges
1/2 teaspoon vanilla
1/4 cup dark rum or brandy

Chop chestnuts into three or four pieces. In a saucepan, combine water, sugar, corn syrup and vanilla. Bring to a boil and add 1 orange rind and chestnut pieces. Simmer, partly covered, until syrup is reduced by one half, about one hour and 30 minutes. If you have a crockery cooker, set it on low. Cover, leaving a slight opening for steam to escape and let sauce reduce overnight.

Pour the chestnuts and syrup into clean jar and let cool. Stir in brandy. Cover tightly and store in refrigerator. This chestnut sauce is a good keeper. To serve, warm slightly and spoon on top of vanilla ice cream. Sprinkle generously with grated orange rind.

Makes 2 cups.

Meditation On An August Garden

One of the joys of a garden is searching the rows on a green and gold August morning and deciding what to make for lunch. There is so much satisfaction in this direct link between nature, the provider, and you, the first beneficiary. You can just about taste the solitude as you select the fruits of the harvest–no shopping carts scraping your ankles, no loudspeakers demanding price checks, no surly clerks scolding you for invading the express line. (Does anyone really know whether three identical cans of soup count as one or three items?) Imagine not having to go anywhere beyond a few steps to the garden for the makings of your next meal. Who needs an express line?

A garden is the place, said William Wordsworth, "Where the heavy and the weary weight/Of all this unintelligible world,/Is lightened."

Of course, there will always be a few nervous blue jays jay-jaying overhead.

But there is also the better-mannered company of the goldfinches breakfasting at the stand of sunflowers. And the monarch and swallowtail butterflies waltzing around the zinnias.

Over in the vegetable patch the first tomatoes are blushing red enough to eat. They are heated by the sun and there the salivating warmth is yet another garden delight.

Three weeks ago, our friend, Steve Hall, brought us a basket of his first tomatoes. Seven miles from here, down in the Ashuelot (pronounced ASH willit) Valley where Steve lives, everything ripens sooner than up here at 1,200 feet. This year, Steve wrapped a few of his tomato seedlings with the new "water walls." As it turned out, the little water-filled teepees made little difference—all of Steve's plants began bearing fruit at the same time. But then summer arrived two weeks early this year. Still the teepee idea is still tempting. I may order them yet.

There is no hurry. After all, I just caught up with tomato cages last spring. Introduced twenty years ago, these inexpensive wire supports increase the yield, save space and discourage pests and disease. I no longer have to pound tomato stakes into clay–an exercise that always reminds me that our garden sits on a granite mountain.

In this August garden, I see lush bouquets of basil, shiny green sweet peppers, purple-flowered oregano, and plump onions vying with weeds for expansion space.

For today's lunch, *piperade* comes to mind. These spicy scrambled eggs originated in the Basque country. The flavors–onions, garlic, peppers, olive oil, tomatoes, parsley, basil and thyme seem so right for an August day. For a moment, I regret that my eggs are not as fresh as everything else in this *piperade.* Someday perhaps, I will keep a hen. Probably the same day I plant my own peaches, popcorn and chickpeas.

Right now, I drop a bit of butter into a whole-wheat pita and warm it while cooking the vegetables and eggs. I stuff the pita halves with the *piperade,* pour a glass of cold milk and plop down under a maple tree. I am content.

I think about summer cooking and the luxury of planning a meal while standing knee-deep in an overflowing garden. What a joyful dilemma to choose among dill, chives, mint, sage, summer savory, parsley and oregano to enhance the less assertive summer squashes and cucumbers.

A garden lunch for one is simple to conjure even on a hot, August day. What to make for dinner is not so easy. For inspiration, I look to sun-soaked places like Italy, southern France, Spain and Morocco. That's where summer's best dishes seem to originate: the pastas sauced with fresh vegetables and herbs, the grilled kebabs, the bulgur and couscous salads, the stuffed eggplant, peppers and squashes.

How about a cold but spicy gazpacho that air-conditions the body and spirit? Or *salade nicoise, fatoosh* salad, or a juicy tomato sauce cooked by the heat of the sun?

The reds, yellows, and greens of the high-summer vegetables offer such a cornucopia of colors that my sauté pan becomes a palette an artist could envy. More than once, I am tempted to blurt out, "Quick, Edward, come see these colors before they change again. But I usually leave Edward in peace–storing his own thoughts or the winter's firewood.

Each gardening year brings at least one discovery. Last season, it was fresh coriander. Until then, coriander meant a few stale seeds leftover from pickling. And a jar of ground coriander I bought for some unmemorable, unrepeatable dish. When fresh coriander appeared in newspaper recipes that sounded good enough to clip, I decided to try it. However, I was usually confused by the parenthetical "Chinese parsley" that followed any mention of coriander. Was the cook supposed to locate a Chinese grocery and ask for parsley?

I considered ordering some coriander seeds from an herb specialist. But you know how that goes. Ninety-five cents for the seeds and six dollars for shipping and handling. Then I spotted coriander seeds in the hardware store. Coriander turns out to be very simple to grow. In fact, coriander is so cooperative that I grew two crops in a single season. And the following spring more coriander popped up by itself. With nothing to lose, I transplanted some of the volunteers to other spots in the garden where they flourished. My only complaint about coriander is that its volunteer seedlings often mislead me into thinking my parsley seeds have germinated, which they never have.

Coriander's pungent odor and flavor enhance the flavors of Caribbean, Asian and Indian food. It also appears in Mexican cooking where it is called cilantro. I use it a scrumptious peanut sauce for pasta that calls for one-half cup of the fresh herb. This dish is similar to Szechwan cold noodles in spicy sauce, a specialty introduced to me by my niece, Bridget Love.

Each gardening season has its disappointments, too. The packet of precious *nicotiana* that spilled as I hurried to finish planting between May rain showers. The *nicotiana* seeds disappeared into the muddy ground and that was that. The Chinese cabbage sprouts that Edward picked prematurely, mistaking them for lettuce. But those were accidents. What about the green beans that were supposed to climb up sunflower stalks but only foundered in their shade? Just another fantasy of some garden writer.

None of that really matters. As I stand in this August garden, I am overwhelmed by it all–the sky, the clouds, the light, the varied greens of the forest's edge, the chatter of the garden critters and the flight path of the birds. I savor each for what it is at this moment. Next month, next hour, even the next moment, each blossom, bird or cloud may assume a different shade, note, rhythm, shape.

Perhaps that is why I never bothered to wage a global war or pursue office politics. I am too busy attending to the universe right here in my August garden.

In the summer, when we eat salads almost daily, I make our house dressing by the quart. It is handy, inexpensive and free of all those funny-tasting flavors and flakes. I mix and store the dressing in a Mason jar with calibrations. For leak-proof shaking, top jar with a lid from a peanut butter or mayonnaise jar. Vary dressing with a squirt of fresh lemon juice, 2 teaspoons good mustard, 1 table-spoon sesame seeds or 2 teaspoons dried tarragon.

OUR HOUSE DRESSING

1/3 cup cider vinegar
2/3 cup olive oil
1 clove garlic, peeled and quartered
1 tablespoon low-sodium soy sauce
Fresh ground pepper to taste

Put all ingredients in a jar, cover and shake. Store in refrigerator. Let come to room temperature before mixing in salad.
Makes 1 cup dressing

Fattoush, a Syrian peasant salad, made with pita bread is refreshing on a hot summer night. The combination of mint and coriander cools the spirit. It is important to salt and drain the cucumbers. Otherwise, the salad's special texture and flavor will be lost.

FATTOUSH

1 6-inch pita
1 lemon
1 large cucumber
4 tomatoes
1/2 cup chopped scallions or other mild onions
3 tablespoons fresh parsley, finely chopped
3 tablespoons fresh mint, finely chopped
2 cloves garlic, finely chopped
1/2 cup olive oil
Salt
Freshly ground pepper
Butterhead lettuce leaves

Dice cucumber. Sprinkle lightly with salt and let drain 30 minutes to remove excess water. Chop tomatoes, mince garlic and juice lemon. Toast pita and break into 1-inch pieces and place in bowl. Sprinkle with lemon juice. Add other ingredients and mix well. Serve immediately on lettuce lined plates.

Makes 4 servings.

Too many cucumbers? Here is a good way to use them up. This dish is inspired by the refreshing cucumber-yogurt salad that is called *raita* in northern India and *cacik* in Turkey. I substitute vinaigrette for yogurt because it shows off the colors of the herbs and vegetables.

CUCUMBER SALAD

4 medium cucumbers
1/2 cup chopped purple onion
1/2 lemon
4 tablespoons fresh mint
4 tablespoons fresh parsley
Salt
Freshly ground pepper
1/2 cup vinaigrette or Our House Dressing

Peel, quarter and slice cucumbers. Grate rind and juice lemon. Combine cucumbers, onion, lemon juice and grated rind, mint, parsley and dressing. Toss lightly. Taste and add salt and freshly ground pepper. Chill for at least 1 hour. Serves 6.

Note: you may substitute 1/2 to 1 cup yogurt for the vinaigrette.

Mexican restaurants are rare in New Hampshire. When I get a summertime craving for Mexican, I make this salsa and slurp it up with tortilla chips. It's just right for an August night and great fun served at the backyard picnic table. Provide baskets of warm chips, lots of napkins and several bowls of salsa.

TOMATO SALSA

4 large red tomatoes
1 medium onion, chopped
3 tablespoons chopped fresh parsley
3 tablespoons chopped fresh coriander
2 teaspoons ground cumin
Red pepper sauce
Salt and freshly ground pepper

Peel tomatoes by dropping in boiling water. Remove with a slotted spoon when skins crack–about 1 minute. When cool enough to handle, slip off skins. Chop tomatoes and place in a bowl. Stir in the onion, parsley, coriander and cumin. Taste. Slowly add red pepper sauce until it is hot enough for your taste. Taste again and add salt and freshly ground pepper. Store in refrigerator. Bring to room temperature before serving.

Makes about 2 cups.

A refreshing dinner salad for evenings when it's too hot to cook and the garden is bursting with vegetables.

SALADE NICOISE WITH CHARDONNAY DRESSING

1 pound small red potatoes
1 tablespoon olive oil
1 pound fresh green beans
1 bunch leaf lettuce, preferably red-tinged
20 cherry tomatoes, halved
1/4 pound Kalamata olives
1 large green pepper, sliced into thin rings
1 purple onion, sliced into thin rings
2 cans (6-1/2 ounce each) best quality chunk tuna
4 medium eggs, cooked and sliced
1 small can anchovies, drained
Fresh tarragon, basil or flat-leafed parsley for garnish

Prepare the Chardonnay dressing. Scrub potatoes and cut into quarters. Bring a medium-size saucepan of water to boiling. Add potatoes and cook until just fork tender about 12 to 15 minutes. Drain.

Trim beans and steam until just crunchy. Toss briefly in ice water to stop cooking and retain color. Toss with 1 tablespoon olive oil.

Line 4 large glass plates with lettuce. Lightly drizzle dressing on top. Divide and arrange the potatoes, green beans, tomatoes, olives, pepper, onion, tuna chunks, eggs and anchovies. Drizzle with dressing. Sprinkle chopped herbs on top of salad. Serve at room temperature. Makes 4 serving.

CHARDONNAY DRESSING

1/4 cup Chardonnay
1/2 cup good quality olive oil
Salt and freshly ground pepper
1 large clove garlic, quartered

Combine Chardonnay, olive oil, salt, pepper and garlic clove.

The Berry That Bounces

It is difficult to imagine Szechuan *kung pao* chicken without the heat and bite of a chile pod. Or a plate of spaghetti without a tomato-rich marinara sauce. Or a *pomme soufflé* without the potatoes. Or a Hungarian goulash without a fresh paprika.

But that is the way it was before the chile, the tomato and the potato were introduced into the cuisines of Europe and Asia. All three foods were cultivated by the indigenous peoples of the Americas. However, it was not until the sixteenth century that European traders began carrying native American foods to other continents.

Most American seeds and plants traveled well and adapted to diverse soils and climates all over the world. And food–in lands like India, China, Thailand, France and Italy–was never quite the same again.

But one important native American plant has yet to take root in other lands. The American cranberry, *Vaccinium macrocarpon* has refused to grow almost anywhere except the acidic, moist peat bogs of North America.

Take Ireland, for example. You would think cranberries would multiply like kudzu in Ireland's peat bogs. But efforts to grow the berries in Ireland failed miserably. The clouds and rain that carpet the Irish countryside with green velvet produced only an anemic, pale berry. It takes long sunny days to ripen the berries to a profitable shade of deep red. How deep? How red? Well, cranberry color is not determined by a quick glance. Both color and the eventual price of the berries are computed by extracting 12 different pigments from the berries. The concentration of each pigment adds up to a precise, objective measure of the fruit's color.

In Holland where the sun often shines, there is a single spot where North American cranberry vines took root and continue to flourish. According the legend, a ship loaded with berries sank off Holland's Island of Tershcelling in 1844. Up popped a cranberry plantation. The fact is that Yankee Clippers and whaling ships did carry barrels of vitamin C-rich cranberries to prevent scurvy among their crews.

For years, no one really cared whether the cranberry would grow beyond the east coast from Nova Scotia to North Carolina and out to Wisconsin and the Pacific Northwest. As long as there were enough berries for sauce to serve with the Thanksgiving turkey. Enough berries to produce quivering cranberry jelly that slid onto the serving dishes with a great plop.

Like that other American native, the turkey, the cranberry only appeared at Thanksgiving. Sixty years after the first batch of canned cranberry sauce rolled out at South Hanson, Massachusetts, the Cape Cod cranberry growers had another inspiration. How about a cranberry cocktail solo or in combination with other fruits like apple or raspberry? How about promoting these juices as refreshing, healthy alternatives to soft drinks? As everyone now knows, the world was ready for new juice flavors and the berry market boomed.

Then came the cranberry Margarita, a spirited drink that combines a native American berry, with tequila, a native American spirit. When this Margarita took off at a California restaurant chain, owner Warren Simmons of Napa Valley decided to run a month's special on the drink. However, Simmons quickly discovered there were no predictable supplies of large amounts of cranberry juice. Like maple syrup, the size and quality of the cranberry harvest depends on the weather. "It's a crap shoot. You don't count your money until the crop is in the barn," says one Cape Cod grower.

Hoping to emulate Brazil's booming orange juice trade, Warren Simmons invested $20 million to start Cran Chile, a cranberry plantation in Valdivia, Chile. There in Chile's volcano-ringed central valley, University of Wisconsin cranberry expert, Elden Stang, supervised the planting of 30 million cranberry plants that originated as tiny shoots propagated in a Wisconsin lab. When the honeybees avoided Valdivia's rainy weather, Stang planted fields of blue-blossomed bee balm and attracted Chile's giant orange bumblebees and pollination was assured. "At first, people here thought we were totally crazy. But I was convinced from the start this was a good place," said Professor Stang. Time will tell whether the finicky cranberry with its demand for water and exacting amounts of nutrients will thrive in Valdivia.

The Native Americas cultivated the potato, chile and tomato but they were content to pick the cranberry from the wild for food, medicine and dyes. The Cape Cod Wampanoag's and South Jersey Leni-Lenape called the cranberry *ibimi* or "bitter berry." Elsewhere, the locals called the cranberry *sassamanesh*. The English settlers noticed that the berry's pink blossom resemble a crane's head and named the fruit "cranberry." I wonder why they simply did not ask the Wampanoag, Pequot or Passamaquoddy people, "What is the name of this fruit?"

In any case, the bitter berry was more than food to Pakimintzen, the chief of the Delaware tribe, who used cranberries as a symbol of peace. I like to think that Pakimintzen's memory is honored when I prepare a cranberry relish for our feast of gratitude, Thanksgiving.

The Native Americans valued the cranberries' antiseptic powers and used berry poultices to draw poison out of wounds. As early as 1672, English writer John Josslyn reported on the health benefits of cranberries in a book called *New England Rarities Discovered.* Josslyn reported the berry was "excellent for preventing scurvy and for reducing the heat of feavers."

In folk medicine, cranberry juice is used to prevent bladder and urinary tract infections. Antibiotics, of course, are the cure for such infections but I always figured that a daily glass of cranberry juice could not hurt. In winter, a mug of hot cranberry juice with a few cloves and raisins warms the hands and the spirit. In the summer, a glass of cranberry juice with a splash of sparkling water makes a refreshing gardening break.

However, new evidence from Harvard Medical School indicates cranberry juice does inhibit infection by preventing troublemaking bacteria from anchoring themselves on bladder walls. Cranberry juice contains hippuric acid, a bacterial growth inhibitor. The berries are also an excellent of vitamin C and iodine and also contain vitamins A, B complex and beneficial traces of quinic and benzoic acids.

Cranberry farming can also heal the planet. On Cape Cod, Massachusetts growers are preserving more than 61,000 acres of precious open space that includes 12,500 acres planted with cranberry vines. This vast system offers an ideal refuge for many plant and wildlife species. The cranberry wetlands system filters ground water, recharges aquifers and controls floods by retaining storm runoffs.

The cranberry farmers use flooding and sanding, fish fertilizer, and natural enemies like nematodes to control insects and propagate the vines. Some growers are leaders in a new approach, IPM, which stands for integrated pest management. IPM includes a careful monitoring of threats to the crops and using pesticides accordingly. Spraying can be cut back as much as 75 percent by checking for predators like blackberry fire worm, cranberry weevil, fruit worm and cranberry girdler. One single enemy, frost, can wipe out a season's crop overnight. That is why the growers keep tuned to a weather station, and if frost is predicted, turn on the sprinklers.

People who grow anything at all learn to accept both happy surprises and stunning losses. But in 1959, many cranberry growers were hit by a loss so devastating, that they were forced out of business. Forever. Just weeks before Thanksgiving, the U.S. Department of Health, Education and Welfare advised consumers not to eat cranberries that year. The government said a weed killer used on part of the Oregon and Washington crop had caused cancer in laboratory rats.

It turned out, however, that humans would have to eat 15,000 pounds of treated berries daily for several years to get the equivalent of the lab rat dose. The herbicide, aminotrazole, earlier had been approved by the U.S. Department of Agriculture. But as Massachusetts growers doused their entire crops with kerosene and hauled them to the dump, they considered the irony that 1959 had been a great cranberry harvest. Shortly after the 1959 berry bungle, aminotrazole was again declared safe.

Today, there is a new and perhaps final threat facing Massachusetts' largest crop. Where cranberries now grow, developers envision vacation condos, tennis courts and golf courses lining the beaches. Selling the family cranberry bog is a tempting idea; you get to be an instant millionaire and leave behind an unpredictable way of life. But despite the pressure, the 750 grower-owners of the Ocean Spray cooperative are determined to resist.

These Yankees live and work in a tradition-steeped industry where some of the most vigorous cranberry vines were planted as long ago as 1850. And in an industry where "bounce test" for a fresh berry has not changed since it introduced around 1815. Each berry must bounce over a four-inch high board or it is discarded.

The first printed recipe for cranberry sauce appeared in Amelia Simmons' *American Cookery* in 1797. Her 1812 edition included a recipe for cranberry tarts with the fruit sweetened and spiced and baked in puff pastry. The year, 1812, was also the first year cranberries were cultivated.

Looking beyond the Thanksgiving menu, the Ocean Spray Cooperative challenged some of the world's most innovative chefs to create new year-round cranberry dishes. Chefs from Brussels, Paris, Stockholm and Tokyo created recipes for appetizers, soups, entrees, and salads all based on the tart red berry.

Robert Vifian, chef-owner of Tan Dinh, a Vietnamese restaurant in Paris, pickled cranberries to serve with his king crab rolls that he described as a "very traditional, very classical Vietnamese dish." He used whole berry sauce and cranberry cocktail for his sweet and sour pork. For dessert, he garnished coconut pudding with candied cranberries. Cranberries fit neatly into Vietnamese cooking, Vifian said. "We insist on having a red touch in dishes. It can be cranberries or carrots. Red is supposed to bring good luck. That is why we are so fond of it."

A symbol of peace to the Delaware tribe. A good luck charm for the Vietnamese. What more could we ask of our native berry?

This version of cranberry relish retains the tartness of the berries and is a nice contrast to the heavier dishes of Thanksgiving menus.

CRANBERRY RELISH

1 large orange
4 cups fresh cranberries
1 cup sugar
Pinch salt
1 tablespoon fresh grated ginger

Put orange and berries through coarse blade of a food grinder. Or fit the steel knife blade into the bowl of a food processor. Process orange until chopped into 1/8-inch pieces. Add cranberries and sugar and process until berries are coarsely chopped and ingredients are mixed. Let stand at least an hour before serving.

Store in refrigerator for up to 2 weeks. Makes 3 cups.

CRANBERRY HAZELNUT PIE

2 cups cranberries
1-1/3 cups sugar
½ cup hazelnuts coarsely chopped
2 tablespoons orange juice
2 eggs
¾ cup butter, melted
1 cup unbleached all-purpose flour

Preheat oven to 325 degrees. Put cranberries in a well-greased 10-inch pie plate. Sprinkle with 1/3 cup of the sugar, the hazelnuts and the orange juice.

Combine the eggs, butter and remaining sugar until just smooth. Stir in the flour. Spread the batter over the berry mixture. Bake for one hour or until the crust is golden. Serve warm or cold with whipped cream or ice cream, if desired.

Makes 8 servings.

An easy but oh-so-good way make chicken. According to the Jamaica Travel and Culture website, there are two theories about the origin of the word "jerk." The first holds that the work originated in the Spanish word, "*charqui*," used to describe dried meat. The second theory holds the name derives from the practice of jerking (poking) holes in the meat to insert spices. Today, the noun jerk, describes the seasoning used in jerked food and verb, jerk, describes the cooking process.

CRAN JERKED CHICKEN

1 teaspoon ground allspice
6 cloves garlic, peeled crushed
2 tablespoons chopped, peeled fresh ginger
2 tablespoons dark brown sugar
1 teaspoon chopped, seeded jalapeno pepper
1/4 to 1/2 teaspoon ground hot red pepper
1/2 teaspoon salt
1/3 cup olive oil
1/3 cup sliced green onion
1/4 cup red wine vinegar
2 tablespoons lime juice
1 chicken cut into 12 pieces
(2 legs, 2 thighs, breasts cut into
4 pieces, wing tips removed, wings halved

In a food processor combine allspice, garlic, ginger, brown sugar, jalapeno pepper, red pepper, salt, oil, green onion, vinegar and lime juice. Whirl until smooth.

Place chicken pieces in a large, non-reactive pan and rub with vinegar mixture. Gently lift skin and rub vinegar mixture under skin. Cover and refrigerate 2 hours.

Preheat oven to 400 degrees. Lay chicken in a broiler-proof pan that will hold pieces in one layer. Bake 35 minutes. Broil 4 inches from heat 4 to 5 minutes until lightly crisped.Makes 4 servings.

The savory flavors of this sauce make it a good accompaniment to roast turkey, chicken, pork or chilled sliced meats.

SPICY CRANBERRY SAUCE

1/4 cup water
1/4 cup fresh lemon juice
1/2 cup onions, finely minced
1 cup sugar
1/4 cup red wine vinegar
1-1/2 teaspoons ground allspice
Salt and freshly ground pepper to taste
1 pound cranberries

In a heavy saucepan, mix water, lemon juice, onions, sugar, vinegar and allspice. Bring to a boil, lower heat and simmer for 15 minutes. Add the cranberries and cook until all berries pop–about 10 minutes.

Makes 2 cups. Keeps up to one month refrigerated in a covered container.

Here's a cheerful drink for a cold, gray day. I keep it warm on top of the wood stove where its spicy aroma greets guests who have climbed the ice mountain to our door.

CRANBERRY WARMER

1 (48-ounce bottle) cranberry juice cocktail
1 teaspoon cinnamon
1/2 teaspoon allspice
1/2 teaspoon cloves
1/4 cup raisins
1/4 cup slivered almonds

Pour the cranberry juice into a large kettle. Stir in spices, raisins and almonds. Bring to a boil and simmer gently for 10 minutes. Taste and add more spices if desired. Keep warm over low heat.

Makes 8 6-ounce servings.

SIMPLICITY

One way to simplify things is to eat the way the locals do. I wish I had known that when I was a young bride, keeping house in Jerusalem. I exhausted myself searching the *souk* for familiar things like canned tomatoes and frozen orange juice. If I had known, I would have cooked like my Palestinian neighbors with ingredients available fresh in the food stalls of the Old City–creamy yogurt, olives in barrels of brine, cracked wheat, lemons, pine nuts, almonds, herbs and pita. But I was a child of the 19508 and foodstuffs came in packages.

Eating locally in the Western Hemisphere includes cooking two native foods that are almost nutritionally perfect–the potato and the bean. Each of these foods can be prepared simply or elaborately. In busy times like planting or remodeling, I bake a few pounds of potatoes or cook a pot of baked beans. I do not have to think about cooking again for a few days.

The Native Americans undoubtedly bred certain potato and bean varieties to simplify storage. Both can be stored in a cool place for months without a care or a kilowatt. I think about this whenever I feed the sourdough starter or rinse the tofu.

The Bean Supper, Saturday Night On The Town

Back in the 1920s, one of the best buys in our town was the community baked bean supper. I know because our neighbor, Jane Allen, gave me a copy of a supper flyer from her mother's scrapbook. The supper, sponsored by the Community Needlecraft Club, was held August 8, 1929 at the Chesterfield, New Hampshire, Town Hall. Admission? Sixty cents.

A few weeks later the stock market crashed and the Great Depression swept over New England. Suddenly, many Yankees were living much lower on the hog. On any Saturday night there were more people dining out at the bean suppers than at the country club.

Well, here we are many decades later and again the New England economy has soured. It does not matter what you call it–a recession, depression or downturn–the effects are the same. Factories have shut down. Our department store has closed and Woolworth's has deserted us. Boarded storefronts line our downtowns. Neighbors who one day have a good job, find themselves unemployed the next. When the only available work is beyond the region, people sell their houses at a great loss and move on.

In all this, the Saturday bean supper endures. Take, for example, the supper sponsored by the United Church of Winchester, New Hampshire. This particular supper has been held on the first Saturday of the month for at least 50 years and was recommended to us by people who dine regularly on the church supper circuit.

Edward and I sampled the Winchester bean supper one August night. The young minister greeted us, took our names and told us we were welcome to look at the sanctuary while we waited for the next sitting. Upstairs, the sanctuary was hushed and cool. The early evening light filtered through the red, blue and yellows of the stained glass windows. As I read the names on the windows, I felt at one with the people who had sung and prayed there a long time ago. If you must wait to dine, this is one civilized way to do it—no smoke, no noise, no harried servers—just you and your thoughts and a certain presence.

At our sitting—the second of three that evening-about one hundred people were served. We sat across from an engineer, who had been "outplaced" by IBM. The engineer brought his elderly mother and a guest from Boston, proving that even a jobless man can take people out to dinner if he knows where to go. The Winchester supper cost five dollars and included baked beans, coleslaw, white and whole wheat dinner rolls, hot dogs and potato salad. Cheerful servers brought fresh platters of food and offered second helpings and a choice of beverages. For dessert, there was an assortment of pies: apple, blueberry, peach to name a few.

At community suppers, the cooks, servers and clean-up crew are volunteers. The modest profits from our church and community suppers buy library books, playground equipment, church steeple repairs, or emergency aid to people in other places–a flood in Iowa, an earthquake in India.

Of course, there are more efficient ways to raise money but our suppers flourish for other reasons. In our town, we catch up with our neighbors and the local news at the community supper. These events also offer the elderly, the single or lonely an affordable way to break bread with others. Singles are seated at tables with other people where they can visit or eat in silence. Yankees have a way of letting people be. You can buy leftover beans packed in a pint carton to take home. Or you can volunteer to deliver a pound of beans to a neighbor who cannot get out.

That is the way things are done in nearby Westmoreland, New Hampshire, explained Lois Leach, a nurturing cook and a faithful reader of a newspaper column I used to write. She often sent me encouraging notes, a cookbook from her collection, or a recipe to share with my readers.

Mrs. Leach gave me a recipe for baked beans used by most of the town's cooks when they contribute a pot of beans to a community supper. "So many people speak of the fine beans we all make," Mrs. Leach wrote. "In fact, for Old Home Day in August, three of us made eight pounds apiece in those old Westinghouse two-piece cookers and we could not tell them apart."

Of course, not every bean supper listed in the local newspaper is palatable. The first supper I attended was one of the dreariest meals I have ever eaten—canned baked beans served with slabs of brick red ham.

The supper was held in a metal building with overhead lighting that cast a purplish pall over all of us, already pasty-faced from the sun deprivation of late winter. I went to this supper to research this essay and came away hungry and depressed. But Edward persisted. When I was out of town, he gamely dined at other Saturday night suppers around the region.

He sampled the turkey, chicken pot pie, spaghetti, and strawberry and blueberry suppers. But we both concluded the "BE-in SUP ah" is the most popular and the probably best. After all, this is New England and like most cooks in this land, we use the prefix "Boston" when referring to a pot of beans. The biggest city in our region is nicknamed Bean Town.

The first written recipes for a dish called "Boston Baked Beans" appeared in Lydia Maria Child's 1882 cookbook, *The American Frugal Housewife –Dedicated to Those who are not Afraid of Economy*.

Boston baked beans could also be called Micmac or Narragansett baked beans after the indigenous peoples who introduced the European settlers to the native American bean, *Phaseolus vulgaris*. At the time the only bean available in Europe was the fava or broad bean, a spring vegetable that is best when eaten fresh. Dried, the fava bean is a favorite feed for horses. Someone once gave me a pound of dried fava beans and I simmered these stone-hard beans for hours. When they would not yield to time nor heat, I dumped them into the compost heap where they landed with a thud.

The Native Americans taught the settlers to cook the local beans with maple syrup, bear fat and tomatoes. The newcomers adopted the maple and meat flavorings but rejected the tomato as poisonous. When the Europeans finally accepted the tomato's role in baked beans, at least one fortune was made with the Native American formula. Back in 1891, Gilbert and Frank Van Camp of Indianapolis figured out how to package, preserve, and market pork and beans in tomato sauce. Today, a can of pork and beans, one of America's first convenience foods, is still a handy pantry staple. I know one hostess who mixes unheated canned baked beans with hot dog relish and plops the mixture onto a Ritz cracker for an appetizer, a company special I find appalling.

All over the Americas, the native people grew many kinds of beans. According to the carbon tests done by botanical archeologists, beans were stored in the caves of Peru as long ago as 5000 B.C.E. *Phaseolus*, (fah SEE oh lus), the American bean genus, includes 4,000 different species, and each will grow almost anywhere. In the days of seasonal migration, the high-energy beans were easy to store and carry. The plants themselves are good neighbors in the garden enriching the soil wherever they grow with nitrogen-fixing bacteria.

Among the Native Americans, there were even bean specialists. The Papago of southern Arizona were called ''the bean people'' because of their extensive cultivation and use of beans. Unfortunately, the Papago were frequently attacked by the Apache. The Papago preferred growing beans to fending off bullies so they signed a treaty with the United States to help them keep the Apache out of their fields, villages and lives. In 1986, the Papago drafted a new constitution and changed their tribal name to Tohono O'odham.

Meanwhile in New England, the Puritans discovered that baked beans were a convenient way to observe the Sunday no-work rule. Some sources say that the Puritans baked the beans on Saturday and ate cold beans on Sunday, certainly an unappetizing prospect on a cold winter day. Other sources say the beans were kept invitingly warm in the beehive oven, the crockery pot of its day.

Bullies and religious rules aside, beans offer top nutritional value for your food dollar. First, beans are a rich source of fiber, which is essential to a healthy intestinal tract. One-half cup of baked beans contains 9.8 grams of fiber, one third the daily intake recommended by the National Cancer Institute. A lack of dietary fiber has been linked to such serious diseases as heart disease, colon and rectal cancers, diverticulitis, varicose veins and obesity.

Second, beans also contain large amounts of the B vitamins. One half cup of beans contains 110 calories and seven grams of protein. That is equivalent to the protein in one ounce of lean beef. However, bean protein lacks two essential amino acids, which are the protein's building blocks. But you can get those building blocks if you combine rice, grains, meat or dairy foods with your beans.

The United States Department of Agriculture has always lumped dried beans in the relatively high-fat, high-cholesterol meat, poultry and egg group. However, the amount of fat in beans is negligible. When the food pyramid, a graphic tool sponsored by the USDA to teach nutrition, was introduced in 1992, beans, lentils and dried peas were grouped with the meat. Why? Because the beans, lentils and dried peas have *always* been in that category, a USDA spokesman said. Well, at least since 1926, he added.

The National Dried Bean Council wants beans re-assigned to the bread, cereal, rice and pasta group. Beans would become one of the choices in the six to eleven daily servings of the bread group. The bean council uses the term *pulses* to distinguish beans from legumes like alfalfa, mimosa and peanuts.

While some people debate pulses and food pyramids, volunteers in little towns all over New England are busy organizing next Saturday night's bean supper.

When I wrote a weekly newspaper food column, I invited readers to nominate the best community bean suppers in this corner of New Hampshire. Jane Dunn of Harrisville wrote, "We have church supers the third Saturday of each month at Wells Memorial School This has been a steady date for the last 21 years first for the Chesham Baptist church and later for the Combined Churches of Harrisville and Chesham"

Elizabeth J. Piper of Winchester noted, "Baked beans are still a New England specialty to many people. Look at the large attendance at the family style baked bean suppers served at the United Church of Winchester on the First Saturday of each month. The menu includes three kinds of beans that are popular in this region–yellow eye, pea and soldier. Many people who grew up with Saturday night baked beans come from miles away to enjoy our suppers."

The pineapple, a symbol of hospitality, is a universal New England motif, appearing in carvings over doorways, in quilt blocks and in stenciling on stair risers. At bean suppers, coleslaw is often served with the baked beans. This version offers the welcoming note of pineapple.

PINEAPPLE COLESLAW

1 medium head firm white cabbage
1 8-ounce can crushed pineapple, drained
2 medium carrots, grated
½ cup fresh lemon juice
¼ cup olive oil
¼ cup cider vinegar
½ teaspoon curry powder
1 teaspoon honey
1 teaspoon finely chopped fresh parsley
Salt and freshly cracked pepper to taste

Cut the cabbage into quarters. Remove core and tough outer leaves. Shred using a food processor or a grater.

Mix the cabbage, pineapple and carrots in a large bowl. Whisk together the lemon juice, olive oil, cider vinegar, curry powder and honey. Pour over the cabbage mixture. Mix gently. Add parsley and mix again. Add salt and pepper to taste.

Refrigerate at least one hour. May be made the day before serving.

Makes 8 cups.

NANCY S. WRIGHT'S BROWN BREAD

¾ cup sifted all-purpose flour
1-½ teaspoons baking soda
 1 teaspoon salt
1 cup yellow corn meal
1-1/4 cups whole wheat flour
¼ cup shortening, melted
¼ cup vinegar
1- ½ cups milk
½ cup seedless raisins

Nancy's original recipe called for baking the bread in 1-pound coffee cans. Since she gave me the recipe, the coffee can has shrunk incrementally to an 11-ounce size. Well, some canned vegetables still come in 1-pound cans so you can use that size.

Sift flour, baking soda and salt. Stir in cornmeal and whole wheat flour.

Combine molasses, shortening, vinegar and milk.

Pour milk mixture into flour mixture and stir just until blended. Stir in raisins.

Pour into three well-greased 1-pound cans. Fill 2/3 fill distributing batter evenly. Smooth the surface. Cover tightly with foil. Place cans on a rack in a deep kettle. Add boiling water to half the can's height. Cover. Set over enough heat to keep water boiling gently. Steam for 3 hours, checking water level occasionally. Add additional water to keep it at halfway level.

Makes 3 loaves.

FITZWILLIAM COUNTRY STORE BAKED BEANS

1 pound navy beans
1 teaspoon salt
¼ pound salt pork
1 tablespoon dry mustard
¼ cup brown sugar
1/3 cup molasses
1/3 cup catsup
1 onion, quartered
½ teaspoon garlic powder
Pinch dry ginger
1 tablespoon vinegar

Wash beans and soak six hours or overnight. Parboil until skins can be blown off, about 20 minutes. Preheat oven to 300 degrees. Pour beans and cooking water into a bean pot. Add salt, salt pork, mustard, brown sugar, molasses, catsup, onion, garlic powder, ginger and vinegar.

Stir well and bake for six hours. Remove cover and continue to bake an additional hour to brown surface. Add more water if necessary. Water should just cover the beans. Serve with coleslaw or carrot and raisin salad and brown bread, ham or frankfurters.

Makes six servings.

This recipe originated with Marjorie A. Hudson of Westmoreland, New Hampshire, and was sent to me by Lois Leach, who wrote, " This recipe is used by *many* cooks in town."

WESTMORELAND BAKED BEANS

2 pounds soldier beans
1 teaspoon baking soda
1 small onion
½ pound salt pork, cut into 1-inch squares
½ pound brown sugar
¼ cup molasses
1/3 cup maple syrup
½ teaspoon ginger
2 teaspoons salt
2 teaspoon dry mustard
½ cup hot water

Soak beans overnight in cold water. In morning, drain, cover with fresh water and add 1 teaspoon baking soda. Parboil until tender or until skin lifts when you blow on a few in a spoon. Do not let beans get mushy.

Drain in a colander and rinse gently with cold water. Quarter the small onion and place in the bottom of a bean pot or large heavy casserole. Pour in half of the beans and top with the salt pork. Pour in the rest of the beans. Add sugar, molasses and maple syrup. Dissolve salt, ginger and mustard in hot water and pour over beans. Add cold water to cover. Bake in a 250 to 300-degree oven for 6 to 8 hours.

Makes 12 servings.

WINCHESTER BAKED BEANS

1 pound (2 cups) dried Great Northern or navy beans
Cold water
2 ounces salt pork or 3 slices bacon
 I medium onion, peeled and sliced
6 tablespoons molasses
1 tablespoon cider vinegar
2 teaspoons dry mustard
Grind fresh pepper
Boiling water
½ teaspoon salt

Put beans in a large pot and cover with cold water. Soak overnight. Drain. Place beans in pot and cover with 6 cups fresh water. Bring to a boil and simmer for 30 minutes. Beans are cooked when one can be crushed easily between thumb and forefinger.

Drain beans, reserving liquid. Cut salt pork or bacon into ½- inch pieces. Put half of the pork or bacon and half of the onion into a heavy, 2-quart ovenproof pot. Add beans.

Preheat oven to 300 degrees. Mix molasses, vinegar, mustard and pepper with 2 cups boiling water. Pour over the beans. Press remaining salt pork or bacon and onion slices into beans. Add just enough bean soaking liquid to cover the beans.

Cover and bake 4-1/2 hours, stirring occasionally. Add more water if beans begin to dry out. Twenty minutes before beans are done, stir in salt. Continue baking beans uncovered so beans will form a crust.. Serve warm or cold.

Makes 4 generous servings.

A Personal Pot Of Baked Beans

Now you would think that making a pot of Yankee beans is a simple matter. Soak the beans, cook until tender, add more water, molasses and salt pork and bake. However, there are procedural partisans at every step of the way. I discovered that when I asked the readers of my newspaper column to share their baked-bean secrets.

Good cooks, bean-proud, wrote letters rich with feelings. "Bake the beans until they smell good," advised one cook. "Don't measure maple syrup. Just pour it on," said another. 'Don't throw out the pickle juice–dill or sweet-it doesn't matter. Just toss it into the bean pot."

Each cook had her own technique for making the best beans of them all.

Each cook insisted hers was the only method that worked and explained why. No matter. I concluded that how you cook your beans is not as important as what is in your heart when you do.

Before I could share that conclusion or the bean secrets with my readers, I left the newspaper business. But I saved the correspondence. I treasured these hand-written notes, many on flowered stationary. I switched careers twice more and a decade passed before I returned to that bean pot file. Surprisingly, the letters retained their warmth and appeal. I cannot part with them even though I have long since worked out my own favorite pot of beans. I have learned that baked beans are not difficult to make. But plan on forty eight hours lead time. The actual labor takes less than thirty minutes.

But let's hear from the experts, the New Englanders who grew up on baked beans. First, I asked the cooks what kind of bean makes the best batch. "The only proper beans are the white pea bean or the navy bean," wrote Polly Dugan of East Swanzey, New Hampshire. "The northern white bean is also fine. Personally, I like to change off to kidney, pinto or yellow eye beans but this is heresy among the purists."

"Soldier beans are the best," wrote Lois Wright of Gilsum, New Hampshire. Her declaration appeared on the back of a picture post card showing her town's impressive stone arch bridge. Lucille Davis of Fitzwilliam, New Hampshire, said she prefers Jacob's cattle beans. "My husband raises about ten pounds a year for baked beans." Jacob's cattle are white and heavily stained with crimson. The crimson color disappears during baking but raw Jacob's cattle beans make a brilliant display in a pantry jar.

Mrs. Davis added, "Yellow eyes would be my next choice. My mother, who at ninety years of age, was still known for her excellent beans–especially at a church supper–always used the small pea beans. Probably because my father preferred them"

That thread runs through the bean commentary. Women cook the kinds of beans their husbands and children like–even though they may have different personal favorites. Wilma Horton of Keene, New Hampshire, wrote, "Baked beans are something I have had a lot of experience with. When my kids were home, they were a Saturday night special. My favorite is the navy pea but my family prefers yellow eye or soldier beans."

Joyce J. Searles of Spofford, New Hampshire, wrote, "I don't know just how great my experience is in the art of baking beans but everyone who has eaten my beans enjoys them. I prefer yellow eye or pea beans."

As a bean novice, I discovered the many different shapes and colors of beans–yellow eye, Jacob's cattle and scarlet runner–and all available at the ordinary supermarket. I even saw a package of Maine-grown Jacob's cattle on a shelf in the Food Hall at Harrods in London.

No matter what kinds of beans the Yankee cook bakes, she often makes two pounds at a time. Said Polly Dugan, "They keep well in the refrigerator, at least until Sunday morning when all of the family is at home. With our three children all away at college, I freeze a few batches and the beans freeze beautifully. "

The next issue is soaking. Some cooks hold that quick soaking–cover beans with water, bring to a boil, boil two minutes, remove from heat, soak one hour and then simmer until tender–is the best way to prepare beans for baking. On the other hand, a *Los Angeles Times* food writer recently declared soaking beans a total waste of time.

However, my correspondents favored the long soak. They argued that the quick soak is insufficient because most available beans are older and drier than they should be. Further, the long soakers point out that no-soak or quick-soak beans rarely absorb enough water. In trying to hurry my beans, I have noticed that individual dried beans do not absorb water at the same rate. In the end short-soak beans take longer to cook and they cook unevenly–they are either undercooked or mush.

The next issue is the soaking water. The first school believes you should discard the soaking water because you will also discard the oligosaccharides (sugars) that make beans hard to digest and cause uncomfortable gas. Not so, says the opposition. What you are doing is throwing important nutrients out with the bean water.

Then there is baking soda or sodium bicarbonate. Some cooks add baking soda to the soaking and cooking water to prevent the formation of gas. Other cooks say the baking soda destroys some nutrients. Joyce Searles noted that she uses baking soda "to take the snappers out of the beans. But I won't guarantee that it will"

Wilma Horton added, "Yes, soda should be added to the cooking water. If I forget the baking soda, we all know it. "

The latest expert advice on gas suggests if you gradually increase the amount of beans you eat, your body will adapt accordingly. That is probably reasonable advice for most people. Chewing slowly and well will also help minimize gas. There is always Beano, a product that has brought relief to many bean eaters. A sprinkle of Beano on your dish of beans will neutralize those oligosaccharides.

There is no debate at all about how to cook the beans. Everyone seems to agree that beans should be brought slowly to a boil and then cooked over low heat. Too much heat applied too quickly will split the beans and turn them to mush. A bean is cooked when it can be crushed easily between your thumb and forefinger.

Next is the choice of sweetener to flavor the beans. When maple syrup and molasses were plentiful, they were the standard sweeteners for a pot of beans. These days, when New England cooks do use maple syrup, they use the cheaper Grade B. Or brown sugar.

Most baked bean recipes call for a slab of salt pork or bacon. One old woodstove cookbook suggests baking a partridge in your pot of beans to add a gamey flavor. This bird is plentiful up here where it is heard more often than it is seen. In season, the male partridge drums away in a steady rhythm to alert interested lady partridges. A partridge of either gender will startle the woods walker out of his or her meditative state by taking off like the bird equivalent of a 747. I, for one, am unlikely to flavor my beans with one of these magnificent birds. But if I change my mind, I will need more specific advice about grabbing this elusive bird from its forest hideout and thrusting it into my bean pot.

Classic salt pork is easier to come by although it is getting pricey. In these days of fat gram awareness, most cooks hesitate to toss a pound of salt pork into the bean pot.

"I used about one-quarter to one-half cup of diced fat back since salt pork has risen so sharply in price," wrote Polly Dugan. "The fat back is about the same as the salt pork, just remove the tough rind. I have cut way back on the pork in the beans to reduce our fat consumption. I dice the pork finely so a small amount distributed throughout the pot gives the flavor of a much larger lump."

To bake beans, my readers favored the oven, a pressure cooker, a slow cooker or the bean hole, the traditional Native American method. Here's how it is done: dig a hole, line it with rocks, build a fire and let it burn until the rocks are red hot, insert an iron pot filled with beans, pack more red-hot rocks around the pot, cover the pot with soil and bake for ten to twelve hours. 'Mmmm, ole bean hole beans," wrote Jane Blood of Keene, New Hampshire. "Who needs an oven?"

Well, yes, but even a hard-working researcher like myself would hesitate to cook up a batch of bean hole beans. First, if you dig a bean hole in New Hampshire between November and April you will need a jackhammer to penetrate the frost in the ground. Instead, some summer I will drive up to South Paris, Maine where the Annual Bean-Hole Festival attracts three thousand hungry people who devour tons of bean-hole beans cooked in huge iron pots. Each pot holds five hundred servings of beans. Also on the menu are hot dogs, sauerkraut, brown bread, pickles, relishes and homemade pies.

But most New England cooks bake their beans indoors in smaller quantities and don't need a derrick to hoist their pots around the kitchen. "I used to bake them in the traditional bean pot all day long in the oven but rising electric bills put a stop to that," explained Polly Dugan. "I tried a slow cooker with a lovely thick crock and hoped for the best and it was. The slow heat evenly encircles the crock and turns out as fine a batch of baked beans that ever came out of a colonial brick oven."

Ruth A Fuller of Winchester prefers using the oven. "1 do not like the slow cooker beans. They are too wet. I bake mine all day in a 250-degree oven. You just have to keep checking the water."

The secret to baking a good pot of beans, said one cook, is to keep them covered with water while baking and remove the lid during the last hour of baking.

Nancy Wright of Keene wrote that she had a lot more success with her pressure cooker than with baking beans all day long in the oven. "In these days of high energy costs, the pressure cooker is cheaper than either a gas or electric oven." She soaks one pound of small California beans for six hours and then parboils them for twenty minutes. She puts the drained beans into a pressure cooker with a slice of salt pork, two whole onions, two tablespoons molasses, a sprinkling of pepper, one teaspoon salt and a half teaspoon dry mustard. She covers the beans with water and cooks them at fifteen pounds pressure for thirty five to forty minutes.

I recently bought a pressure cooker and discovered I could cook two pounds of pre-soaked navy beans in ten minutes after the cooker came to a boil and reached fifteen pounds pressure. To save energy, I brought the ingredients to a boil in a large pot on top of the woodstove before transferring them to the pressure cooker and finishing the cooking on top of the electric stove. At first, there appeared to be too much liquid but as the beans cooled, they absorbed the liquid and the texture was just right.

Saturday night has been baked bean night in New England for a long time. Mrs. C.F. Trueax of Fitzwilliam, New Hampshire, offered her recipe for "Country Store Baked Beans," which are sold on summer Saturdays at the Blake House Museum in Fitzwilliam "I grew up in an old New England family," Mrs. Trueax explained, "and baked beans were served every Saturday with coleslaw, baked ham, hot dogs or kielbasa, brown bread, corn muffins or homemade white bread with Indian pudding for dessert."

All the bean cooks mentioned the ultimate bean treat: a Monday sandwich made with leftover beans. Wilma Horton wrote, ''Even though I know this will probably gag you, beans are also good cold for a sandwich. I have warmed up a black roll from the bakery and filled it with beans and no matter how it sounds, it is delicious. "

Gag? Not at all Wilma. In fact, I remember racing home from grade school on Monday afternoons anticipating a baked bean sandwich on squishy white bread. With gobs of ketchup leaking onto my hands, I chomped away my despair over finding the square root of anything.

Faith Trueax also has baked bean sandwich memories. "Monday's lunchbox or after-school snack consisted of a baked bean sandwich: cold beans on white bread with mayonnaise, and a little bit of salt and pepper."

And Ruth Fuller's description of her Monday sandwich brought tears to my eyes. ''I used to bake two pounds of beans for our Sunday night supper. And oh! Above all, a bean sandwich on Monday with a slice of raw onion."

What a fine way to start off a new week.

Wilma Horton, who gave me this recipe, describes it as, "the best baked bean recipe in the world." When Wilma and her husband ran a service station that was on my route home from work, I actually looked forward to buying gas. A quick stop at the station got me a full tank and a good measure of cheer from Wilma.

UNCLE JOE'S BAKED BEANS

1 pound baked beans
1/8 teaspoon baking soda
¼ pound lean salt pork
1 cup sugar
1 tablespoon dry mustard
1/8 teaspoon pepper
1/8 teaspoon ground ginger
3 tablespoons molasses
½ cup hot water

Cover beans with cold water and soak overnight. Drain beans and discard water. Put beans in a large pot and add baking soda, salt pork and fresh water to cover. Bring beans to a boil, lower heat and simmer beans until skin cracks when you blow on it.—about one hour.

Drain and rinse the beans. Place the salt pork on the bottom of the baking pot. Add the sugar, dry mustard, pepper, ginger and molasses. Pour in ½ cup hot water and mix well.

Add the beans to the pot and enough cold water to cover. Bake at 350 degrees until they smell good. Then lower the heat to 200 degrees and bake at least six hours more. Do not stir.

Makes six servings.

"Serve these wonderful beans with hot dogs or ham, a cabbage salad with pine-apple and raisins, bran muffins, homemade pickles and a custard or pumpkin pie for dessert," suggests Lucille Davis. And don't discard that sweet pickle juice. "I usually add about a cup of sweet pickle juice to my beans. It makes them taste great and uses something you would otherwise throw away," Mrs. Davis said.

LUCILLE DAVIS' BEST BEANS

2 cups dry beans
½ cup dark brown sugar
1 teaspoon salt
1 teaspoon dry mustard
2 tablespoons catsup
½ pound salt pork or fat trimmed from a ham
¼ cup molasses

Cover beans with cold water and soak overnight. Drain, cover with fresh water and parboil until skins burst. Drain. Put beans into a pot with a lid. Add the brown sugar, salt, mustard, catsup and molasses. Add hot water to cover. Cover pot and bake for 8 hours in a 250-to-300-degree oven. Check beans occasionally and if they get dry, add hot water, a little at a time. Makes six servings.

JOYCE J. SEARLES' BAKED BEANS

1 pound pea beans
½ teaspoon dry mustard
4 tablespoons molasses
½ cup brown sugar
Pinch ginger
4 small onions, halved
¼ pound salt pork
½ cup maple syrup

Pick over beans and soak in cold water overnight. Parboil until tender or until shells break away from beans. Drain and rinse the beans. Pour one half the beans into an ovenproof pot with cover. Add mustard, molasses, brown sugar and ginger to beans. Top beans with salt pork and onions.

Add remaining beans and pour maple syrup on top. Add water to cover. Cover pot and bake at 325 degrees for six or seven hours.

Check beans periodically to make sure they are covered with water. Less water may be added toward the end if you prefer less juicy beans. Makes 6 to 8 servings.

I began making baked beans regularly when I bought a pressure cooker. My favorite baked beans are now done in about 15 minutes, which saves a lot of time and energy. The beans may seem soupy at first but as they cool they absorb the liquid and the sauce becomes silky. Of course, I was wary about the possibility of my pressure cooker exploding and taking my kitchen ceiling with it out through the roof. My hesitations disappeared when I discovered the manufacturer had a toll-free number staffed by helpful women out there in Wisconsin to talk the novice through the process.

PRESSURE COOKER BAKED BEANS

2 pounds yellow eye beans
Water
¼ cup diced salt pork
4 medium onions, chopped
4 cloves garlic, minced
1 tablespoon minced fresh ginger
¼ cup molasses
¼ cup brown sugar
1 tablespoon dry mustard
¼ cup cider vinegar
¼ cup catsup
2 teaspoons salt
7 cups water

Cover beans with water, cover and soak overnight. Drain beans. In an eight-quart pressure cooker, mix together the salt pork, onions, garlic, ginger, molasses, brown sugar, dry mustard, vinegar, catsup, salt and water. Add the beans and mix.

Cover and follow manufacturer's instructions for sealing and operating pressure cooker. Bring cooker over medium high heat to 15 pounds pressure and then lower heat and cook for 15 minutes. Remove cooker from heat and reduce pressure according to manufacturer's instructions.

Makes 8 servings.

NOTE: The salt pork actually has a practical function besides flavor in pressure cooked beans. It reduces foaming of the liquid that could clog the vent. If you prefer vegetarian baked beans, substitute 3 tablespoons of olive oil for the salt pork. Author Lorna Sass has written many fine cookbooks on cooking with a pressure cooker. I admit I have at least four of her books and have given several as gifts. One reason is that her recipes are always very, very good.

This version of Boston brown bread goes together quickly because it is baked rather than steamed. If you don't have buttermilk on hand, use ordinary milk. Stir two tablespoons of lemon juice or vinegar into two cups milk and let stand for 5 minutes before adding to dry ingredients.

BOSTON BROWN BREAD

1-1/2 cups all-purpose flour
1-1/2 cups rye flour
1 cup yellow corn meal
1 teaspoon baking soda
1 teaspoon salt
1/3 cup raisins
2/3 cup chopped walnuts
½ cup molasses
2 cups buttermilk
Butter

Preheat oven to 375 degrees. Spray a 9-by-5-by-3-inch loaf pan with non-stick cooking spray.

Stir together all-purpose flour, rye flour, corn meal, baking soda and salt. Stir in raisins and walnuts. Beat in molasses. Add buttermilk and stir just until mixed. Bake in a preheated 375-degree oven for about one hour or until a cake tester or wooden pick inserted in center comes out clean.

Cool on a rack for 5 minutes. Loosen sides of loaf with a knife and turn out onto a rack. Brush top with melted butter. Serve warm.

Makes 1 loaf

As Perfect As A Potato

When I was a child potatoes seemed like such a dull food. Something we had to eat before we were allowed to leave the dinner table. I dawdled over a few bites of boiled potatoes, the last step in "clean your plate and then you may be excused from the table." I was not a fussy eater but I had no appetite for the very vegetable I now find comforting, nourishing and even intriguing to prepare. But back then, unmoved by my parents' tales of the potato famine back home in Ireland, I slipped my potatoes to Trixie, our grateful cocker spaniel, who waited under the table for a handout.

As a teenager, I discovered that the French fries served at our local Greek restaurant were an irresistible after-school snack. We sprinkled the fries with vinegar or dipped them into ketchup and made a serving last for hours of boy-watching to the tune of the McGuire sisters wailing "Sincerely." The fries or six plays on the juke box, each cost a quarter, the wages for one hour's babysitting.

When my growth spurt abruptly halted, the fries bulged into extra body fat. And just as suddenly, I was in college, working nearly full-time and the idle hours of high school were no more.

I do not remember any college food courses that included the study of potatoes, although they are a nearly perfect food. No history professor revealed that the potato and its thousands of varieties were developed in this hemisphere by the indigenous people of the Andes. Or that after the Spaniards introduced the potato to Europe, this single vegetable saved entire populations when famine struck or war broke out. The one thing I was certain about turned out to be false: that potatoes were fattening. It never occurred to me that the fat source might be gobs of sour cream or chunks of melting butter. Instead, I simply quit eating potatoes.

Decades later, I began craving potatoes. Not the greasy, lard-soaked fries of my youth or flour-and-fat laden scalloped potatoes we baked in the 1950s. Instead, I craved the newer versions that emphasized the potato's flavor—mashed potatoes with skim milk, a bit of butter and lots of garlic. Or grilled potatoes brushed with olive oil and sprinkled with rosemary. Or my friend Margritt Richter's *Himmell und Erde*—heaven and earth—mashed potatoes mixed with applesauce and topped with a bit of crumbled bacon. As a child in Germany, Margritt's grandmother won her heart with this dish.

Like the New York City chef who sells an $8.50 "power" potato, roasted over apple wood chips and drizzled with extra virgin olive oil, I, too, can finally appreciate the potato for itself. Consider this from the Department of Agriculture, "If a person's entire diet consisted of potatoes, he would get all the riboflavin, one and one half times the iron, three to four times the thiamine and niacin and more than ten times the amount of Vitamin C that the body needs each day.

But in nineteenth century Ireland, millions whose diet did consist of mostly potatoes died a terrible death. Not because of potatoes but because of politics. Beginning in 1845, a series of blights destroyed the potato crop, the staple of the Irish diet. By 1850, Ireland had lost 3.5 million people to starvation, disease and emigration. My ancestors fled to America. They were the lucky ones. The mass graves at places like Killary Harbor on the west coast of Ireland tell the story of the others.

Ironically, at the time of the famine, there was an abundance of other foodstuffs on hand in Ireland—sufficient to feed twice the population. However, England ordered the livestock and the grain stores shipped out of Ireland under armed guard. In other European countries where the potato blight also struck, food exports were banned and the stores fed to the hungry. The descendants of the potato pioneer breeders—the indigenous people of the Andes—also suffered under armed oppressors. When the Spanish arrived in 1531, the Incas were already cultivating seventy different potato crop species, the equivalent of all crops developed by their farming counterparts in all of Europe. Within the potato species (*Solarnum tuberosum*) alone, the Andean farmers cultivated 3,000 different varieties. This was done by transforming a harsh, uneven terrain, with countless microclimates into fertile, productive farmland. Thanks to the ingenuity of the Andean farmers, the potato became the economic basis for several great empires, ending with the Incas.

But the Inca's wealth was too tempting for the invaders. The Spanish stole the gold and silver, enslaved the people and almost as an afterthought, took a few potatoes back to Europe where they were promoted to cure impotence. Despite the appeal of that cure, the potato was slow to catch on. In France, it was alleged to cause leprosy. But a French man, who survived on potatoes alone in a Westphalia prisoner of war camp, returned home and became the vegetable's champion. In fact, French potato dishes are often named Parmentier in honor the army pharmacist who recognized the potato's nutritional value. Meanwhile, in Russia, the potato was dismissed by one Orthodox sect, because it was not mentioned in the Bible. Even so, vodka was invented in Russia using the starchy potato as it base. Later, that other American native, corn, was used to distill the favorite spirit of all the Russias and Poland, too.

But in the end, the potato had a far greater effect on the world than all the plundered silver and gold. This funny looking tuber turned out to be the miracle food the world was waiting for: a consistent source of cheap food that could sustain nations.

The potato yields more nutritious food faster on less land and in more varied climates than any other major crop. One acre of potatoes yields fifty percent more calories than an acre of grain. The potato grows in a variety of soils that are otherwise not productive. Once mature, the potato does not need extensive milling or special storage. It can be used immediately or can be stored up to a year.

Today in the mountains surrounding the Urubamba Valley, the Quechua people of Peru raise many kinds of potatoes using ancient tools and methods. Dr. Carlos Arbizu of the International Potato Center of Lima points out that even Peruvian farmers with tiny plots raise a variety of potatoes without expensive fertilizers or pesticides.

Andean cooks can choose from a dozen different kinds of potatoes even at small village markets. Each kind of potato has its champions. Some local experts insist the deep yellow *amirilla* is the best-tasting potato in Peru. But the people of the Inca capital city of Cuzco hold that the *ccompis*, a round white-fleshed potato is the best of the bunch. Other locals prefer the *lamellina,* which has a smooth creamy texture like an avocado.

Centuries ago, the Andean farmers developed a kind of insurance against crop failure. Using freeze-dry technology, they invented *chuno,* a potato staple that resembles a piece of plastic foam. Chuno lasts for years without refrigeration and is a main ingredient in *chairo,* a specialty soup of the Andes.

But life is harsh in the mountains of the Urubamba Valley where there is neither electricity nor running water in many villages. Social and economic pressures, creeping development and terrorist attacks on farmers have driven many families into the slums of Lima.

But scientists like Dr. Carlos Ochoa, Peru's most famous potato explorer, refuse to let the ancient potato species disappear. In the last forty years, Dr. Ochoa at some personal risk, has recovered eighty of the 230 wild potato species that were about to be lost to disease, development or the spreading desert. The International Potato Center's seed collection includes 300 different species and 4,500 varieties. The center's scientists are now combining wild and native potato varieties to produce high-yield disease-resistant crops.

And it is just in time because the potato blight is back. Modern strains of the 1840s fungus that wiped out the European potato crops are threatening the current potato crops on almost every continent. Experts believe the best long-term defense is the creation of new, resistant varieties. "We have been steadily creating new varieties for years," says Dr. Alvin Reeves, a potato breeder at the University of Maine. "But the blight will give us new impetus."

Here in the United States, most of us can buy just two types of potatoes—the high-starch russets for baking or deep-frying or the Eastern all-purpose potatoes that we used for everything from pancakes to salad.

The total American crop includes no more than twenty varieties. Limiting ourselves to a few kinds of potatoes raised with tons of pesticides and fertilizer would seem to make us vulnerable to large-scale blight.

But there is hope. Tastes change. Who would have imagined that one day Americans would buy more bottles of salsa than ketchup? Potato-wise, even in an ordinary super-market, consumers can now buy the yellow-flesh Yukon Gold or the Yellow Finn.

People who dine in New York City can sample several unusual potatoes at the Gourmet Garage, which offers Caroles, Russian Bananas, Rose Finns and 13 other va-rieties of potatoes.

However, if you want to cook that kind of potato variety at home, you probably have to raise the tubers yourself. One source, Ronniger's Seed Potato Catalog of Moyie Springs, Idaho, offers 80 varieties of potatoes in a rainbow of red, rose, yellow, and blue. red-gold, white blue-white and many more colors. If potato beetles are your bugaboo, consider this advice from New Hampshire Extension specialist Doug Routley: A heavy mulch of pine needles around your plants will discourage these ravenous insects.

If you are a garden-free couch potato who wants a little variety in your spuds, con-sider this offer by the New Penny Farm of Presque Isle, Maine. During the eight-month potato harvest season, the New Penny Farmers will send you five pounds of a different potato variety every month—from All Blue to Russian Banana. Not everyone can claim membership in a potato species-of- the- month club. Some folks must be content with membership in Mensa or a best- seller-of- the- month club.

I relish a once-a-summer splurge on a great potato salad with good mayonnaise and lots of hard-cooked eggs. But if you must watch the fat, substitute a fat-free mayonnaise and use only the whites of the hard-cooked eggs.

ONE OF THE GREAT POTATO SALADS

5 pounds all-purpose potatoes
2 tablespoons cider vinegar
2 tablespoons olive oil
2 tablespoons sugar
2 tablespoons salt
2 cups celery, finely chopped
6 hard-cooked eggs, sliced
¼ cup chopped parsley
8 ounces chopped pimientos
½ cup minced onion
1 10-ounce jar sweet potato relish
2 tablespoons Dijon mustard
1 quart mayonnaise
1 5-ounce jar prepared horseradish

Fill a large pot with cold water. Peel and slice potatoes and place in the cold water to prevent browning. Bring a large pot of water to boiling. Drain potatoes and place in boiling water, return water to a boil, lower heat and continue to boil just until fork tender. Begin checking for doneness after 12 minutes after potatoes have begun to boil. Drain cooked potatoes.

Meanwhile, whisk together vinegar, olive oil, sugar and salt and gently toss with warm potatoes. Cover and refrigerate until thoroughly chilled.

Add celery, eggs parsley, pimientos, onion and pickle relish to chilled potatoes. Mix horseradish and mayonnaise. One hour before serving, toss potato mixture with as much of the horseradish-mayonnaise as desired.

SAVORY POTATO SKINS

4 baking potatoes
3 tablespoons butter or margarine, melted
1-1/2 teaspoons Cajun seasonings
1 teaspoon ground cumin
1/2 teaspoon chili powder
1 cup chopped onion
1/4 cup plain low-fat yogurt

Quarter potatoes lengthwise. Remove all but a ¼-inch layer from each quarter. Reserve potato flesh for another use. To prevent browning, cover with cold water. Cut potato quarters in half crosswise. Arrange on a microwave and broiler-proof platter. Cover with plastic wrap and microwave on high for 6 to 8 minutes.

Meanwhile, mix melted butter with 1 teaspoon Cajun seasoning (recipe follows), cumin, chili powder and salt. Mix yogurt with ½ teaspoon Cajun seasoning.

Carefully remove wrap from potato skins. Brush butter mixture over the skins and sprinkle the chopped onions on top. Potato skins can be prepared ahead to this point.

Broil 3 inches from the heat until lightly browned. About 3 to 6 minutes. Serve with yogurt for dipping.

Makes 32 skins.

When I was a beginning cook, I bought a cookbook that had a mysterious ingredient, *Beau Monde Seasoning*, in every other recipe. It was very frustrating because no other cookbook or cook could tell me what that ingredient was or where I could get it. So I just left it out. Thus, I am including the formula for Cajun seasoning for beginning cooks. After making a few thousand dishes, you will discover which ingredients are essential and which are not.

CAJUN SEASONING

1 tablespoon paprika
1 teaspoon onion powder
1 teaspoon garlic powder
1 teaspoon cayenne
¾ teaspoon fresh ground pepper
½ teaspoon dried, crushed
¼ teaspoon dried thyme, oregano crushed

Combine paprika, onion powder, garlic powder, cayenne, pepper, oregano and thyme. Mix well. Store tightly covered in a cool, dry place.

Makes about ¼ cup seasoning.

When Corning introduced a line of white platters that could go from the micro-wave oven to the standard oven or to the broiler, I rejoiced. Before this handy item was available, I used a microwave dish to cook the potatoes and then trans-ferred them to a foil lined broiler pan to brown them. We love these roasted potatoes that are fragrant with rosemary. And they are so quick and easy to make.

LOWER FAT FRIES

4 baking potatoes
1 medium onion
2 teaspoons dried rosemary
Olive oil cooking spray
Salt
Freshly ground pepper

Cut potatoes in half crosswise. Stand each half on its flat end and slice lengthwise into 8 wedges. Cut onion lengthwise into wedges. Spread potatoes and onions on a microwave and broiler-proof platter. Cover with plastic wrap and microwave on high for 6 minutes. Platter will be very hot. Carefully lift one corner of wrap to let steam escape. Remove remaining wrap.

Lightly coat potatoes with cooking spray. Sprinkle with rosemary. Broil 3 inches from heat for 8 to 10 minutes until browned.

Makes 2 large servings.

When mother made this salad years ago, the flavor came from bacon, vinegar and sugar. We children relished the sweet-sour taste. Now that we are eating lighter, here is an updated version that is also tasty. Serve this warm dish with sautéed boneless breast of chicken, a green salad and steamed winter squash pureed with orange juice and a bit of apple sauce.

WARM GERMAN POTATO SALAD

2 pounds red potatoes
½ cup chopped red onion
2 minced garlic cloves
¼ cup olive oil
1 tablespoon dried rosemary
2 tablespoons cider vinegar
2 tablespoons finely chopped fresh parsley
Salt and freshly-ground pepper

Quarter the potatoes lengthwise but do not peel. Cut crosswise into ½ -inch pieces. Cover with boiling water, bring to a boil, lower heat to medium and cook for seven minutes or until tender but firm. Drain thoroughly. Put potatoes in a heatproof serving bowl and place in a warm oven.

Meanwhile sauté onion and garlic over medium low heat. Stir in rosemary and cook just until onion is softened. Toss potatoes with onion-oil mixture to coat adding more oil if necessary. Sprinkle with vinegar. Season to taste. Dust with parsley. Serve at once.

Makes 4 servings.

For garlic mashed potatoes, add 3 peeled garlic cloves when you boil the potatoes and mash them with the potatoes.

SKINNY MASHED POTATOES

2-1/2 pounds red potatoes
1/4 cup hot skim milk
1/2 teaspoon salt
1/4 teaspoon freshly ground pepper

Peel and quarter potatoes. Place potatoes in a 5-quart saucepan. Add water to 1 inch above tops of potatoes. Bring to a boil over high heat. Reduce heat and simmer covered for about 20 minutes until potatoes pierce easily with a fork. Remove from heat and drain.

Place potatoes in the large bowl of an electric mixer. Begin to break up potatoes at medium-low speed. As potatoes break up, increase speed to medium high. Add milk, salt and pepper; mix until smooth. Serve immediately.

Make 6 servings.

ABUNDANCE

Take one look at the serving table at a potluck party and you will see abundance. If you invite me to a potluck, I will cook the best dish in my repertory and present it with all the splendor of a magazine cover. And when dinner is announced, all the guest cooks gather around the table to inspect what the others have done.

But what about leftovers? Who has the rights to the leftovers? If you bring your splendid cherry cheesecake to my potluck, please bring any leftovers with you. On the other hand, when I bake bread, I make an extra loaf for the hostess. She has done most of the work and made the rest of us happy.

Once when I was on a between-jobs-tight-budget, I was invited to an extravagant party by a couple celebrating the purchase of a very extravagant gift. I brought a savory dish of *tabbouleh*. It came almost entirely out of my garden and cost me little. But at the party there was an abundance of everything. As we departed, I stopped at the food tent and scooped up my untouched *tabbouleh*. We ate it for a week afterward. May Miss Manners forgive me.

A Gardener's Rubies

Why would anyone grow radishes when an entire bunch sells for 39 cents—even in mid-winter? I cannot answer such a reasonable question. Instead, every March, I lug fertilizer, shovel mulch and squish tiny seeds into the earth. In a mud-brown off-again-on-again spring, radishes are my sign of hope. I plant them between snow squalls and a few weeks' later, heart-shaped leaves pop up.

I am content with one, maybe two radish crops per summer. Yes, I know about those gardeners featured in *Mother Earth News* who compute the moon phases, National League Standings and weather forecasts and raise crop after crop of radishes all the way to Thanksgiving.

That would be too complicated for me. My radishes are over and done with before I must weed, water or preserve them. Long before root-guzzling cabbage maggots locate my crop.

I grow just enough radishes for in-garden snacking, several salads, and a few for radish roses in case the garnish mood strikes.

However, one spring I went out of control. While browsing in one of the last FW Woolworth stores in America, I came across a seed sale. The store was in Raleigh, North Carolina, and there radish season was already history but up North it was only April and there were still patches of snow in the woods. I bought four packs each of Cherry Belle and Early Red Globe. At eights each, I figured I had saved $1.07 a packet. Each contained 300 seeds, a fact I chose to ignore in the heat of saving $8.56.

I planted the seeds and counted the 21 days until harvest. Of course, 21 days is a seed-packet promise like "easy to grow" or "does well in any soil." Actually, the radishes took 35 days to mature.

That spring was cold and rainy, even for Northern New England. But such depressing weather is perfect for growing mild, plump radishes. Beach weather—warm, sunny and dry—produces radishes that are woody, tongue-burning hot and quick to bolt to seed.

But that year I pulled up handfuls of crisp, well-formed, scarlet bulbs. It was soon clear there were more radishes than Edward and I could eat. Even at 2.3 calories per radish. I began carrying a radish bouquet on every errand to town. Garden-free people like our good Postmaster April McDonald accepted this bounty as it were the sacred gold radishes the Greeks offered Apollo.

However, at the dentist's office where one would expect approval for high-fiber, pesticide-free living, receptionist Ellie Rhoades responded to my offering with "Oh, no!" She had a radish overload of her own.

In all that red round abundance, I discovered only one recipe to deal with the excess—radish soup. Perhaps I am the only person who has ever planted 2,400 radishes to feed a family of two. I'll never know because radishes do not make the news unlike the president's dogs or cats or a zucchini squash the size of a sumo wrestler.

Like squash, each different kind of radish has its season. Our most familiar radish—the round red kind—is a spring radish. So is the slender white icicle radish. These spring radishes flourish in the cool weather.

The summer radish is a larger, carrot-shaped radish that can take the heat but the winter radish needs cool weather to mature. Like Hubbard or acorn squash, the winter radishes are good keepers if stored in a cool place. The winter radish is an important diet staple in Asia, India and Africa. In fact, this radish represents more than 25 percent of Japan's total vegetable crop.

The skin of the winter radish comes in many colors—black, red and violet are just a few. However, the flesh is always white. The winter radish family includes many sizes and shapes. For example, *Sakurajima* Mammoth, matures to a beach ball-size 60-pounder.

African and Asian cooks peel the winter radish and then boil it or steam it like a turnip. It is also pickled or grated into salads, soups and dipping sauces. In China, exquisitely carved winter squashes decorate each table at important banquets.

In Korea, the white radish starred in *kimjan,* a harvest ritual of preserving vegetables in brine. Entire families assembled as a stream of farmers' carts loaded with white radishes and cabbages pulled into the city's open air market where the stalls were already hung with chiles, garlic and green onions.

A frenzy of bargaining was followed by peeling, chopping and salting. The resulting preserved vegetables or *kimchi*, were packed into porcelain jars to provide vegetables for the long, cold season ahead.

American cooks are most familiar with the long white winter radish called daikon that is grated and added to stir-fry along with gingerroot.

One year I planted the daikon April Cross Hybrid described by the Park Seed Company as "60 days. An outstanding giant Japanese or Daikon type radish with hybrid vigor. Grows to a huge 18 inches and up to three inches in diameter and yet its white flesh remains crisp and mild with a touch of sweetness. Excellent fresh with a dip, in salads or pickled. Slow to bolt, holds well in the garden or continued harvest."

That was the year seed germination was uneven at best. Then came a prolonged drought followed by too much rain. But the unexpected success of my April Cross Hybrid was thrilling. Even if the huge roots had never developed and they did—the plants appealing foliage would have been reward enough. Each leaf radiates like a flower petal from the top of the root. The white flesh is sinus clearing hot but that may be blamed on this acidic New England soil or the unseasonable weather.

In any case, I pickled some of the April Cross in Szechuan style and braised a few in the Hangchow style. Both satisfied my craving for Chinese food set off by memories of Chicago or San Francisco.

There was a time that Americans did not limit themselves to radishes like Cherry Belle. The 1888 Burpee seed catalog listed 15 different spring radishes—from the white-tipped violet oval to the creamy Lady Finger. Burpee's also offered the summer radishes, Golden Globe and Giant White Stuttgart. For winter keeping, the 1888 catalog suggested China rose, Mammoth White Russian and Round Black Spanish.

A packet cost five cents, a pound 75 cents. And shipping was free! In fact, the catalog urged you to send your cash by registered mail. The fee for registered mail was ten cents and in return, Burpee would give you an extra ten cents worth of seeds.

Today's taverns serve salty popcorn to promote thirst but in other times and places, radishes did that job. Ben Johnson sent his characters to an offstage tavern "for a bunch of radish and salt to bring out the taste of the wine." In Bavarian beer halls, pungent white icicle radishes accompany each stein of beer.

In Westmoreland, England, the first radish crop calls for a celebration. Each May 11, the villagers feast on radishes served with buttered brown bread and washed down with the strong local ale.

Perhaps I should have invited our neighbors over for a radish supper the year I over-planted. The neighbors would have quickly appeared had I also let it be known that in Renaissance England, radishes were used to cure melancholy, rheumatism and warts.

But I was thinking small and instead bought two gadgets to carve radish roses. Unfortunately, each tool complicated a simple task and eventually joined all the other poorly designed gadgets in the free shed at the dump.

I have since discovered two simple radish garnishes that require no special tools. First, spinners: slice off the stem and root ends from a round radish. Slice radish crosswise into thin slices. Make a slit in each slice from center to one edge. Gently push one slice into another at their slits. They fully intersect to form a spinner, a playful garnish for stuffed eggs or sandwiches.

To make radish fans, use oval radishes. Trim ends but leave one leaf attached. Make a series of crosswise cuts along the radish but do not slice through. Drop in ice water and refrigerate for several hours. The radishes will fan out while you are not looking.

And what about cooking a spring radish? Well, the purists say that there are two foods that should never be cooked—grapefruit and radishes. However, you can use spring radishes instead of canned water chestnuts in stir-fry. The radishes may taste better than the canned water chestnuts, which are overpriced, over salted and over processed.

Or serve tiny steamed whole radishes with a bit of butter. For a milder yogurt or sour cream dip, substitute grated radishes for horseradish—no relation. Grated radishes add a pungent spark to hot dogs and burgers. An otherwise sensible Shaker cookbook suggests serving creamed radishes in a spinach ring. Back in the 1950s, I, for one, had my fill of anything served in a rice, potato or gelatin ring.

After your crop has bolted, you can rescue all those flea-sized radish seeds. Then sprout them for winter salads, a tip offered by *Organic Gardening*. How many radish seeds will you need for a crop of sprouts? A billion? Two, maybe.

In other whimsy, consider the new Easter Egg Radish. It pops up in a rainbow of pastels: reddish purple, lavender, pink, rose, scarlet and white. You won't find this radish at the usual produce counter, so if you want to impress your friends, you will have to grow your own. Just let me know how you coordinate the arrival of the radish crop with the moveable feast of Easter.

All radishes—spring, summer and winter—belong to the species of *Rhapanus sativus* and are members of the mustard family which explains why they sometimes bite back. The eye-watering horseradish –*Armoracia rusticana* belongs to an entirely different species.

I have never planted horseradish because I have heard all about it from people who have. They planted it to relieve their sinuses and now have a weeding headache that will not go away because horseradish spreads faster than kudzu. Of course, I did not know any of this when I planted my bargain radish seeds. It could have been worse. I could have planted 2,400 horseradish seeds.

This is a handy solution to the garden overflow. Almost any combination of vegetables suitable for pickling will work with the basic spicy liquid. I have also used zucchini, yellow summer squash, red bell peppers, or green beans in combination with the vegetables listed below or as a substitute or some of them. You may also adjust the red pepper, sugar and salt to your taste.

SZECHWAN PICKLE

2/3 pound daikon
4 medium carrots
3 medium cucumbers
2 inches fresh ginger root
3 garlic cloves
2 cups shredded cabbage
2 quarts water
2 teaspoons salt
2 tablespoons Szechwan peppercorns
1 tablespoon sugar
2 tablespoons rice wine or dry sherry
¼ cup white vinegar
1 tablespoon red pepper flakes

Peel daikon and slice into 1/8-inch rounds. Peel carrots and slice into matchsticks ¼-inch by 2 inches. Leave peels on cucumbers and slice into 1/8-inch pieces. Peel garlic and quarter. Peel gingerroot and slice into 1/8-inch pieces. Place all vegetables including the cabbage into a large non-reactive bowl such as stainless steel or glass.

Bring water to a boil. Remove from heat and stir in the salt and sugar until dissolved. Add the peppercorns, rice wine, vinegar and red pepper flakes.

Pour the water mixture on top of the vegetables and mix thoroughly. Water should just cover the vegetables. Add more boiling water if necessary. Cool. Refrigerate in jars with tight-fitting lids.

Makes about 3 quarts.

In a bountiful garden year, I always need recipes for fresh vegetables. This brightly-colored salad features three of my favorite garden vegetables and includes the savory aroma and flavor of sesame oil. Serve with grilled steak, chicken or fish. To make a julienne or matchstick cut, slice vegetables into pieces 2 inches long by ¼-inch thick.

SHANGHAI SALAD

1-1/2 cups daikon, peeled and cut into julienne
1-1/2 cups carrots, peeled and cut into julienne
1-1/2 cup cucumbers peeled and cut into julienne
1-1/2 teaspoons salt
¼ cup rice or white vinegar
3 tablespoons sugar
2 teaspoons sesame oil

Place each vegetable in a separate bowl and sprinkle each with ½ teaspoon salt. Let sit for 2 hours. Rinse vegetables with cold water and drain well.

In a large bowl, whisk together vinegar, sugar and sesame oil. Add vegetables and toss thoroughly. Refrigerate until serving. Can be made up to 3 days ahead.

Makes 4 servings.

Fiddleheads are fern shoots that local collectors pick from the banks of the Connecticut River. These are not just any fern but are the edible ostrich fern, *Matteuccia struthiopteris*. The fiddleheads sell for about $3.99 a pound at our supermarkets. This salad is colorful and spring like. Serve with spinach fettuccine tossed with chickpeas and slivers of ham.

SPRING RADISH SALAD WITH FIDDLEHEADS

2 cups fiddleheads
1 clove garlic, minced
½ teaspoon Dijon mustard
2 tablespoons lemon juice
½ cup olive oil
1 teaspoon light soy sauce
Salt and freshly ground pepper
1 small onion
2 large bunches radishes, thinly sliced
Sprinkle of sesame seeds
1 yellow bell pepper, cut into julienne

Rinse fiddleheads several times. Steam for 8 to 10 minutes. Rinse with cold water to stop cooking. Drain and pat dry. Radishes may be sliced ahead of time and refrigerated separately in a plastic bag. Use food processor to slice radishes if desired.

Whisk together garlic, mustard, lemon juice, olive oil, soy sauce, salt and pepper. Toss dressing with fiddleheads, onions and yellow pepper. Refrigerate.

Just before serving, add sliced radishes to fiddlehead mixture and toss gently. Sprinkle with sesame seeds.

Makes 6 servings.

When I was based in Chicago, I discovered that no backyard barbecue, street fair or football game was complete without a serving of "brat," short for authentic bratwurst sausage. There are many small butcher shops in Illinois and Wisconsin that make their own high-quality bratwurst—even low-fat versions. To prepare bratwurst, soak it in beer overnight, pierce each sausage a few times with a sharp knife and grill 15 to 20 minutes. Onions usually accompany bratwurst but here is a radish relish that is often used. It works on hot dogs, too.

BARB'S RADISH RELISH FOR BRATWURST

1 6-ounce bag radishes, coarsely chopped
2 tablespoons honey mustard
2 green onions
1 tablespoon sour cream
1 tablespoon fresh minced parsley

In a small bowl, combine radishes, mustard, onions, sour cream and parsley. Do not prepare relish more than two hours ahead because radish flavor will become overpowering.

Makes 1 cup.

These days our New Hampshire supermarkets do stock ingredients like oyster sauce and fresh ginger. But sometimes, I need ingredients like red sumac. That is when I am grateful my stepson Peter lives in New York. He is a fine cook and understands when I ask him to bring me the dried shrimp that is essential to braised daikon. This dish goes well with grilled chicken, pork or beef.

HANGCHOW BRAISED DAIKON

1 daikon or giant white radish
2 teaspoons dried shrimp
1 tablespoon rice wine or sake
3 tablespoons oil
3 tablespoons low-sodium soy sauce
1 chile pepper, seeded and minced
1 teaspoon minced fresh ginger
¼ cup ground pork
1 cup water
1 thinly sliced green onion

Soak dried shrimp in lukewarm water for 30 minutes. Drain and chop finely.

Peel radish and slice lengthwise into ½-inch strips. Slice strips on the diagonal into 2-inch pieces. Whisk together rice wine and soy sauce. Heat oil in a large skillet and stir in ginger and chile pepper. Cook and stir for 30 seconds. Add dried shrimp, pork, radish, wine-soy mixture and water and stir until thoroughly mixed.

Cover, lower heat and simmer for 5 minutes or until radish is tender. Makes 4 servings.

The Kitchen In My Mind

"Now, first I'd like to see your kitchen," said the earnest young interviewer from New Hampshire Public Radio. "I always look at food writers' kitchens." I pointed to the small, dark room that could be mistaken for a pantry. "Hmmmm," said the young man. "Well, let's do this outside."

I know he was disappointed. He had driven an hour from the city of Concord, New Hampshire and I know what he was looking for—the kind of country kitchen I have dreamed about ever since I moved here. My dream kitchen, like everyone else's dream kitchen reinvents itself from moment to moment.

For example, when I face a mountain of dishes, the mind installs a dishwasher. When Edward and I trip over each other at breakfast, an island with its own sink appears. And as in all daydreams, this kitchen plan never addresses the realities like electrical connections and plumbing.

The kitchen of my mind is certainly spacious, with a large table, flanked by benches, with counter space measured in miles. The counters are so spacious that I can display my doll-size antique cast iron stove. The little black stove sits on a white solid surface counter and at night I flick on a pin point spotlight over the little stove for a night light. Each cabinet has doors that open wide and slide back out of the way like they way they do in "entertainment center" furniture. That way, every ingredient and tool is in full view and at hand for the working cook. Then when the meal is done, the cabinets are shuttered for the night.

Next to the huge, dreamy fireplace an ample chair for Edward and another for me. As I peel and chop I explain the importance of fresh basil. Or he explains the orbiting of multiple star systems. Or we agonize over the latest spate of violence in the news from the real world.

In the corner, there is a softly-lit banquette with cushy, overstuffed seats and a table topped with smoked glass. A sleek little desk holds my kitchen computer so I can make notes as I test recipes.

I won't have a cookbook shelf in my kitchen because I revere my cookbook collection and want to keep it as tidy as possible. Of course, some cookbooks don't contain a useful recipe but the stories or photographs are worth revisiting. Other cookbooks spend a lot of time in my kitchen and are spattered with the evidence. These are the basics by Betty, Fanny and Irma.

My fantasy kitchen has a walk-in pantry with wine racks and selected preserves lit up like stained glass in a cathedral. Stacks of matched china, crisp linens and polished sliver are always fingertip ready for dinner.

My mind's refrigerator has neither photo murals nor gadget-y ice water fountain. No grinning geese decorate every potholder, canister or coffee mug.

The kitchen of my mind contains no potpourri cooker steaming with the authentic fragrance, New England Wildflower Field, packaged in Seoul. And none of the fashionable clutter prescribed by big city editors for country kitchens: no tin ware, no tole ware, no fiesta ware.

There is nothing trendy in my fantasy. I made that mistake once in real life with an avocado green refrigerator. Avocado was a popular decorating magazine's color of the year. For me, it was the color of about one month. And I despised it for the next 239 months. Our current refrigerator is now a pure, versatile, happy immaculate, ever-loving white.

To its credit, my real kitchen has exposed ceiling beams, a tribute to the farmer who built this house two centuries ago with hand tools and native pines. Such beams aren't much use beyond displaying a few herbs and holding up the second floor, and they limit the options for improving the lighting in this kitchen but we love them anyway.

For years, I grumbled about cooking in my own shadow. Then we installed a light over the sink—and we forget to turn it on.

My kitchen has a handy peg board that stores everyday utensils. The board is neither magazine worthy nor museum quality but it keeps the pots, pan and tools sorted out. And I know that Julia Child's pegboard with each pot outlined in black is enshrined in the Smithsonian Institution.

I have scant cabinet space for storage. So we stow canned goods, potatoes, onions and picnic supplies in milk crates under the dining table and the top of the refrigerator holds old canning jars filled with staples like split peas, corn meal or pinto beans. The colors of the staples themselves—green, yellow, red—sometime inspire a meal all by themselves.

We have a new window over the sink. Its diamond panes make me feel like the mistress of a castle when I check for chickadees in the morning or white-tailed deer in the evening. When the August heat and humidity oppress, the window admits a passing breeze from the south.

Despite its size, my kitchen attracts guests at the slightest aroma. I used to be annoyed when visitors lifted saucepan covers or peered into an oven. I have since learned tolerance.

The vast literature on kitchen renovation indicates that most of our kitchens are inadequate to begin with. I don't know why this has to be. Surely, the giants of technology could perfect the place where we generate the fuel that drives mankind. And isn't the kitchen the emotional center of the household? But serious kitchen design is seldom introduced into house building. Home economists can present facts about traffic flow, job-specific work centers and the Major Appliance Triangle but workflow in most kitchens is as about efficient as the Bermuda Triangle.

In college, I had to design a complete kitchen. The assignment overwhelmed me. At our house, the layout of the kitchen was a given, an unchanging fact like the Golden Rule or Spam. The refrigerator did not fit in the kitchen so it was installed in the back entrance hall. The stove did fit into our small kitchen. While my mother stood at the stove and stirred her pots, traffic from three rooms and the entry converged behind her. My parents painted, papered and sewed curtains but no one we knew knocked down a wall.

Me design a kitchen from scratch? I turned to a neighbor. If women had been allowed to have careers in the 1950s, Christine Gannon could have been a prosperous decorator. She was that good. Lucky for me, she had just redone her kitchen. She handed over her flooring samples, countertop samples, wallpaper samples, fabric samples, even her pink-dusk paint chips. I made a collage of them on top of her floor plan. Mrs. Gannon and I earned an A for the course.

Real custom kitchens are seldom an option for most people. What comes with the house is what you live with. Most cooks adapt in small ways: a shelf for the food processor here, a cart for the microwave there. Major appliances are replaced only when they sputter and die.

A nearby custom kitchen I envy has more cabinet space than a school lunch program. It has two pantries and his and her sinks in primary colors. Each small appliance has its own little garage with a push-button overhead door. The irony of such a kitchen is that the people who own it don't cook at all and depend on gourmet kitchen takeout and the best caterer in town.

Space has always been a kitchen issue. "Largeness of dimension is the first requirement of any kitchen," wrote Isabella Beeton in her 1859 *Household Management*. Mrs. Beeton also primly advised, "The kitchen be sufficiently remote so that family members, visitors or guests not perceive the odor incident to cooking, or hear the noises of the culinary operation."

But some things change and the popularity of today's open kitchen design indicates that we now value the aromas, the sounds, and the company.

Sometimes Edward watches as I work on the 21-by-27 inch expanse that is my total counter space. "You deserve a better kitchen that his," he says. Our friend, Terry Cox, agrees. He builds fine kitchens with exquisite cabinets. "When you do your cooking video, Pat, you will need a better kitchen than this," says Terry. Both men are right.

And that radio interview went well—out in the dooryard over warm bread and fresh butter. The birds of June sang the background music and Madame Nhu, our Siamese cat, made an occasional comment, later aired on New Hampshire Public Radio. That young man was right about our kitchen. It worked well for a farmer's wife back in 1815 but it is not the sort of laboratory a cookbook writer needs.

So I'll just keep dreaming up my ultimate kitchen while you stir up these realities.

This special dessert is a good way to celebrate the apple harvest. If you don't have applejack for the sauce, substitute rum or brandy.

APPLEJACK APPLE CAKE

1 cup sugar
1-1/2 cups flour
¼ teaspoon baking powder
1 teaspoon baking soda
1 teaspoon cinnamon
1 teaspoon nutmeg
½ cup softened margarine
½ cup milk
1 egg
2 cups peeled, finely chopped apples
½ cup chopped nuts

Spray a 9-inch-by 13-inch cake pan with non-stick vegetable coating. Stir together sugar, flour, baking powder, baking soda, cinnamon and nutmeg. Mix in apples and nuts. Cream shortening and sugar. Beat in egg and milk. Stir in the flour mixture mixing well. Pour into prepared pan and bake in a pre-heated 350-degree oven for 35 to 40 minutes or until a toothpick inserted in the center comes out clean.

Serve warm or cold with applejack sauce.

Makes 12 servings

APPLEJACK SAUCE

½ cup butter
½ cup heavy cream
½ cup sugar
1 teaspoon vanilla
1 tablespoon applejack

Gently heat butter, cream and sugar together until sugar dissolves. Stir in vanilla and applejack. Pour over individual servings of cake.

This recipe goes together quickly because it is done in a food processor. For a crispy crust, mist loaf with a spray bottle of water two or three times during baking.

LIGHTER RYE BREAD

¼ cup dark brown sugar
1 cup water
1 tablespoon butter
1 teaspoon salt
1 tablespoon caraway seeds
2 to 2-1/2 cups all-purpose flour
1 cup rye flour
1 package active dry yeast
Cooking spray
1 egg
1 tablespoon cold water

In a small saucepan, mix together sugar, water, butter, salt and caraway seeds. Bring to a boil. Cool to 120 degrees.

Meanwhile, fit food processor with a steel blade. Put 1 cup of the all-purpose flour, the rye flour and yeast into the work bowl. Pulse twice to mix.

Add cooled water mixture to bowl. Process until smooth. Add enough of the remaining flour—pulsing on and off—until dough forms a ball that cleans sides of bowl. Let dough rest 5 minutes in bowl. Then, if dough is still sticky add all-purpose flour by the tablespoon and pulse until dough is smooth.

Turn dough onto a lightly floured surface. Shape into a ball. Spray a bowl with cooking spray and place dough in bowl. Spray dough. Cover loosely with plastic wrap and let sit in a warm place (85 degrees) until doubled, about 1 hour.

Punch dough down. Shape into a ball and place in a greased 8-inch round cake pan. Spray lightly with cooking spray. Cover with plastic wrap and let stand in a warm place until almost doubled, about 45 minutes.

Heat oven to 400 degrees. To prepare egg wash, mix 1 tablespoon cold water with 1 beaten egg. Using a pastry brush, spread egg wash over surface of loaf. Freeze surplus egg wash for next baking session.

Bake about 30 to 35 minutes until loaf is evenly brown and an instant-read thermometer inserted in center of loaf reads 190 to 200 degrees.

Remove from pan and cool on rack. Makes 1 loaf.

When the dessert maker bowed out a few hours before our potluck dinner, I had to improvise. A 40-minute drive to town was out of the question. But I did have an ample supply of cocoa and some tiny jars of raspberry jam from a gift.

PANTRY CHOCOLATE CAKE

1-1/2 cups flour
2 cups sugar
1-1/2 teaspoons baking soda
½ teaspoon salt
¾ cup canola oil
1-1/2 cups water
2 teaspoons vanilla
¼ cup raspberry jam
Easy chocolate icing

Preheat oven to 350 degrees. Spray a 13-by-9-inch pan with nonstick vegetable cooking spray. In a large bowl, stir together the flour, sugar, baking soda, cocoa and salt. Beat in oil, water and vanilla. Pour into prepared pan. Bake for 30 to 35 minutes or until a toothpick inserted in center comes out clean.

Cool cake in pan for 10 minutes. Remove cake from pan and place on a rack. Warm jam slightly to thin and apply with a pastry brush to top of cake. Frost with chocolate icing.

Makes 15 servings.

EASY CHOCOLATE ICING

6 tablespoons butter, melted
6 tablespoons hot coffee
6 tablespoons cocoa
1 teaspoon vanilla
3 cups powdered sugar

Combine butter, coffee, cocoa and vanilla in a bowl. Beat until smooth. Gradually beat in enough sugar until icing reaches a smooth and spreadable consistency. Frost top of cake.

This rich lemony bar offers s sweet-tart ending to a dinner. The recipe is from Roberta Liston, a flight attendant from Saginaw, Michigan, who has made it so often that she recites it from memory.

LEMON BARS

2 sticks soft butter
½ cup powdered sugar
2 cups flour
2 cups sugar
4 eggs
¼ cup flour
¼ cup fresh lemon juice
2 teaspoons lemon extract

Preheat oven to 350 degrees. In a food processor bowl, mix together butter, powdered sugar and 2 cups flour. Spray a 9-by-13-inch pan with nonstick vegetable spray. Pat butter-flour mixture into pan and bake for 15 to 20 minutes until edges are light brown.

Meanwhile, make the filling. Place the sugar, eggs, ¼ cup flour, lemon juice and lemon extract in the food processor bowl. Process until mixed. Pour over the hot crust and bake for 25 to 30 minutes or until toothpick inserted in center comes out clean. When cool, cut into bars.

Makes 16 bars.

This is a wonderfully moist cookie that I have been baking since I was a teenager. I like to mix the batter when I have time and freeze to bake later. A stockpile of dough (as opposed to baked cookies) is unlikely to inspire midnight raids on the freezer. I serve the baked cookies in a large glass apothecary jar decorated with a seasonal bow or decoration.

OLD-FASHIONED OATMEAL RAISIN COOKIES

1 cup (2 sticks) butter or margarine
1 cup firmly-packed brown sugar
1/2 cup granulated sugar
2 eggs
1 teaspoon vanilla
1-1/2 cups all-purpose flour
1 teaspoon baking soda
1 teaspoon cinnamon
1/2 teaspoon salt
3 cups quick-cooking or old-fashioned oats
1 cup raisins
1/2 cup chopped nuts

Bring butter or margarine to room temperature. Heat oven to 350 F. Beat butter and sugars together until creamy. Add eggs and vanilla and beat well. Stir together flour, baking soda, cinnamon and salt. Beat into butter mixture.

Add oatmeal, raisins and nuts and mix well until all ingredients are combined.

Drop by rounded tablespoonfuls onto ungreased cookie sheet. Bake for 10 to 12 minutes until just golden brown. Remove with a pancake turner to a wire rack Cool completely. Store in an airtight container. Makes about 50 2-1/2-inch cookies.

Potluck Feelings Shared

We who had been doing potluck suppers for years had to smile when *The New York Times* finally discovered them.

Of course, *The Times* editors did not use the word 'potluck.' 'Cooperative dinners,' they said. The newspaper noted that career people, singly or in tandem, have scarce time these days to prepare an entire dinner party. So it is now okay to delegate parts of the meal to the guests.

The Times described a woman banker ordering Guest A to bring a bottle of viognier; Guest B, a three-grain baguette; Guest C, a quart of chocolate mousse; Guest D, a bouquet of anemones and so on until her menu was completed.

Cooperative? Sounds more like KP orders in an up-scale gulag.

Such rigid directives leave no margin for surprises–the fun of potluck. And what if the bakery had only four-grain bread left that day? Would a written excuse from the baker be acceptable? Or should the guest simply call in sick?

Up here in Northern New England, people have shared the food–and the cooking– for centuries. Our guidelines are casual. Traditionally, the cooks bring the best dishes in their specialties. Quality can vary but nobody minds. The point is the gathering, the sharing.

New Englanders also call their shared meals "covered dish suppers." By any name, potluck events inspire flexibility. If the salad maker-elect has jury duty, the host has to make do. Or when it becomes clear that latecomers are not coming at all, you put on a pot of rice or toss a salad.

As in everything else, there are fashions in potluck. At one time, you could count on at least two pots of meatballs in a faddish grape jelly sauce. Yes. Or a canned green bean-mushroom soup casserole topped with deep-fried onion rings. Yes. Mercifully, such mediocrities went out of style with excessive salt, sugar and fat.

I plead guilty to a scalloped potato casserole made with a canned cream of chicken soup. It was called a potluck but I knew that most of the guests would be drinking their dinner. I do not like to make food for people too numbed to appreciate it. I should have trusted my feelings and said no in the first place. Instead, I was marooned up on my hill by an unpredicted, fast-moving ice storm. The entire county lost power and I heard later that potluckers sat in the dark eating cold food and toasting each other.

Mention potluck and people want to know if it is related to potlatch. In spirit, it is. Potlatches were feasts given by Native Americans of the Pacific Northwest. In the Nootka language, potlatch means 'to give.'

My friend, Mary Campbell, who lives in Southfield, Michigan, gets together every month with a group of women to cook lunch according to the Gourmet magazine centerfold. One month's menu: Warm shrimp and scallop salad with roasted red pepper vinaigrette, roast goose with sausage, fennel and current stuffing, wild mushroom and port gravy, sautéed potatoes and celery root, Brussels sprouts with shallot butter, black forest cake and eggnog ice cream. The wines include Meursault Clos de la Barre, Domaine des Comtes Lafon '83 and Quady's Essenscia. The hostess prepares the main dish and the other guests volunteer to cook the other menu items. "We are women who like to cook, who like to try new recipes and we really enjoy our get-togethers. Each December, we prepare dinner instead of lunch and invite our husbands," Mary said.

Every so often, New Hampshire poet Jim Kates hosts a mammoth, county-wide, multi-generational potluck. "Bring anything you like," he advises his guests. And somehow it never turns out to be all salads or all desserts. The diversity of potluck unfolds magically.

While I am not as uptight as the hostess of that Manhattan gulag, nor as fancy as Mary and her gourmet group, I am not as casual as Jim. When I host a potluck, I make the main dish. This sets the theme. It is also good insurance against no-shows–likelihood in New England weather. Then I call five friends; when they ask what they can bring, I let them select appetizer, vegetable, salad, bread or dessert.

If I am invited to somebody else's potluck, I am doubly delighted. I can test a recipe-in-progress and have a good time, too. They usually want my breads. So we get to drive to dinner in a car filled with the aroma of warm bread. I can also feel the uncommon appreciation of people savoring homemade bread.

The hostess of the first New England potluck I ever attended, ordered me to bring a pound of hamburger. I did what I was told. But I felt cheated that I could not splurge on special ingredients or create something interesting for a new audience.

What makes a good potluck dish? For one thing, it has to be portable. Over country roads. Or city potholes.

One humid August day I carried a blueberry dessert up a footpath to a clearing at the top of a hill where we had been promised a spectacular view of the Green Mountains of Vermont. Suddenly, a mosquito jammed her hypodermic into the back of my thigh. I swatted. I stumbled. My food basket and I tumbled down the path. Somehow my blueberry dessert survived. The other guests even called for encores–of the dessert, not the fall.

A potluck dish made with feeling can also be made with simplicity. Avoid dishes that require special serving tools, space or time. Simplicity is itself an authentic feeling. Haste and congestion are anti-feeling.

I learned that from "Bananas Foster," a New Orleans ice cream dessert that is topped with sliced bananas sautéed in butter and flamed with banana liqueur and rum. Our book group had read *All the King's Men* by Robert Penn Warren we decided on a southern menu. My Bananas Foster took major last-minute fussing. Worse, its dramatic flames were invisible in the bright June evening.

Of course, potluck doesn't have to be dinner. Consider a brunch, a happy-hour with hors d'oevres or a dessert buffet.

Not everyone approves of potluck. One guest told an etiquette columnist about an invitation that included an order for a birthday cake to serve 30 and a liter of wine. The columnist fulminated that potluck was getting out of hand and invited guests were being treated as servants and how about non-meal entertainment instead of potluck at gunpoint.

I agree there are times when potluck doesn't feel quite right.

For instance, I don't think it appropriate when I am staging a dinner to honor a particular person, perhaps for a particular kindness. Or the time I gathered friends to help heal the impact of a community tragedy.

Sometimes I'm inspired to do all the cooking simply to celebrate a bountiful garden. To potluck or not to potluck–it's guided by feeling.

Perhaps potluck is closer to the way we actually live. Closer than hiring a caterer, taking guests to dinner or waiting until we win the lottery and can entertain Martha Stewart style. In these days of two-earner families, portable meals carried home from the deli or the pizzeria are becoming standard. Mail order houses are now retailing insulated space-age food carriers. Mine is still an ash basket woven right here in our county.

Sharing homemade or even takeout dishes may be the only way some of us can break bread with friends in the busy years ahead. There is something comforting about the kind of person you can ask to bring a dish. It defines a friend. Potluck gives us back the time, energy and occasion to feel the greatest feeling of all–each other's company.

What can I bring? How about a savory spread for nibbling? This chicken liver pate is just right with drinks. It's simple and fast to prepare.

CHICKEN LIVER PATE

¼ cup peanut oil
½ pound chicken livers, trimmed, rinsed
½ cup chopped onion
1 hard-cooked egg, chopped
1 tablespoon brandy
Crackers or light rye party bread

Pat the livers dry with a paper towel. Heat the oil in a skillet until hot but not smoking. Cook the livers and onion until the liver is no longer pink within. Put liver mixture and egg into a food processor bowl fitted with a steel blade. Process just until smooth. Fold in brandy.

Serve with party rye or crackers.

Makes 1-1/2 cups.

This turns out to be my classic contribution to feminist potlucks. In 1979, I took it to a local celebration for Judy Chicago's Dinner Party art installation. I lost the recipe and found it just in time for a feminist potluck in 1999. The ultimate feminist potluck, I suppose, would be a buffet of take-out dishes but how much fun would that be for cooks like me?.

SALLY'S SANTA FE NOODLE SALAD

2/3 cup cider vinegar
¼ cup olive oil
1 teaspoon Worcestershire sauce
1 teaspoon hot pepper sauce
1 teaspoon ground cumin
1 teaspoon salt
½ teaspoon sugar
½ teaspoon ground pepper
1/3 cup non-fat plain yogurt
1 pound ditalini or other small pasta
1 cup chopped celery
½ cup chopped green bell pepper
½ cup chopped red bell pepper
8 green onions, sliced
1 4-ounce can green chiles, drained
1 15-ounce can black-eyed peas, drained and rinsed
2 cups frozen corn, rinsed with cold water, drained
½ cup pitted black olives, sliced
¼ cup pimiento-stuffed green olives
2 tablespoons fresh coriander, chopped

Whisk together vinegar, olive oil, Worcestershire sauce, hot pepper sauce, cumin, salt, pepper and sugar.

Cook pasta in boiling, salted water until *al dente.* Drain thoroughly. Gently toss pasta with vinegar mixture. Add celery, green pepper, red pepper, green onions, chiles, black-eyed peas, corn, black olives and green olives.

Taste for seasoning and adjust if necessary. Cover and refrigerate overnight to allow flavors to blend. Check seasonings again before serving. Sprinkle with fresh coriander.

Makes 12 servings.

My friend, Cheryl Burrows, totes this dish to potluck suppers where it quickly disappears. The recipe originated with her mother, Helen, of Merrymeeting Lake, New Hampshire. This dish may also be served as dessert. It doubles nicely and can be frozen up to two days before serving.

HELEN PHIPPS' FROZEN FRUIT SALAD

1 cup heavy cream
1 cup sour cream
1 tablespoon lemon juice
¾ cup sugar
1/8 teaspoon salt
1 9-ounce cans pineapple chunks, drained
1/3 cup maraschino cherries
¼ cup chopped nuts
2 bananas sliced
Lettuce

Whip cream. Gently mix the sour cream, lemon juice, sugar, salt, pineapple, cherries, nuts and bananas. Fold sour cream mixture into the whipped cream. Pour into a 9-inch square pan and cover with plastic wrap. Freeze.

Remove from freezer 15 minutes before serving. Cut into nine portions and serve on crisp lettuce.

Makes 9 servings.

This dessert uses a surprising combination—apples and rhubarb—for a superb flavor. It's a fine dessert to tote to a potluck. Pack a balloon whisk for last-minute cream whipping. And don't forget to refrigerate the cream on arrival. This was my contribution to a dinner following a discussion on Carl Jung.

MEMORIES, DREAMS, REFLECTIONS AND A RHUBARB APPLE DESSERT

1-1/2 cups flour
¾ cup butter
6 tablespoons brown sugar
3 eggs
1 cup brown sugar, packed
6 tablespoons flour
2 cups rhubarb, cut into ¼-inch pieces
1 cup peeled, diced apple
¾ teaspoon almond extract
¾ cup slivered almonds
1 cup heavy cream

Preheat oven to 350 degrees. Cut together flour, butter and 6 tablespoons brown sugar until crumbly. Press mixture into 9-inch-by-13-inch pan.

Mix the eggs, 1 cup brown sugar, flour, rhubarb, apple and almond extract. Spoon onto the crust. Sprinkle almonds on top. Bake 35 to 40 minutes. Serve warm or cold. Cut into squares and top with whipped cream. Serves 12 to 14.

BLUEBERRY CRUMBLE

½ cup plus 2 tablespoons butter
1-1/4 cup flour
¼ cup brown sugar
½ cup coarsely chopped walnuts
1 pint blueberries
1 tablespoon flour
1 cup sugar
1 teaspoon baking powder
2 eggs, beaten
½ cup unsweetened shredded coconut
1 tablespoon lemon juice
Powdered sugar

Preheat oven to 375. Grease a 13-by-9-inch pan. Mix the butter, flour and brown sugar. Press into the bottom of prepared pan. Sprinkle walnuts on top. Bake for 12 minutes.

Meanwhile, toss the blueberries with 1 tablespoon flour. Mix the sugar, baking powder, beaten eggs, coconut and lemon juice. Stir in the blueberries. Spread the blueberry mixture on top of the hot crust and bake for 20 minutes.

Sprinkle lightly with powdered sugar. Cool on a rack. Cut into squares.
Makes 20 2-1/2 –inch squares.

INDEX